A GAME-CHANGING REVELATION

The Hidden Ancestry of America & Great Britain

Volume Two

Every scribe instructed concerning the kingdom of heaven is like a householder who brings out of his treasure things new and old.

Matthew 13:52

First Printing: September 2014 (V2)

ISBN: 978-1-937735-82-1

Legends Library Publishing, Inc.
Rochester, NY

Inquiries to: info@legendslibrary.com
Phone: 877-222-1960
Website: www.LegendsLibrary.org

Cover design by Alisha Bishop

A GAME-CHANGING REVELATION

The Hidden Ancestry of America & Great Britain

Volume Two

Stephen J. Spykerman

Legends LIBRARY

New York

ACKNOWLEDGEMENTS

༺❦༻

First of all I am indebted to Lord Michael Allenby for his initial help and interest in this project. I shall always remember our several encounters at the House of Lords and his kindness in showing me all the heraldic splendour of the Palace of Westminster in 2004. A special thanks to him for his fulsome and most generous foreword.

Special thanks must go to my precious wife for her outstanding loyalty, forbearance and love. She has been a great sounding board and a wonderful help, especially with the editing and arranging of the case notes.

I am also indebted to Margie Kinikin, who without a doubt must be the fastest proof reader in the West. Her work has truly been a blessing.

A special accolade must go to the writings of Mr W.H. Bennett, E Raymond Capt. Howard Rand, and Isabel Hill Elder, as all of them have been of great help and inspiration to me.

The contribution made by my dear Orthodox friend Yair Davidiy, must also be acknowledged, as without his ground breaking and most extensive research all authors attempting to write on this subject would be the poorer.

Grateful thanks and my deepest appreciation go to Mary Ellen Picchi and her team, whose dedicated support for this project has made a difference which, though it may be hard to evaluate, is none the less more than substantial.

Finally, I would like to thank and compliment Alisha Bishop for creating the beautiful cover design for this book. It is just what the doctor ordered!

CONTENTS

࿇

FOREWORD

༄༅

By:

The Viscount Michael Allenby of Megiddo

House of Lords - London

It is a particular pleasure to write this foreword to Stephen Spykerman's revolutionary new book, *The Hidden Ancestry of America & Great Britain,* as it is a subject that has fascinated my family for a long time. What makes reading this work exciting is that on several fronts it totally overturns long held views of our nation's roots. Clearly, the roots of the Anglo-Saxon and Celtic peoples have never been delved in so deeply, and the reader is in for a whole range of unexpected surprises.

There cannot be many people in the world today who have not thought about their own personal ancestry. Most of us are able to research back a few generations or even a few hundred years. However, tracing back the ancestry of our nation takes one into a much greater and more complex dimension altogether. Logic alone tells one that if it is possible to trace back our own personal ancestry one ought also to be able to do the same for the nations of our birth.

The author affirms that our Anglo-Saxon and Celtic ancestors are descended from the Ten Lost Tribes of Israel. Speaking for myself, I found the idea of interest, yet nevertheless endeavoured to approach the book with a degree of scepticism, whilst at the same time keeping an open mind. At the end of my reading, I have to say that I was staggered at the evidence the author has brought to light, and although some people may quarrel with certain of his assertions, there is no doubt that the evidence is overwhelming. Showing us the true origins of our nations that have lain dormant for such a long time, the writer has empowered us to change our perceptions about the fabulous history of our peoples in a most meaningful way. Some of the incredible detail produced in this fascinating work is simply enthralling. Full credit must be given to the carefully chosen illustrations that play a pivotal part in this astounding work. The reader cannot fail to be impressed by revelatory explanation given to every aspect of the colourful heraldry of Great Britain and America. To look at the heraldic emblems of our respective countries' in a new way is truly an eye opening experience!

The book is constructed on a simply easy to follow framework of just twelve major testimonies or signs, with each chapter comprising a sign. The historical chapters about the formation of the United States of America and the early years of the British Empire are especially fascinating. The way the author brings both prophecy and history to life is nothing short of amazing. To think that both the American War of Independence and the Civil War were prophesied in the Bible is an incredible thought. The book fills one with awe about the destiny of our nations and one becomes convinced that both America and Great Britain have benefited from an invisible benefactor. Understanding the true identity of our nations also greatly clarifies much of our history. This is especially so regarding the reasons why there should be a 'special relationship' between Great Britain and the United States of America.

My message to you, the reader, is to put aside your preconceptions and weigh for yourself the content of this book. Please don't come to any conclusions until you have read the entire work and then consider your verdict – on the evidence, and without bias.

"The Hidden Ancestry of America and Great Britain is essential reading for every thinking Anglo-Saxon, Celtic and Jewish person in the world. You can be sure that your worldview will never be the same again!

"All truth passes through three stages—

First, it is ridiculed;

Second, it is violently opposed;

Third, it is accepted as self-evident."

Arthur Schopenhauer (1788-1860)

INTRODUCTION

☙❧

Who are the Americans & the British?

In Volume One we clearly stated our premise and the fact that we were inspired by the example of Galileo, the great 15th century astronomer. It is important at this stage that we have a brief resume of the specific purpose for this work.

What is our premise?

Our premise revolves around Abraham being designated a 'Father of Nations'. The question that flows from this statement surely is: How many nations is Abraham the father of? It is commonly accepted that both the Jewish people, as well as the Arabic desert tribes are his descendants. The question is; are the Jews, together with a dozen or so Arab nations, the only peoples that have descended from Abraham? Might there be others? Could it be that America and Great Britain have descended from this same patriarch, or is that too farfetched to even consider? What we have here is a revolutionary idea every bit as politically incorrect and unacceptable to our modern twenty-first century society, as was Galileo's idea to his society in the fifteenth century. Do you want to know the answer? If you do, let us boldly follow in Galileo's footsteps and courageously state our seemingly impossible premise that the British and American peoples are indeed the descendants of Abraham.

The fact is that secular history does not confirm any relationship that connects modern day Americans and Britons with Abraham or his son Isaac. If it did, we would all know about it, as we would have been taught it at our schools as part of our normal curriculum. Yet, once we start out from the premise that, despite all the evidence to the contrary, it may nevertheless still be true that America and Great Britain and her Commonwealth kin have descended from Abraham through his son Isaac, we are bound to enter into wholly uncharted territory. Like Galileo before us, we are going against the mainstream of accepted knowledge ready to conquer entrenched frontiers of prejudice.

A most ancient secret

When speaking of Britain and America's hidden origins we are talking about a secret that is already some 4,000 years old. It is a secret of most ancient roots and independent nationhood. The incredible message of this book is that the English and the other tribes that make up the British Isles, as well as her American and Commonwealth cousins, are a people every bit as ancient as the Egyptians, Persians and Babylonians of old. Can you imagine that? Why should this surprise us? We have already seen considerable evidence of this in Volume One of this book. In this second part you are set to discover that the British and the American people originate from a civilization that is much older than that of ancient Greece or Rome! The revelation of this hitherto largely hidden knowledge will forever change our perspective of who we really are as a people.

Our quest is to assemble as much evidence as we possibly can muster to make our case. To this end we have called on twelve witnesses to present their case for us. Four of those have already provided convincing and in places irrefutable evidence from history in Volume One of this book. In this Part Two you will be presented with further Game-changing Revelations that will astound you. One of the keys used in our assembling of the evidence is what is known as, *The 'Law of Probability.' According to this law, if the same thing happens just once it is an accident, if the same thing occurs twice it is a coincidence, yet when the same thing turns up three times in a row or more it has meaning.*

In ancient times one could get a conviction on the evidence of just two or three witnesses, but if one can bring twelve independent witnesses and then find that their testimony is in complete agreement; then the fact of the case is established beyond any shadow of doubt. This book's aim is to take the reader step by step through each of the twelve witnesses or signs in the hope that the incredible identity of all the Celtic and Anglo-Saxon peoples may be proved beyond doubt. For reasons of simplicity the twelve witnesses or signs are divided into twelve separate chapters. For ease of understanding, all twelve signs are first of all summarized, as when these witnesses are taken together, they set the United States of America and Great Britain, together with her Canadian, Australian, New Zealand and South African cousins, most conclusively apart as Israelite nations.

Here then follows a resume of these inspired and most accurate testimonies of twelve prophetic witnesses, who will describe what the people of the House of Israel were to do and become, and how they are to be recognized in the 'last days' (Genesis 49:1).

THESE TWELVE SIGNS DEMONSTRATE THE MAIN CHARACTERISTICS THAT WILL IDENTIFY THE LOST TRIBES OF ISRAEL TODAY:

- *Israel was to become a 'great' nation.* (Jeremiah 31:35-37; Genesis 12:2)

- *The Israelites were to reassemble in a 'new' home.* (Amos 9:9; 2 Samuel 7:10)

- *Israel was to inhabit 'islands' and 'coastlands' located 'northwest' of Jerusalem.* (Isaiah 49:1)

- *Israel was to become a 'nation' and a 'company' (commonwealth) of nations* (Genesis 35:11; Genesis 48:19)

- *Israel was to become a 'military' superpower.* (Deuteronomy 33:17; 15:6; Genesis 49:23-24)

- *Israel was to possess the 'gates' of her enemies* (Genesis 22:17 and 24:60)

3

- *Israel was to acquire 'great' wealth & become an economic giant* (Genesis 27:28-29 & Deuteronomy 15:6 & 33:13-16)

- *Israel was to have a very 'large' population* (Genesis 22:17)

- *Israel was to be a 'Royal Kingdom'* (2 Samuel 7:12-16 and Jeremiah 33:17)

- *Israel was to be recognized by the Emblems of a 'Lion' and a 'Unicorn'* (Numbers 24:8-9 & Deuteronomy 33:17)

- *The Israelites were to be unaware of their true origins* (Deuteronomy 32:26; Isaiah 1:3)

- *Israel's Birthright inheritance was to be deferred* (Leviticus 26: 18,21,24,28)

Having summarized these twelve honest witnesses and faithful signs we can get started in earnest on our wonderful quest. This exercise is much like doing your own ancestral research, only on a much grander scale. For many it can be a most exciting journey of discovery, as they piece together every bit of evidence they have so painfully dug up. When you start on the project you may only have a few family rumours about great ancestors of noble birth. You want to find out if it is true? The question you ask yourself is: Can it be proved? Would it not be rewarding for you subsequently to discover that your ancestry is even more amazing and glorious than you could possibly imagine? This is the journey we are now embarking on, so come along and let us discover the amazing secrets of Britain and America's incredible and most illustrious past. Let us together discover the real truth about their hidden pre-Celtic and Anglo-Saxon ancestry.

As four of the above witnesses have already given their account in Volume One, we will now start with the fifth testimony.............

CHAPTER ONE

৵৽৽

5th Sign
Israel was to become a 'military' superpower

"You shall reign over many nations, but they shall not reign over you."
(Deuteronomy 15:6b)

"His glory shall be like a firstborn bull, and his horns like the horns of the unicorn; together with them he shall push the peoples to the ends of the earth; they are the ten thousands of Ephraim and the thousands of Manasseh."
(Deuteronomy 33:17)

"Joseph is a fruitful bough, a fruitful bough by a well; his branches run over the wall. The archers have bitterly grieved him, shot at him and hated him. But his bow remained in strength, and the arms of his hands were made strong by the hands of the Mighty God of Jacob."
(Genesis 49:22-24)

In 1905/6 the British Empire was at its zenith. It ruled over an empire that comprised much of the world, its territory covered thirteen million square miles. It ruled over a full one quarter of the human race from an island no greater than 121 thousand square miles. By way of contrast the Roman Empire at its height ruled over a territory of only 2.5 million square miles, and thus the British Empire was more than five times larger than the empire of ancient Rome. Is this not extraordinary! It also ruled over more than four times the population. It truly was, and still today retains the record of having been, the greatest empire the world has ever seen! The territory she ruled over was nearly 108 times larger than her own country, yet her army was surprisingly small. In the world rankings of the time, based upon the peacetime strength of the regular forces of the major armies of the world of that day, the British army ranked eighth. The Russian, French, German, Turkish and Austrian armies were all considerably larger. All the same, she was able to deal with any emergency in her far-flung empire in the most efficient way, frequently using local indigenous auxiliary forces to support her regular troops. It was not so much the size of the British Army that made the difference, but the quality of her leadership, training, equipment and men. This was demonstrated by the fact that, although the army was only the eighth largest in the world as far as manpower was concerned, Britain ranked third in terms of annual expenditure. For instance she spent considerably more on her armed forces than France, whose army was nearly four times larger.

Britannia Rules the Waves

Where Britain really scored over the other nations was in her magnificent navy. Britain needed a powerful navy to protect her commercial interests around the world. The British naval planners of the day worked on the axiom of British naval policy that the Royal (British) Navy should at all times be equal in strength to the combined fleets of the next two largest naval powers. In 1907, at the height of her empire, she possessed 60 battleships and 125 cruisers, against the 61 battleships and 77 cruisers of the combined navies of France and Germany.

"Fear God and Dread Naught!"

Much like her American brother and global superpower successor today, Britain too had a vast technological advantage over her rivals, as she was the first naval power to introduce the 'Dreadnoughts'. The name of this formidable ship was derived from the motto *"Fear God and Dread Naught"*, a saying that perfectly expressed the sentiment of the Victorian age. The 'Dreadnought' was a new type of ironclad battleship, which, because of the exceptional power and reach of her mighty guns, effectively rendered all the other modern navies obsolete. Apart from these first class battleships and cruisers mentioned, Britain had a further 239 torpedo boats, gunboats, destroyers and submarines. In case of war Britain had several reserve fleets stationed at her naval dockyards, totalling a further 158 ships, including many battleships and cruisers. In addition to these the British possessed nine naval stations abroad, plus 39 coaling stations, where ships could replenish their stores of fuel, which gave her enormous strategic advantage.

One of the supreme highpoints of the British Empire was the celebration of Queen Victoria's Diamond Jubilee. She was the royal figurehead of empire, the Great White Queen to many of her foreign subjects, remote and 'half divine.' As part of the celebrations the Empire staged a consummate exhibition of raw power in what has since become known as the Spithead Review. The Royal review of the fleet at Spithead took place just four days after the Jubilee procession in London on June 26, 1897. This naval review was claimed to be the largest assembly of warships ever gathered at anchorage, and it must have been a truly awesome sight. In lines seven miles long more than 170 ships, including 50 battleships, lay dressed for inspection by the Prince of Wales and his guests. Most of the fleet was less than ten years old, and all of them were gloriously ablaze with brass and bunting. For the benefit of the visitors from rival powers it was carefully publicized that not one of the ships on show had been withdrawn from a foreign station! It was truly fair at that time to say: "BRITANNIA RULES THE WAVES!" There was no one around then who dared challenge her awesome might.

POSITION OF THE FLEET AT SPITHEAD ON THE 26TH JUNE 1897

(image of map showing position of the fleet at Spithead)

Let nations bow down to you

(courtesy Queen Victoria Diamond Jubilee Scrapbook)

Part of the 'Birthright blessing' was: "*Let peoples serve you, and nations bow down to you*" (Genesis 27:29). This has certainly come to pass both in war and in peace. Many nations have bowed down to Great Britain especially in the heyday of her empire. Since that time many nations have had absolutely no choice but to bow down to her brother and successor, the United States of America.

One of the most recent examples occurred at a time when the British fleet was much depleted, and had become a mere shadow of its former self, yet even so, she still was able to enforce her will by force of arms. The case in question was Britain's daring recapture of the Falklands Islands in the 1982 Falklands War, when Britain by force of arms forced the Argentine government to concede defeat.

Even more recently was the Gulf War, where Saddam Hussein and his Iraqi occupying forces *'were made'* to leave Kuwait. The two sons of Joseph, America and Great Britain led the grand military alliance that comprised Operation 'Desert Storm'. Ever since that victory, for the following twelve years, and despite Saddam's defiance, his air force was forbidden to fly over much of his own country, as a result of a 'No Fly Zone' ORDER by these same two sons of Joseph. Then in the Second Gulf War, these two sons of Joseph, in the teeth of the most ferocious global opposition, have once again intervened to force their will upon Iraq's evil regime.

Thus once again the world witnessed the extraordinary affinity between Britain and the United States of America. Whenever a major crisis occurs to threaten the stability of the world these two nations have demonstrated over and over again they have not only the power but also the will to act together to overcome the threat.

The terrorist attack of September 11 on the twin towers of the World Trade Center and the Pentagon changed the face of the world. Commentators generally agree this terrorist attack has changed many of the parameters in the way nations will conduct their affairs in the future. One thing has not changed is that in a time of crisis the United States can usually count on the support of Great Britain. The account of history clearly shows that the reverse is also true, as America too has supported Britain in her hour of greatest need, as she rallied to Britain's aid in both World Wars.

On September 11, 2001, in a gross act of outrageous Islamic fundamentalist terrorism, as the two airliners were flown into the twin towers of the World Trade Center in Manhattan, mass murder was committed in front of a worldwide TV audience. Most of the dead were American. The shock to the American psyche was enormous, as for the first time since the foundation of the Republic 'Fortress America' had been breached.

As the whole of America was traumatised by the immense shock, British Prime Minister Tony Blair declared that Britain stood shoulder to shoulder with the American people. He offered total support including Great Britain's armed forces in the global fight against terrorism. As President George W. Bush rallied his nation, Tony Blair did the same on British shores, and history repeated itself, as these two sons of Joseph – America and Great Britain – were once again united in a common purpose to defeat the foe. As President Bush gave his benchmark speech to the nation in the specially called joint session of Congress, there sitting in the Congressional Gallery was a solitary head of a foreign government. It was Tony Blair, the Prime Minister of Great Britain, who alone of all the leaders in the West had taken the trouble to be present in solidarity with President Bush, and the American people. His presence served as a singular symbol of the unequivocal support of the British people for America in her time of distress. It was almost as if Mr. Blair represented 'family' on this most traumatic of all occasions for America. As President Bush acknowledged Blair's presence, referring to Britain as America's closest friend and ally in the world, the Prime Minister received a spontaneous ovation from the assembled leadership of the American government. The occasion was watched by the whole of the American nation, and excerpts of the speech were beamed all over the world. Other nations also offered help and support for America's war on terrorism, but no other nation has been as supportive as Great Britain. Even the Queen demonstrated her support with a marvellous gesture, when at Buckingham Palace during the changing of the guard ceremony the American National Anthem was played. This too was broadcast and commented upon all over America. With tens of thousands of Americans stranded in London in the immediate aftermath of the disaster, this act of royal support, together with countless other acts of individual and corporate kindness, demonstrated once again that blood is thicker than water and that the English-speaking people instinctively know whom their true friends are.

Anglo-Saxon blood brothers

This mutual support between the British and the Americans has, as we have already seen, a fundamental cause which goes much deeper than sharing a common language or heritage. The close affinity between Britain and America is based on the fact that they are truly 'brother' nations, who descended from the two sons of Joseph, Ephraim and Manasseh. It is this kinship, more than anything else that explains the *'special relationship'* that exists between Great Britain and the United States of America. The bond between America and Great Britain is based upon a blood relationship. The relationship is instinctive simply because it is in the very fibre of the Anglo-Saxon and Celtic peoples. These two nations received the lion's share of the Birthright blessing of the Covenant that the Creator God made with their patriarchal ancestor, Abraham, some four thousand years ago. It is as a result of this divine favour that these nations have become the natural leaders of the world, and it is only they, when push comes to shove, who have the moral fibre, the will, as well as the necessary power, to withstand evil in this world. Thus they have seen off the Kaiser of Germany in World War I, utterly defeated Hitler's Third Reich and the Emperor of Japan in World War II, brought about the implosion of the Communist Soviet Empire in 1989, and whether they will yet vanquish the global terrorist threat of fundamentalist Islam remains yet to be seen. The signs so far by no means look good, especially with the lack of leadership and the rank spirit of appeasement coming from the present occupant of the White House. America, after the blood-soaked debacles of her wars in Iraq and Afghanistan seems to have lost all confidence in her power. The outside world perceives that America's will is broken, and she appears to be in wholesale retreat. Nevertheless, history has taught us that in a time of extreme danger and crisis that these Anglo-Saxon and Celtic brothers 'know' that only 'family' will do. We must not forget that Canada, Australia and New Zealand share the same ancestry. On that fateful day, September 11, when all American airports were closed, the

Canadians stepped in freely to host countless redirected American, British and other aircraft from all over the world. Then Canada, Australia and New Zealand, like Britain, all promptly offered to send troops, ships and aircraft to Afghanistan to fight Bin Laden and his Taliban protectors. For more than a century these freedom-loving sons of Joseph, this Israelite 'family' of nations, have always come together to overcome the threat posed by totalitarian regimes bent on world conquest and domination.

Only trust your family

Another telling example of the kinship between America, Great Britain and her Commonwealth partners Canada, Australia and New Zealand, is their joint involvement in 'ECHELON', the global spy satellite system. ECHELON is a secret worldwide intelligence-gathering operation, and it is the greatest surveillance network the world has ever seen. The U.S. National Security Agency (NSA), has created a global spy system, codenamed ECHELON, which is able to intercept and analyse virtually every phone call, fax, email and telex message sent anywhere in the world. The interesting point is that the USA, in seeking allies for this project, has not sought the assistance of nations such as France, Germany, Italy, or Japan, but has instead enlisted the aid of Great Britain, Canada, Australia and New Zealand. Thus it seems as if almost by instinct, the modern day descendants of Joseph, Ephraim and Manasseh, in matters concerning their national security, are only prepared to trust the members of their own family. We must not forget that Canada, Australia and New Zealand share the Ephraim roots of Great Britain, and that they too are the descendants of the Ten Tribes of Israel.

ECHELON is controlled by the NSA and is operated in conjunction with the UK Government Communications Head Quarters (GCHQ) in Cheltenham, England, the Communications Security Establishment (CSE) of Canada, the Australian Defence Security Directorate (DSD), and the General Communications Security Bureau (GCSB) of New Zealand. These national security organizations are bound together under a secret agreement they entered into in 1948 in the aftermath of the Second World War. Their intelligence signals proved invaluable in countering and eventually defeating the Soviet Union during the Cold War. The current focus of the system is the war against global terrorism, with the threat coming from fundamentalist Islamic terrorist organizations and countries such as Afghanistan, Iran, Saudi Arabia, Iraq, Syria, Sudan and Libya.

In the late 1990s the existence of ECHELON was disclosed to the public, triggering a major debate in the European Parliament and, to a lesser extent, to the United States Congress. France has been especially vociferous in accusing the Anglo-Saxon spy network of commercial espionage against major French and other EU corporations. At French instigation, the European Parliament has been asking questions as to whether ECHELON communications interceptions violate the sovereignty and privacy of citizens within the European Union. In 1996, a detailed description of ECHELON was provided by New Zealand journalist Nicky Hager in a book titled *"Secret Power – New Zealand's role in the International Spy Network"*, which was cited by the European Parliament 1998 report titled, "An Appraisal of the Technology of Political Control" (PE 168.184). *1 As a result of this campaign, the European Parliament voted 367 – 159 to adopt 44 recommendations on how to counter the ECHELON system. Great Britain was put under considerable pressure by France, as well as by other EU members, who pointed out the inconsistency in her participation in ECHELON, whilst at the same time being a full member of the European Union. Britain at the time forcefully resisted all attempts to persuade her to withdraw from ECHELON. As a matter of fact, it is as a result of this EU campaign that this highly secret, worldwide intelligence-gathering network has become public knowledge.

As a result of the disclosures of the former NSA contractor Edward Snowden, who in 2013 referred to Echelon as "FIVE EYES", which perfectly describes the Anglophonic alliance of five nations,

Snowden described the "Five Eyes" as a "supra-national intelligence organization that doesn't answer to the laws of its own countries. Documents leaked by Snowden in 2013 revealed that the "Five Eyes" have been intentionally spying on one another's citizens and sharing the collected information with each other in order to circumvent restrictive domestic regulations on spying. Despite the impact of Snowden's disclosures, the general consensus among experts in the intelligence community holds that no amount of global outrage will affect the "Five Eyes" relationship, which to this day remains the most powerful espionage alliance in world history. *2

Is it not extraordinary that the nations comprising the secret ECHELON/FIVE EYES alliance are the modern nations of the tribes of Ephraim and Manasseh? The combined efforts of those "Five Eyes," representing the five nations of the U.S., UK, Canada, Australia and New Zealand appear to be a shadowy, but very real alliance of the entire House of Joseph in the modern world. Is it not interesting that, without even being aware of their common Israelite origins, these nations have naturally gravitated into a very close security alliance? It seems that, when it comes to their national security, these modern day descendants of Joseph are prepared to trust only their immediate family.

Joseph's forgiving heart

When we go back to Israel's ancient history book, we find that Joseph's brothers hated him because he had confided his dreams to them. In these dreams Joseph was portrayed as ruling over them even to the point where his brothers were bowing down to him. They were envious of him because he was their father's favourite son and this had been especially highlighted when Joseph was given a beautiful coat of many colors. According to some rabbinical sources, Joseph's coat was in a tartan pattern. This coat was not just a very fine garment it also represented a certain rank and status. As their hearts burned with envy his brothers ended up selling Joseph into slavery in Egypt. Actually, their first intent had been to murder him and they had thrown him into a pit planning to kill him later on. When a trading caravan passed by they had a change of heart and decided to sell their brother as a slave instead. They told their father Jacob that Joseph had been killed and his body torn up by wild animals. As evidence, they showed Jacob Joseph's colorful coat of authority, which they had covered in the blood of a goat (Genesis 37). They kept up this charade for a full 21 years, deceiving their father, whose grief knew no bounds. Jacob had already lost his beloved wife Rachel, Joseph's mother, when Benjamin, the youngest of his twelve sons, was born.

As God would have it, Joseph prospered in Egypt, and from being a slave who ended up in Pharaoh's prison, he was raised up to become the ruler of all Egypt, second in power only to Pharaoh himself. It was through his God-given ability to interpret Pharaoh's dreams, in which he prophesied seven years of plenty followed by seven years of famine, that Joseph acquired his position of supreme executive power in Egypt.

Egypt in those days was the greatest superpower in the ancient world, and Joseph's stewardship of Egypt's economy during the years of plenty proved an astounding success. For seven full years he stored up all the surpluses in vast warehouses he built, then when the seven years of famine started, other nations, tribes, and clans came to Egypt to buy grain. As the universal drought and famine took hold Joseph ended up feeding not only Egypt, but also much of the then known world as well. This is how Joseph's own brothers came to stand before him to petition him for food for their households and their clan. Despite the fact that Joseph had power of life and death over them, as his brothers *bowed down* before him he was ready to forgive them for the cruel way they had treated him and their father Jacob. He not only forgave them but he invited them to come and live in Egypt, and he then magnanimously cared for them and their families. Thus Joseph saved the lives of his own brothers, as without his intervention they most certainly would have all perished in the seven-year famine (Genesis 45 – 47).

Victorious brothers in arms

To continue the subject of other nations bowing down to the sons of Joseph, let us look at the last century. An especially graphic example is to be found in the Armistice followed by the humiliating Treaty of Versailles at the end of the First World War in 1918, when Germany was forced to *bow down to Great Britain and the United States of America, as well as to France.*

At the end of World War II, after the hard-won victory of the Allied Forces over Germany and Japan in 1945, **the greater part of the world's population was subject to either the British Empire or the United States of America**. During World War II the British Marines wore a badge depicting half the globe, whereas the American Marines wore a similar badge that pictured the other half. Between them these two brother nations-in-arms controlled much of the world either as colonies and protectorates or as occupied territories. Nations such as Germany, Austria, Italy and Japan *'bowed down to them'*. Yet, surprisingly, the allied Anglo-Saxon brothers in arms in their hard won victory demonstrated the most extraordinary mercy towards their conquered and vanquished enemies. Without knowing it, they exhibited one of the key characteristics of their forefather Joseph.

Anglo-Saxon mercy

There is a further modern-day parallel here, as Joseph's descendants Ephraim and Manasseh, alias Great Britain and America, saved their Israelite brothers in the Second World War. Norway, Denmark, the Netherlands, Belgium, Luxembourg and France are all nations of Israelite descent. The Nazi war machine had overwhelmed them all. They had lost their independence, and their only hope of deliverance lay in the mighty efforts of their Israelite brothers, America and Great Britain, assisted by her Commonwealth compatriots. Thus it was the sons of Joseph yet again who saved their brethren.

In the same spirit of Joseph, the most outstanding example of mercy and magnanimity was America's act of restoring the damaged economies of her former enemies, Germany and Japan, through her Marshall Aid plan. People say the Americans only did it out of pure self-interest, and as a defence against the onslaught of the Communist juggernaut to the east. This might have been true had there been no alternative! However, there were many other options available, one of which would have been the ruthless subjugation of the German and the Japanese people through permanent occupation. The Allies most certainly had the power, as both Germany and Japan were totally at their mercy. They could have easily annexed Germany at that time. It is what the Germans themselves would have done! The Japanese too, had shown that they had no qualms about doing just this to the countries they overwhelmed. The Russians also demonstrated that they would hold on to conquered territory and turn them into Russian satellites. The Allied Forces not only had the military might but also the right in international law to do so!

America's act of giving her defeated enemy her own territory and government back was an extraordinary act of mercy and magnanimity. For her then to pour in billions of her own dollars to restore her enemy's economy had never been heard of before, in all the history of the world. Never before had victorious conquerors treated their vanquished foe in such a benign way. Also, after America and Britain had conquered much of Germany in World War II, allied airmen from Britain and America flew their mercy missions 24 hours around the clock to feed their former German enemies in the Berlin Airlift of 1948. The Russians had cut the corridor into West Berlin, which was situated deep in Russian-occupied East Germany. Nothing could get through overland to the citizens of West Berlin, who faced starvation and inevitable surrender to the Communist giant to the east. The American and British pilots risked their lives flying the Berlin Corridor in the face of Russian threats to shoot them down. They did this for their defeated German enemy just three years after the bitter war against the Nazis had ended. They did this to save Berlin of all places, the very seat of Hitler's evil empire. They did this at a time when the whole world stood aghast after the true horrors of the Holocaust had become public knowledge. President J. F. Kennedy came to Berlin to make his famous declaration: *"Ich bin ein Berliner!"* Thus he 'drew a line in the sand', making it crystal clear to the Soviet Union that the Western Alliance, led by Joseph's modern day descendants, America and Great Britain, would resist Russian attempts to take over West Berlin. In direct consequence the Russians were *forced to back down* from the confrontation they had started. Thus the Russians too, like the Germans, Japanese and the Italians before them, were forced to *'bow down'* before the modern day sons of Joseph.

There was nothing magnanimous in victory about the conduct of the Communist partner in the wartime Western Alliance. The Russians in Eastern Europe behaved in stark contrast, as the nations they liberated from their Nazi conquerors soon discovered to their cost that they had exchanged a Nazi yoke for a Communist one. The Soviet Union held on to its conquered satellites, including East Germany, for over 45 years, until through economic necessity she had no choice but to let them go. The contrast between Israelite and Gentile mind-set could not have been greater.

The most recent example of this extraordinary magnanimity has been the handover of the British Crown Colony of Hong Kong to Communist China. When the British originally acquired Hong Kong, it had been an opium and malaria-infested rat-hole that was going nowhere. Under British rule it became one of the greatest financial and commercial centers of the world. Hong Kong prospered under the freedom-loving and free market administration of the enlightened British colonial government to become one of the most successful economies in the world. Yet when the British government handed over their colony to the Chinese in a marvellously dignified ceremony, they left over sixteen billion Pounds sterling in the colonial exchequer. It was a rare and most superior gesture of magnanimity and Imperial largesse that is so quintessentially British.

It was a gesture that portrayed the 'oh so British' belief in fair play and doing the decent thing. I dare say the Chinese could not believe their good fortune. As the Communist regime in Beijing could not by any stretch of the imagination be described as a friend of Britain, one would be hard pressed to find any nation that would have been quite so generous to an enemy.

The world's only Superpower

At the end of World War II America and Great Britain were in possession of the greatest collection of military hardware and power the world has ever seen in all of its recorded history. As America faced a two-front war on the seas its Navy grew tremendously. In 1943, the Navy's size was larger than the combined fleets of all the other combatant nations in World War II. By years' end in 1945, the United States Navy had added nearly 1,200 major combatant ships, including 27 aircraft carriers and 8 battleships, and had over 70 percent of the world's total tonnage of naval vessels of a 1,000 tons or greater. At its peak the U.S. Navy was operating 6,768 ships on V-J Day in August 1945, including 28 aircraft carriers. *3 In the D-Day invasion of German occupied France, an awesome armada of 6,939 vessels sailed from British ports to the Normandy beaches. This force included 1,213 naval combat ships, 4,126 landing craft, 736 ancillary craft and 864 merchant vessels. The invasion fleet deployed on June 6 was an inspiring and impressive sight. An American bomber pilot looking down at the fleet, observed, "We could see the battleships firing at the coast. And literally you could have walked, if you took big steps, from one side of the Channel to the other. There were that many ships out there." But the sight of the approaching armada frightened the Germans stationed on the coast. One German officer marvelled, "It's impossible...there can't be that many ships in the world."*4 Thus as the power of the British Empire began to wane after the Second World War, a new Anglo-Saxon military superpower arose to take her place. Britain's brother, Manasseh, the American fellow Israelite people, had already come to her rescue twice in both world wars, and both times her intervention saved the day. With the fearsome explosion of the atom bomb on Hiroshima in 1945, a new, militarily awesomely powerful nation had made its terrifying *début* on the world stage. Ever since that time the American brothers of *'good old England'* have militarily dominated our planet. The U.S. Navy, with her giant aircraft carriers like floating cities in the sea, her nuclear submarines, her Tomahawk and Attack cruise missiles and huge fleet of warships, patrols the great oceans and seas of the globe. No army in the world can withstand her invisible Stealth bombers and her precision guided Joint Direct Attack Munitions and bombs, as well as her fearsome fleets of Apache Attack helicopters with their deadly Hellfire missiles. Her sinister pilotless drones are able to spew death and destruction with total precision, strike fear into the minds of her enemies. Her technological lead over the other nations in the development of new weapons is constantly increasing by leaps and bounds, leaving the rest of the world way behind in her wake. Her highly sophisticated satellites can tap into all the secret plans of her enemies at will.

In the late 1990s Kosovo conflict in the former Yugoslavia, she demonstrated that she could even win a war without suffering any casualties, by utilising her overwhelming air power alone. Today, after the break-up of the former Soviet Union in the early nineties, she is the sole military superpower in the world. Her defence budget is a staggering at $640 billion represents 3.8 percent of America's GDB, and is equal to 36.6 percent of the total defence spending of the world. *5 Just as it was in the days of his brother Ephraim's British Empire, when Britannia "ruled the waves", so now we find that with Manasseh's U.S.A. There is no one around who would dare challenge her awesome might. Could all of this just be happenstance? The words of Sir Winston Churchill come to mind:

"He must indeed have a blind soul who cannot see that some great purpose is being worked out here below!"

With just one exception — England never lost a war

The prophet Micah made an astonishing prophecy about the remnant of Jacob *vis-à-vis* her enemies:

"And the remnant of Jacob shall be amongst the Gentiles, in the midst of many peoples, like a lion among the beasts of the forest . . . who, if he passes through, both treads down and tears in pieces, and none can deliver. Your hand shall be lifted against your adversaries, and all your enemies shall be cut off." (Micah 5:8-9)

This prophecy has come true for the English nation, as the English people have never lost a war of note since the Norman Conquest by William the Conqueror in 1066. These Normans themselves were Israelites, being of good Viking stock, originating primarily from the tribe of Benjamin, when William the Conqueror came to England to claim his right to the throne. Thus even the famous conquest of England by the Normans of Normandy, when seen in its proper context, was merely a family affair. Micah's prophesy forms part of the 'Birthright' of the English, and the prophecy that England's enemies shall be 'cut off' has certainly come true.

It was in direct fulfilment of this prophecy that the four invasions planned respectively by Philip II of Spain, Louis the XIV of France, Napoleon Bonaparte of France, and Adolph Hitler of Germany ended in their ignominious defeats. As we have already seen, part of the 'Birthright blessing' was: *"Let peoples serve you, and nations bow down to you"*. But the Divine Covenant contained even stronger words than these, as the further promise given to Abraham and his descendants was:

"Cursed be everyone who curses you and blessed be those who bless you." (Genesis 27:28-29)

Thus when England was attacked it would automatically bring a divine curse upon the aggressor. This can be seen in many of England's most decisive battles, where divine Providence seemed to play a most decisive role, such as in the defeat of the Spanish Armada, the miraculous escape from Dunkirk, the defeat of Rommel at the battle of El Alamein, and the D-Day invasion onto the Normandy beaches in 1944, to name but a few. In all of these battles, together with many others, the advantage was won through the providential assistance of the elements. Sir Winston Churchill made reference to this very thing in a speech he gave in October 1942, whilst addressing mine owners and workers' delegates. This is what he said:

"I sometimes have the feeling of interference. I want to stress that. I have the feeling sometimes that some guiding hand has interfered. I have a feeling that we have a GUARDIAN because we have a great Cause, and we shall have that Guardian as long as we serve that Cause faithfully; and what a Cause it is."

Maybe he was thinking of the 'Battle of Britain', or maybe he remembered the miracle of Dunkirk. When studying the wars and battles of England it becomes obvious that the English have a divine Guardian who especially intervenes, often through the blowing of a great wind or at strategic times through the stilling of the wind and bringing a great calm. The latter happened at Dunkirk, when the notoriously rough seas of the English Channel became exceptionally calm for **four days and nights**, whilst the British expeditionary forces were being rescued out of the jaws of death from Dunkirk's beaches. At the same time, further inland, the foulest of weather immobilized the German *Luftwaffe*, effectively preventing them from attacking the continuous flotillas of rescue vessels.

All of this has a most ancient echo of the time when our Israelite ancestors were making their miraculous escape from another oppressor. We have all heard of the account of ancient Israel's great Exodus from Egypt when nearly **three million Israelites** were able to escape the murderous Egyptian army by miraculously crossing the Red Sea. The God of Israel used the elements against the Egyptian army. He used a Pillar of Cloud to shroud them in a dark mist, as they approached the helpless Israelites trapped at the edge of the Sea. The cloud produced darkness on the Egyptian side and yet it was light on the Israelite side. Then he dried up the Red Sea with a mighty east wind, so much so that the fleeing Israelites were able to cross the Sea on dry land. Then when the Egyptian army were permitted to pursue their quarry again, as the Pillar of Cloud had lifted towards early morning, the Lord caused water to gently seep back so that the Egyptian chariot wheels became stuck in the mud. The moment the last Israelite had safely reached the other shore, he caused the waters to return with a great and mighty wind and the entire Egyptian army perished in the depth of the sea. After their miraculous escape from their Egyptian oppressors, Moses led them in a song of victory. As the children of Israel were singing to the Lord with great joy, celebrating the victory over Pharaoh, they sang:

The LORD is a MAN OF WAR; the LORD is his name. Pharaoh's chariots and his army he has cast into the sea . . . **You blew with Your wind, the sea covered them; they sank like lead in the mighty waters."** (Exodus 15:3-4, 10 – Emphasis added)

The prophet Isaiah confirms the words of Micah and Moses as he specifically addresses the **'*coastlands*'** or **the Israel in the '*isles*'**, as he writes the following:

"Those who war against you shall be as nothing, as a non-existent thing. For I, the LORD your God, will hold your right hand, saying to you, 'Fear not, I will help you'. . . Behold, I will make you into a new threshing sledge with sharp teeth; you shall thresh the mountains and beat them small, and make the hills like chaff. You shall winnow them, **the wind shall carry them away, and the whirlwind shall scatter them."** (Isaiah 41:12-13; 15-16 – Emphasis added)

Perhaps this is what impressed itself upon Winston Churchill's mind when he was obviously speaking from the heart, he said: *"I have the feeling we have a 'Guardian' "*. According to Isaiah, Churchill was right, as the promise is that *the Lord their God would hold ISRAEL'S right hand and he would help them* (Isaiah 41:13).

The most amazing fulfilment of this prophecy was the destruction of the "invincible" Spanish Armada. Ironically, in official Spanish documents of the time, the invasion fleet was named *'La felicissima Armada'* – 'the most fortunate fleet.' The arch-Catholic Philip II of Spain had been promised a million gold ducats by Pope Sixtus V of Rome. A predecessor of this Pope had previously exhorted his Catholic followers in England to kill Queen Elizabeth I, as anyone who performed this task would be *"received as a martyr in heaven"*. It just goes to show that Islam did not think of it first! Commit murder and you will become a martyr in heaven! There is the whole world and his wife thinking that the Ayatollah Khomeini was the first religious leader to pronounce a *'fatwa'*. Well, never mind, the world obviously got that wrong, as the Popes of Rome beat him to the idea some five hundred years ago!

In the battle against the Spanish fleet the Anglo-Dutch fleet only managed to capture, sink or otherwise immobilize about ten of the 130 ships in the mighty Armada. Admirals Drake and Howard had forced the Spanish fleet out of Calais with fire-ships and managed to drive them towards the Flemish coast intending to get them into the North Sea. The battle at Gravelines began at daybreak and lasted until sunset. The Spanish were completely defeated with some 40,000 casualties, and many wounded. The English cut off their retreat through the Channel and then an Atlantic gale swept the Spaniards into the North Sea. The Armada now numbering 120 ships undertook to sail round Britain via Scotland and Ireland and thus make for safe harbor in Spain. Once the fleet reached the Orkney Islands they were dispersed by a great storm. Some of them foundered. About thirty were afterwards wrecked by gales on the west coast of Ireland. Those of the crews who escaped to the shores were generally killed, and it was calculated that a further 14,000 perished in this way. Less than half of the fleet managed to limp home to Spain, where the defeat of the Armada caused a spirit of depression and defeatism amongst the people. Thus *'the most fortunate fleet'* had not been so fortunate after all!

Historians are almost unanimous in their agreement that this battle in the Channel had been one of the most decisive battles in the history of the world. The Great God of Israel, in order to defend his 'Birthright' people, had sent a wind to carry away this so-called 'Invincible Armada' and a whirlwind to scatter them.

After the defeat of the Spanish Armada, Queen Elizabeth I had a special medal struck with the inscription: *"Deus flavit, et dissipati sunt"* (God blew, and they were scattered!).

These words more than summed up our miraculous deliverance from the evil intent of the Popes of Rome and Philip II of Spain. In the 'Birthright' blessing spoken by Jacob over the sons of Joseph, the dying Patriarch spoke the following prophetic words:

*"The archers have bitterly grieved him, shot at him and hated him. **But his bow remained in strength, and the arms of his hands were made strong by the hands of the Mighty God of Jacob . . . by the God of your father who will help you, and by the Almighty who will bless you."** (Genesis 49:23-25)*

England, above all the nations on the face of the earth, has the matchless record of not having lost a war of any note or consequence. In the last 950 years, England has never lost a war and has never been invaded or subjugated by foreign troops. Maybe this record was also on Hitler's mind, when he wrote his famous book *Mein Kampf*. These are his words:

"The British nation can be counted on to carry through to victory any struggle that it once enters upon, no matter how long the struggle may last, no matter how great the sacrifice that may have to be made, and no matter what means may have to be employed; and all this even though the actual military equipment to hand may be utterly inadequate compared with that of other nations" (Adolph Hitler, *Mein Kampf*, chapter 12, page 25).

You see, sometimes it takes a rank outsider like Hitler to observe the truth about Great Britain's remarkable history. Hitler's words have an almost prophetic ring to them, as the British certainly faced overwhelming odds in 1940, when they stood alone against the Third Reich. Their equipment certainly was no match in terms of quantity or quality, compared to the awesome German war machine that had just rolled all over Europe.

England and France—a Love/Hate relationship

Over the centuries England has had her setbacks on the high seas, as well as on land, and she has lost many a battle, but the fact is that **she has never lost a war**. A most fascinating aspect of English history is that the English ever since the Norman Conquest in 1066, fought thirty wars against France alone, and she won every single one of them. *6 The English and the French seem to have a love/hate relationship that has its origins in the distant past. History testifies to the fact that since time immemorial there has always been an intense rivalry between these two nations. The reason for this is that the ruling tribe of France is Reuben, the firstborn son of the patriarch Jacob, whereas Joseph was Jacob's eleventh son. Reuben sinned against his father, as he defiled his father's bed and he thus disqualified himself from inheriting the leadership position, as embodied in the right of the firstborn. Reuben was passed over and the blessing of the birthright was awarded to his younger brother Joseph instead. The ruling tribe of England just happens to be Ephraim, the younger son of Joseph. This ancient resentment at being passed over has imprinted itself into the DNA of Reuben, and has been simmering in the breasts of his French descendants ever since that time. It is in France's national character to always want to have the pre-eminence, and, history teaches us they really cannot stand it when it goes to either Great Britain or to the United States. Basically they feel that they are entitled to be number one, as somehow subconsciously they seem to sense that the blessing of the birthright should have gone to them.

On occasions the English would lose the first, the second and maybe even the third round in a war against her enemies, but she never lost the last round. Sometimes she won the war only to let her gains slip later on. At other times she won the war only to subsequently lose the peace, but even so, she never lost a war. Could this be true? It certainly is not true of the French, as the English beat them in war countless times – and so did the Germans for that matter. It also is not true of the Germans, the Italians, or the Japanese, as Great Britain defeated them all in World War II, ably assisted by her Commonwealth and American brothers.

The Dutch in the last 500 years have been invaded no less than three times, first by the Spanish, then the French, and finally by the Germans. The Belgians suffered a similar fate only more so, as the Spanish invaded and occupied her for eighty years. Napoleon used Belgium as his military doormat in his pursuit of greater conquests, whereas the Germans invaded them three times. Even Russia has suffered defeats in war at the hands of Sweden, Poland, France, England, Germany, Afghanistan, Chechnya, and just recently she lost even the Cold War against America and Great Britain. The Turks cannot lay claim to this proud record either, as the British fought and dispatched their mighty Ottoman Empire from the face of the Middle East in the aftermath of the First World War. Even the United States of America cannot say she has won every war she has fought, as she lost the Vietnam War, no question! Also she did not really win the Korean War either, as at very best it might be called a draw. Neither has she won the recent War against Terror, in the case of Iraq and Afghanistan. Can it really be true that the English over a period of some nine hundred years have never lost a major war?

Only one exception!

In nine centuries of sublime victories in war there was just one exception! Britain decidedly did not win the American War of Independence. As we have already seen in chapter ten, the prophet Isaiah in his mysterious and rarely understood prophecy stated that *'Manasseh shall devour Ephraim and Ephraim Manasseh'* (Isaiah 9:19-21). Manasseh devouring Ephraim and Ephraim in turn devouring Manasseh cannot mean anything other than war. History records that after a long and bitter struggle America defeated the British, and won her freedom and emerged as an independent and great nation. The European view of Britain's resounding defeat and the loss of America was expressed by none other than the Hapsburg Holy Roman Emperor Joseph II of Austria who – like others – thought the country had *"fallen entirely and forever descended to the status of a second rank power"*. *7 Nevertheless, despite their defeat the British then went on to build the greatest empire the world had ever seen. In fact after the loss of her thirteen American colonies from 1783 the British, in direct fulfilment of God's Covenantal Promise, went on to acquire 103 Imperial Territories. *8 Nevertheless, to only lose one war in nine hundred years is an extraordinary record for any nation to be able to claim. In this unique record we have yet further proof of God's divine favor upon Ephraim. We have historical evidence of God's hand in human affairs in faithfully fulfilling his prophetic word. We have therefore, even in this further proof of the 'Birthright' blessing resting upon the English-speaking descendants of the Hebrew Patriarchs Jacob and Joseph.

CHAPTER TWO

❧❧

6th Sign
Israel was to possess the gate(s) of her enemies

After Abraham had passed the ultimate test of faith by showing willingness to sacrifice Isaac, his only begotten son of the Covenant by his wife Sarah, God made the promise of the Birthright unconditional. The angel of the Lord called out of heaven and said:

*"By myself have I sworn, says the Lord, because you have done this thing, and have not withheld your son, your only son – **blessing I will bless you, and multiplying I will multiply your descendants as the stars of the heaven and as the sand which is on the seashore; AND YOUR DESCENDANTS SHALL POSSESS THE GATE OF THEIR ENEMIES"** (Genesis 22:17 – emphasis added).

Abraham sent the chief steward of his household on a mission to find a bride for Isaac amongst Abraham's relatives. The servant was led to Rebecca, who was the daughter of Bethuel, the son of Abraham's brother Nahor. As he was about to leave with Isaac's intended bride, her relatives spoke a prophetic blessing over Rebecca saying:

*"Our sister, may you become the mother of thousands of ten thousands; **AND MAY YOUR DESCENDANTS POSSESS THE GATES OF THOSE WHO HATE THEM"** (Genesis 24:60 – emphasis added).

This same Rebecca became the mother of Jacob, whose name was later changed to Israel. Thus it is through Rebecca's descendants, through the offspring of Jacob that the unconditional blessing of the 'Birthright' has come down to us today. This is why, in direct fulfilment of prophecy, the Anglo-Saxons have, over a period of four centuries, come into the possession of most of the major 'sea gates' of the world. These sea gates are the vital strategic maritime choke points that give whoever possesses them complete control over passage. Gates are entrances and these sea gates are now called "ports." Gibraltar is one of the best examples, as its fortress is able to control both the entrance and the exit of the Mediterranean Sea. Malta and Cyprus, Alexandria, the Suez Canal, Aden, Somalia, Ceylon, India, Hong Kong, Singapore, Malaysia, Sarawak, Northern Borneo, the American colony of the Philippines, the American controlled Panama Canal and Porto Rico, Papua New Guinea, the Faros and Solomon Islands, Australia and New Zealand, Cape of Good Hope, Newfoundland, Canada, the West Indian colonies plus the Falkland Islands, are just some of these strategic choke points. The incredible fact of history is that Great Britain came into possession of nearly all of the militarily strategic sea gates in the world. Thus in the heyday of her empire she was able to project her global power and impose her will upon the nations of the world.

Britain had more naval stations beyond her own shores than all of the other maritime nations combined. Apart from her mighty naval bases dotted at strategic points around the globe, in 1907 she had no less than 37 coaling stations as well, all of them situated at strategic locations. We only need to look at an early twentieth century map of the world to see how totally the English have fulfilled this prophecy. To quote Daniel Webster's splendid eulogy on Britain's greatness:

"England is a power to which for purposes of foreign conquest and subjugation, Rome, in the height of her glory, is not to be compared; a power which has dotted the surface of the whole globe with her possessions and military posts, whose morning drumbeat following the sun, and keeping company with the hours, circle the earth daily with one continuous and unbroken strain of the martial airs of England."

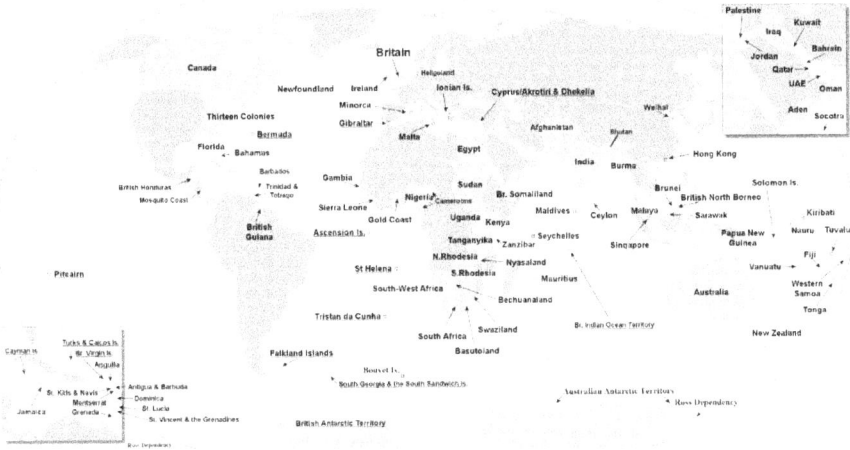

The British Empire
(shown in the lighter tone)
(courtesy The Red Hat of Pat Ferrick, Wikimedia)

Praise from a Frenchman?

To understand the remarkable extent to which this aspect of the 'Birthright' prophecy has been fulfilled, we can do no better than look at the testimony of M. Dupin, an admiring French historian, who in 1826 wrote the following words:

"In Europe the British Empire borders at once towards the north upon Germany, upon Holland, upon France; towards the south upon Spain, upon Sicily, upon Italy, upon Western Turkey. It holds the keys of the Adriatic and the Mediterranean; it commands the mouth of the Black Sea as well as the Baltic. In America it boundaries to Russia, towards the Pole; and in the United States towards the temperate region. Under the Torrid Zone it reigns in the midst of the Antilles, encircles the Gulf of Mexico. In Africa from the center island devoted of yore, under the symbol of the cross, to the safety of every Christian flag, the British Empire enforces from the Barbary States [North Africa] *that respect which they pay to no other power. From the foot of the Pillars of Hercules* [Gibraltar]*, it carries dread to the remotest provinces of Morocco. On the shores of the Atlantic it has built the forts of the Gold Coast and of the Lion's Mountain* [Sierra Leone]*. It is from thence*

31

that it attaches to the soil the freed men whom it snatches from the trade in slaves."

The final line in the above section of Dupin's rare French eulogy of the British Empire is a reference to Britain's pivotal role in the abolition of the international slave trade. In the early 1800s, Christian activists such as Wilberforce turned England strongly anti-slavery, and subsequently the Royal Navy, the only power on the earth with the necessary clout to do so, enforced an end to the African slave trade.

On the same continent, beyond the tropics, at the point nearest to the Australian pole, it has possessed shelter under the very Cape of Storms [Cape of Good Hope]. *From this new focus of action and of conquest, it casts its eyes towards India; it discovers, it seizes the stations of most importance to its commercial progress, and thus renders itself the exclusive ruler over the passes of Africa from the East of another hemisphere. Finally, as much dread in the Persian Gulf and the Aegean Sea as in the Pacific Ocean and the Indian Archipelago, the British Empire, the Possessor of the finest countries of the East, beholds its factors reign over **800** million subjects. The conquests of its merchants in Asia begin where those of Alexander ceased, and where the terminus of the Romans could not reach. At this moment, from the banks of the Indus to the frontier of China, from the mouth of the Ganges to the mountains of Tibet, all acknowledge the sway of a mercantile company* [East India Company] *shut up in a narrow street in the city of London"* *1

When an enemy praises you it is praise indeed. The above words were written in 1826, not long after Napoleon Bonaparte's final defeat at the Battle of Waterloo. It was Britain's control of the seas that had thwarted Napoleon's plans for conquest time and again. He attempted to seize Egypt with the intent of wresting control of the Middle East and from there to gain control over India, that most fabulous of imperial prizes. His dream came to an abrupt end when Horatio Nelson destroyed the French fleet in the now famous Battle of the Nile. "**Overnight, the Mediterranean became an English**

Sea." Napoleon's army, although intact, was stranded in Egypt. Bonaparte could not march to India, which had been his plan all along – without a fleet behind to supply him. He tried to move up through the Levant [Eastern Mediterranean], but a British naval squadron stopped him at Acre. *'If it had not been for you English, I'd have been Emperor of the East,'* he said later; *'But wherever there is water to float a ship we find you English in the way.'* *2 Thus even Napoleon himself, without necessarily meaning to do so, praised the Brits for their naval prowess and supremacy.

"England expects that every man will do his duty"

Napoleon made up his mind to conquer Britain. He raised an army, which he called the *'Army of England'*. In his arrogance he even struck a medal in honour of the conquest of Britain, which as we know never took place, and he even most presumptuously engraved upon the medal, *'Struck at London'*, despite the fact that his army never reached there. The British built a huge chain of defensive towers called Martello Towers and other military defences all around the southeast coast of England. Meanwhile, Admiral Nelson swept the seas in search of the French and Spanish fleets. The enemy was finally located in Trafalgar Bay, off the coast of Spain. A few days before the engagement, Nelson wrote to a friend:

"Here I am watching for the French and the Spaniards like a cat after the mice. If they come out, I know I shall catch them; but I am also almost sure that I shall be killed doing it."

On the eve of the battle Nelson uttered the following prayer: *"May the Great God whom I worship grant to my country and for the benefit of Europe in general a great and glorious victory, and may no misconduct in anyone tarnish it. May humanity after victory be the predominant feature in the British Fleet. For myself, I commit my life to Him who made me, and may His blessing alight on my endeavours for serving my country faithfully; to Him I resign myself and the just cause which is entrusted to me to defend."*

Then on October 21, 1805 the battle began. Every captain in the fleet had received his orders and knew exactly what to do. But Nelson felt there was still something wanting, and from the top of his own ship, the *Victory*, a message was signalled through all the fleet: *"England expects that every man will do his duty"*. The message was greeted with cheer upon cheer from every ship along the line, and every sailor felt his courage rise *3

253	269	863	261	471	958	220	370	4	21	19	24
England	expects	that	every	man	will	do	his	D	U	T	Y

Nelson's famous signal, relayed using Popham's "Telegraphic Signals of Marine Vocabulary"
(courtesy Ipankonin, Wikimedia)

Nelson's premonition of his death in battle proved true, as a French sniper, noticing his magnificent admiral's uniform, shot him and mortally wounded him in the stomach. As the great admiral lay dying, Hardy, the captain of the Victory, was able to bring him the news that victory was theirs. His last words were: *"I am satisfied now, thank God I have done my duty."*

After the battle of Trafalgar, Napoleon's power by sea was utterly shattered, and once again Providence had seen to it that Britain was saved from all fear of invasion. That little ribbon of water between the Imperial France of Napoleon and Great Britain was enough to keep her safe from the threats of the then master of half of Europe.

James Morris in his *Pax Britannica* beautifully sums up the situation that prevailed at the time: "The English posture abroad was habitually one of command. To the educated Englishman responsibility came naturally. No other Power had been so strong for so long, so stable in its institutions and so victorious in its wars; and Britain's naval supremacy really did give the country a measure of universal sovereignty, that immemorial dream of conquerors. In theory no other state could ship an army across the seas without British consent, and in practice the merchant shipping of the rest of the world was largely dependent upon British cables and coaling stations. The presence of the sea, at once insulating the Mother Country and linking it with the Empire, gave the British an imperial confidence. *'I do not say the French cannot come,'* Admiral St Vincent had once remarked; *'I only say they cannot come by sea'* " *4

Reluctantly, France, Spain and the other nations were forced to acknowledge the inevitable fact that British supremacy over the high seas was absolute. Britannia truly ruled the waves!

Just as in all the other aspects of the 'Birthright' blessing given to the Anglo-American sons of Joseph, the blessing came to Ephraim/England first. It was only after Great Britain had established her total dominance and supremacy over the seven seas, that towards the latter part of the nineteenth century, American sea power came to the fore. This enabled the Americans to achieve a quick victory over Spain in the Spanish-American War of 1898. Later on, the Anglo-American dominance of the high seas was crucial in their victory over the Central powers in World War I and the Axis powers in World War II.

America — the world's sole superpower

America, much like Britain before her, has long held military bases all over the world. A number of these are positioned in the territory of her enemies and some of them, like Britain's permanent bases on Cyprus and Gibraltar, are 'sovereign' bases, the sovereign territory of the United States, such as the Wheeler Airbase in Libya, the Guantanamo Bay base in Cuba, and the giant US base on the island of Okinawa in Japan. The USA has over 761 strategic military bases all over the world on every continent and in every ocean. According to the Pentagon's own figures there is a U.S. military presence, large or small, in 132 of the 193 member states of the United Nations. In American 'military speak' it is called 'forward deployment', and the effect of this policy is that there is no place on earth outside of America's reach. She is well and truly continuing in the tradition set by her brother Ephraim before her in the British Empire. They are the 'gates' of her enemies, and these 'gates' or access points give her an enormous strategic advantage. It is interesting to note that only Great Britain and the United States of America have consistently followed this strategy of establishing foreign bases at, or close to, strategic sea gates or military important locations on land. Most people are unaware how utterly unique this is. Neither China, nor India, two of the most populous nations on the face of the earth, has any bases on foreign soil. Japan, the third largest economy in the world, has none. The Russians have a few in their own backyard. Only the former colonial powers of Great Britain and France still have military bases on foreign soil in reasonable numbers. France too is a nation of Hebrew origin, as Reuben, the elder son of Jacob, is the ruling tribe of the French people, and as such the covenantal promise made to Abrahams descendants applies to her too. Yet, Reuben, having defiled his father's bed, lost the blessing of the birthright, which had he not sinned would have been his, as the firstborn son of Jacob. *5 Not counting her bases in Afghanistan, Great Britain has 21 foreign bases leftover as a legacy of her former empire, whilst France still has 20 military outposts in her former colonial possessions.*6

The United States alone has stepped in Great Britain's former imperial shoes, only much more so. The precise number of her foreign military establishments is difficult to figure, as estimates vary wildly between 750 and 1,800. Today, according to published figures by the Pentagon, the American flag flies over 750 military sites in foreign nations and U.S territories abroad. This figure does not include small foreign sites of less than ten acres. Neither does it include over 400 sites in Afghanistan, or indeed those nations where the local governments for domestic political or religious reasons do not wish it to **be known that they have such bases on their soil.**

In the grand scheme of things, the actual numbers aren't all that important. Whether the most accurate total is 900, 1,000 or 1,100 posts in foreign lands, what is undeniable is that the U.S. military maintains, in Chalmers Johnson's famous phrase, "an empire of bases so large and so shadowy that no one – not even at the Pentagon – really knows its full size and scope." *7

Apart from this overwhelming global presence on land, the U.S. Navy has seven fleets, which patrol all the oceans of the world. Her aircraft carriers are the largest ships in the world. The U.S. boasts 11 such carriers, town-sized floating bases that can travel the world to any of more than a 100 ports of call worldwide, from Hong Kong to Rio de Janeiro. *8

Just as it was all prophesied some four thousand years ago, it has all been perfectly fulfilled only and exclusively by Britain and America, those two intrepid latter-day sons of Joseph. God's covenantal promise to Abraham has thus come true in the history of that *"Company/Commonwealth of Nations, and that Great Nation"*, which Jacob spoke about, as he passed on the blessing of the birthright to his two grandsons Ephraim and Manasseh, the two sons of Joseph. *9

Controlling the Gates of space

Remember that God promised Abraham: *"Your descendants shall possess the GATE of their enemies"* (Genesis 22:17). In the past Britain "ruled the waves" and almost all of the major sea-lanes and strategic sea-passes were under British control. The world has moved on since that time and nowadays sea-movement is less important than it used to be. Today it is Space that has become the most important strategic area. It is no accident, therefore, that in fulfilment of the 'Birthright' prophecy, the U.S.A. today possesses total control of Space. Its technology is streets ahead of its major competitors. It has satellites and missiles that can reach any part of the earth, whether for the purpose of attack or surveillance. Through its control of Space the Americans have avenues of entry (Gates) that enable them to observe every move of their potential enemies. Other nations have commanded empires and enjoyed near global power. For example the Ottoman Turkish Empire and even the Russians, Germans, French and Spanish at times have wielded formidable power in the world, where for a time they were unassailable. Yet none of them applied the principle of acquiring and possessing 'gates' as a deliberate and conscious part of their military strategy. This principle, however, has always been an integral part of British and American military planning. The British and American people are the only ones in all of history who have so totally in every detail fulfilled this prophecy. Could this really be yet another coincidence?

CHAPTER THREE

❧❧

7ᵗʰ Sign
Israel was to acquire great wealth and become an economic giant

"Therefore may God give you of the dew of heaven, of the fatness of the earth, and plenty of grain and wine. Let peoples serve you, and nations bow down to you. Be master over your brethren, and let your mother's sons bow down to you. Cursed be everyone who curses you, and blest be those who bless you!"

(Genesis 27:28-29)

"For the Lord your God will bless you just as He has promised you; you shall lend to many nations, but you shall not borrow; you shall reign over many nations, but they shall not reign over you."

(Deuteronomy 15:6)

Joseph's name in the Hebrew language means prosperity, and it follows therefore that his descendants have inherited this same trait. After his treacherous brothers had sold him as a slave, Joseph ended up in the household of Potiphar, who was the Captain of Pharaoh's Royal Guard. This leader of men soon recognized Joseph's extraordinary talent, and thus he put him in charge as the Chief Steward of his substantial household. Genesis 39:2 records the following: *"And the LORD was with Joseph, and he was a **prosperous** man"* (KJV – editor's emphasis). Some of you will be familiar as to what happened to Joseph next. Potiphar's wife took a fancy to this

39

young Hebrew man and wanted him to go to bed with her. However, Joseph strenuously resisted her advances out of loyalty to his master and to God. Do you remember the saying: *"Heav'n has no rage, like love to hatred turned, Nor Hell a fury, like a woman scorn'd"?* Well, Potiphar's wife was no exception, and she cried: *"Rape!"* The result was that Joseph lost his job and was thrown into Pharaoh's dungeon. The prison Governor immediately recognized Joseph's exceptional talent for leadership – so much so, that he put him in charge of all the prisoners. Yet again, *Israel's History Book* records this key attribute of Joseph: in Genesis 39:23 we read: *"The keeper of the prison did not look into anything that was under Joseph's authority, because the LORD was with him; and whatever he did, the LORD made it prosper"*.

Next we see this same Joseph elevated to the position of executive ruler over the entire Egyptian empire, and he ends up feeding much of the known world. What an extraordinary track record of leadership and organizational ability! Joseph certainly lived up to his name of 'prosperity'!

Great Britain and America are the modern day descendants of this man Joseph, and it clearly is no mere coincidence that each of these two nations in turn has held the record of being the most prosperous nation the world has ever seen. One of the key components of the 'Birthright' blessing on Ephraim and Manasseh, the sons of Joseph, was the promise of wealth 'beyond compare'. As early as the 19th Century, the British and American people had between them acquired almost three-quarters of all the cultivated wealth of the world. All other nations combined possessed barely more than a quarter!

If we are to locate the descendants of Ephraim and Manasseh today we need only to look for a Commonwealth of Nations and a Great Nation, that are in possession of the earth's choicest agricultural, mineral and industrial wealth.

Great Britain was a 'prosperous man'

The Scripture, *"The LORD was with Joseph, and he was a prosperous man!"* (Genesis 39:2), could just as easily be applied to Great Britain. In 1800 the British Empire suddenly came of age as it sprang forth onto the world scene. History itself is our witness that for the next 100 or more years it could well be said of her that:

"The LORD was with Great Britain, and he was a prosperous man!"

By this time she had already acquired all of Canada, and a number of other colonies in the Caribbean and West Indies. Gibraltar had been a British fortress guarding the entrance to the Mediterranean Sea since 1704. Sir Robert Clive had already laid the foundations of empire in India, which later on was to become the Jewel in the British Crown. Ceylon was added in 1795, and then, at the turn of the century, came in quick succession Malaysia, Singapore, Borneo, Brunei, Sarawak, and Burma. The expansion of the Empire became an unstoppable process. Possessions literally seemed to fall into Britain's lap all the time. Many of them came to Britain without a shot being fired in anger. Australia, Tasmania and New Zealand acceded to Britain's Imperial Crown in the early years of the nineteenth century. Add to this some sixteen major African territories at strategic positions in the east, west and south of the African continent, and Britain also established her rule over Egypt, Sudan and Somaliland in the northeast, thereby bringing the whole of Africa under her strategic control.

The Imperial red color of the British Empire continuously swallowed more of the world atlas, until it could be said for the first time in the history of the world that *the sun never set on the British Empire!* Up till then in history it had never been possible to say this of any world empire. The Egyptians, the Babylonians, the Greeks under Alexander the Great, and indeed the mighty Roman Empire could never lay claim to this proud boast, and neither has it been possible for any empire since then to match it. By the mid-nineteenth century, Great Britain was in possession of a quarter of all the landmass of the globe and she ruled over 800 million subjects, representing a quarter of mankind. In just a hundred years, it truly had been an awesome progress from a relatively small offshore island to the greatest imperial power the world had ever seen. It most certainly could be said that: *"The LORD was with Great Britain, and he was a prosperous man!"*

The Industrial Revolution

From the middle of the 18th Century there was a marked acceleration in the speed of technological development. The historian and author E. J. Hobsbawm, wrote the following:

"The Industrial Revolution coincided with the history of a single country, Great Britain. An entire world economy was thus built on, or rather around, Britain, and this country therefore temporarily rose to a position of global influence and power unparalleled by any state of its relative size before or since, and unlikely to be paralleled by any state in the foreseeable future. There was a moment in world history when Britain can be described, if we are not too pedantic, as its only workshop, its only massive importer and exporter, its only carrier, its only imperialist, almost its only foreign investor; and for that reason its only naval power and the only one which had a genuine world policy" *1

The British were the pacesetters in this revolution, as most of the great inventions such as the 'flying shuttle', the 'water loom', the 'power loom' and the 'steam engine' were the inventions of British engineers. This in turn led to the age of mass production, where former cottage industries such as weaving and pottery, moved from peoples' homes into huge factories. This was soon followed by the age of the railways, as George Stephenson built *The Rocket*, which was capable of travelling at the unheard of speed of 30 miles an hour. Railway mania soon set in, with the nation's resources being galvanised to build railway tracks across the whole of the British Isles. In 1837 young Princess Victoria saw her first steam train and marvelled at its 'surprising quickness'. Thirty-five years later there were 14,000 miles of railway track, and in that same period passenger traffic had increased by a staggering 1,400 percent.

In all the major cities huge railway stations were built. They were enormously impressive buildings, which subsequently became known as the "Cathedrals" of the industrial age. British engineers then went to build railways all over the world in Canada, Australia, India, Africa and South America, as rapid transport was the essential fuel for the Industrial Revolution. The railroad fired the imagination, and the leading engineers like Isambard Kingdom Brunel and Thomas Brassey became heroes. They were the astronauts of their day. The U.S. too were bitten by the railway bug and started building tracks right across the North American continent from north to south and east to west. Come the early 1900s, the total railway mileage of the U.S. and the British Empire was twice the railway mileage of the rest of the world. *2

The domination of the seven seas

Perhaps the most extraordinary development of all was the way the British merchant fleet dominated the world during the 19th Century and beyond. In 1904, the tonnage of merchant vessels belonging to the British Empire reached 40.5 percent of the tonnage of the world. That same year the merchant navy of the Empire employed no less than 478,320 sailors and crew. It wasn't just that she possessed more ships than anyone else, but also that the quality and speed of her vessels were simply in a different league. In those days Britain enjoyed a huge technological advantage over her competitor nations. In an age when many nations were still transporting their goods in sailing ships, the British Merchant Navy was almost fully converted to steam. Britain possessed nearly two and a half times as many steam powered vessels as America, who had the second largest merchant fleet. She had no less than five times as many steam ships as Germany, who had the next largest merchant fleet. Her position at the turn of the 19th Century was unassailable, as

British vessels earned more than fifty percent of the world's total merchant-shipping turnover. *3

Chief of the Nations

The prophet Jeremiah primarily addresses the Tribe of Ephraim in his 31st Chapter and refers to her as the 'CHIEF OF THE NATIONS'. Ephraim is the chief of the Tribes of Israel, as she is the inheritor of the 'Birthright' promise God made to the patriarchs Abraham, Isaac and Jacob (Genesis 49:13-20; 22-26). The character of Joseph certainly has come out in the British, as they with supreme skill have designed, organized and set in place the systems that even today manage and control the world's global commerce. They did so in banking, in marine insurance, in the design of financial instruments such as gilt-edged securities, in the development of stock markets and in the transfer of shares. Raising extra capital through the issuing of new shares was an English invention, which transformed the international market place and provided the financial fuel for global expansion of trade. They led the world in developing accounting and auditing standards, as well as in corporate governance. They designed and operated the world's commodity markets in which all the world's commodity prices were set on a daily basis, governed by the laws of supply and demand. It was Adam Smith who laid the foundation for our prosperity today in his benchmark book *The Wealth of Nations*. Thus, just over two centuries ago, this Glasgow-born Scottish economist made the link between freedom and the market economy. Even today, in the 21st Century, the principles and yardsticks that underpin the foundations for the free flow of world trade still bear the mark 'MADE IN GREAT BRITAIN'. *4

The prosperity of the British Empire was almost beyond belief. Britain controlled and owned through her colonies, such as South Africa, Australia, Canada, India and Rhodesia, 60 percent of all the gold mined in the world. Through the diamond mines in South Africa she owned and controlled no less than 82.5 percent of the total world output in diamonds. The London Metal Exchange set the world prices for gold and silver, as well as for iron, steel, copper, lead, zinc, bauxite and most other metals and minerals. The London Baltic Exchange set the world prices for tea, coffee, cocoa beans and most other commodities. The London based British South Africa Company, set the world prices for diamonds and precious stones by carefully controlling the supply. Lloyds of London effectively set the world prices for Marine Insurance and she became the world's one-stop-shop for any form of commercial insurance. The London and Edinburgh based Life Insurance market became the largest in the world. The London Stock Exchange dominated world trade and was, comparatively speaking, equal in importance to Wall Street today. The London auction houses, such as Sotheby's, Christie's, Phillips and Bonham's, dominated the world's art market, and thereby effectively determined world prices for art.

As history is our witness, at the turn of the 19th Century, England burst ahead of her fellow nation-states in virtually every category of human economic, military, and political endeavour. By mid-century, the British were so far ahead in economic and industrial development, they could scarcely see who was in second place! Come the 1880s, London, including its prosperous suburbs, had become far and away the largest city in the world with a population fast approaching the five million mark. She had become the first megalopolis of the modern age. The Pound Sterling became by far the strongest and most sought after currency in the world. Britain's global economic domination was absolutely total for nearly 150 years measured from the late 18th Century until approximately the 1920/1930s.

In the Bible, that supreme history book of Israel, we find yet another statement written in the book of Deuteronomy 15:6, where the following promise is given:

"For the LORD your God will bless you just as He promised you; you shall lend to many nations, but you shall not borrow; you shall reign over many nations, but they shall not reign over you."

This promise was made to God's chosen people Israel. How remarkably true it has become of England. In 1881, foreign nations owed Great Britain the staggering sum of £2,800,000,000, and they were continually coming to borrow more. For that time this sum was so immense that it is hard to comprehend. When translated into a sum in some way reflecting the currency values of today, according to the Bank of England there has been an average rate of inflation of 3.6 percent in the period from 1881 to 2012. This means that we are looking at a figure just in excess of Twenty Eight Trillion Pounds Sterling, or around $48 Trillion U.S. Dollars! *5

As loan requests came in from some state or government in the world, it would be so heavily oversubscribed that most British lenders willing to lend would only be allocated a fraction of the amount they had offered. The loans were so enormous that the amount of interest in Britain alone was in excess of six million Pounds in a single month. In those days there was so much unemployed capital in London looking for a suitable home at 2 to 3 percent interest, yet enough borrowers could not be found.

The renowned historian Robert Briffault wrote: *"The world control of industrial and wave-ruling England did not become fully evident to the world until the middle of the 19th Century. The year of the Great Exhibition of 1851 may be regarded as marking the proclamation and recognition of that matchless power and influence . . . That power rested almost exclusively on the fact that England was first in the field of new economic conditions which transformed the world and displaced all other sources of wealth and economic control . . . The chief cause of their (the English) 'muddling through' was that they had more money!"* *6

Thus the prophecy that Joseph's latter day descendants would 'lend to many nations' came to perfect fulfilment. This prophecy of Moses also forecast that Joseph's sons would *'reign over many nations, but they shall not reign over you'.* The British Empire did indeed reign over many nations. Yet, we can see how this has been fulfilled in the realm of money too, as it is clear that *'he who pays the piper calls the tune'.* Wise King Solomon summed it up very nicely when he wrote: *"The borrower is servant to the lender".* Countless nations had become beholden to Great Britain in that they owed her millions, and as such Britain ruled over them indirectly, as she set the rules and called the tune. Yet again, it could be said that: *"The LORD was with Great Britain, and he was a prosperous man!"*

Some sixty-five years later, England's equally 'prosperous' brother Manasseh was able generously to distribute her Marshall Aid to the war ravaged countries of Europe. First Ephraim fulfilled this prophecy, then Manasseh. First the Birthright leader Britain, then America - the older brother following in his younger brother's footsteps, exactly as per God's promise to Jacob some 4,000 years ago, and as repeated by Jacob just prior to his death.*7 What an incredible fulfilment of prophecy! What really stands out is God's absolute faithfulness in keeping his promises to Jacob, the patriarchal father of Israel.

Britain and America's Inventive Genius

A key ingredient of the 'Birthright' blessing passed on by Jacob to the sons of Joseph is the gift of a most inventive mind. This providential gift has imparted in a small measure the creativity of God himself into the sons of Joseph. It is a gift so extraordinarily generous in its proportions that it has really put its recipients in a class altogether of their own. Britain can easily be classified as the most inventive individual nation on the face of the earth! This was certainly true in the early days of the British Empire, as British inventors opened the doors to whole new dimensions of industrial development. For instance in the years from 1701 to 1815, of all the major new inventions recorded in the world, a staggering 65 percent were British in origin. This must surely rank as an all-time world record for an individual nation to hold, as it is a totally unique record that has never been repeated by any nation. Just think what this means!

This little island nation for over a century was responsible for nearly two-thirds of all the major new inventions prior to the industrial revolution. If we count in the American inventions for the same period at 8 percent of the world total, the percentage of Anglo-Saxon inventive dominance rises to 73 percent. It is almost as if the rest of the world did not count! If we bring these figures a little closer to our modern times and measure all of the world's major inventions from 1701 to 1995, we find that these two sons of Joseph, Great Britain and America, between them are responsible for no less than 66 percent of new inventions. Let us pause and think about this for a moment: over the last 300 years Great Britain and America clocked up between them nearly two-thirds of all of the world's major new inventions. What a record to hold – and that over close to 300 years! This is a truly staggering feat. Surely this cannot be a mere accident! It is totally unprecedented and surely yet another amazing proof of the Birthright blessing that has come to these Israelite brother nations. *8

The inventive pendulum swings to America

Once again it is interesting to note that the British had the lion's share of the world's inventions in the early period of their Empire, whereas today the roles are reversed. From 1701 to 1885 the British had more inventions than any other nation on the earth, and America, while lagging well behind her, still managed to come second. However, from 1885 onwards we see exactly the opposite development, with America leading the way and Britain following in second place. To give an example of this, between 1932 and 1995 the United States and Great Britain between them were credited with 77 percent of all the world's major inventions. Britain's share of the total was a mere 22 percent, whereas the USA invented the remaining 55 percent. *9 Is it not fascinating to see the pattern of the Birthright blessing worked out in these two brother nations even in the realm of their inventiveness? Ephraim, alias Britain, achieves her prominence and excellence first, and then Manasseh, alias America, follows in Britain's glorious footsteps and takes over the supremacy. Once again, what a wonderful confirmation of prophecy this is!

The inventive record of the British is truly astonishing. If we just look at the subject of engines alone, it becomes almost a question of: Which engine did they **not** invent? They are credited with inventing the steam engine, the closed-circuit hot air engine, the electric engine, the water-cooled engine, the two-stroke internal engine, the rocket engine, the turbo-jet engine, as well as the turbo-fan engine, just to mention a few. Alexander Graham Bell, an Edinburgh-born Scotsman, who later immigrated to the USA, invented both the telephone and the gramophone. Another Scot, Sir Alexander Fleming, discovered penicillin in 1928. Isambard Kingdom Brunel built the first trans-Atlantic steamship in 1843. Sir Isaac Newton invented the telescope in 1672. In the realm of transport, the British invented the first locomotive, the first railway, the first steamboat, the first motorised bus, and the first tram and built the first underground railway. They also invented the aeroplane, the hovercraft, the Rover safety bicycle as well as pneumatic tyres. The computer and the computer programme are both British inventions, and so is television. Tim Berners-Lee, an Englishman, whilst working on a project in Geneva, invented the World Wide Web. Yes, even the Internet was a British invention! Think of all the huge industries that have sprung from these inventions alone and what incredible prosperity they have created in the world today. For a modern day example, just look at the phenomenal growth of the computer industry! It has become a veritable global economic colossus, which, with the advent of the Internet revolution, is experiencing further explosive growth.

Sir Isaac Newton, as early as 1665, explained the interaction of mass, gravity and acceleration. He also suggested that light was made of tiny particles. A New Zealander by the name of Ernest Rutherford working at Cambridge University is recognized as the father of nuclear physics, best known for demonstrating that atoms are made up of smaller particles called neutrons, electrons and protons. His research assistant from Eastbourne, Sir Frederic Soddy, came to explain the phenomenon of radioactive decay of atomic nuclei, thus paving the way for the development of nuclear energy. Ernest Rutherford, assisted by his German assistant Hans Geiger, also invented the Geiger counter for measuring levels of radioactivity.

From the Age of Steam to the Space Age

The British through their God-given inventive genius have given the world 'The Age of Steam', closely followed by 'The Age of Rail', followed by 'The Age of Motorised Travel', followed by 'The Age of Air Travel', followed by 'The Atomic Age', followed by 'The Age of Telecommunication' and, through her invention of the computer, finally 'The Electronic Age'. The Americans, with some help from the Russians, have since then catapulted the world into 'The Space Age'. What an astonishing achievement! It is a unique record never matched by any other nation. The British and the Americans have their God-given Birthright to thank for this most amazing blessing that has brought them such an advantage over other nations.

Teaching the world to play British games

Britain's inventiveness was by no means restricted to technological development alone, as she also became extraordinarily talented at devising games for our recreation. Football, which today is being referred to as 'the beautiful game', is a British invention and it was formally established in 1848, when the rules of the game were set at Cambridge University. It has more than survived to become a global sport and a huge worldwide industry in its own right.

William Webb Ellis, who was a pupil at Rugby School, invented rugby in 1823, and in 1871, the Rugby Union was formed. Everybody knows that cricket is an English invention, and the game has given immense pleasure to countless millions over the centuries. It is a game especially popular amongst the nations of the British Commonwealth. Golf is a 15ᵗʰ Century game invented in Scotland, and Mary Queen of Scots was the first ever woman golfer. Golf today, like football, has become a global success story, with golf courses sprouting up all over the world. King Charles II, whilst in exile in Holland, developed a taste for yachting and through his advocacy it became the sport of kings.

The origin of shooting as a sport goes back to England too, as it came of age with the institution of live pigeon shooting in 1814. Clay pigeon-shooting was also invented in Britain in 1880. Polo was imported into Britain from Bengal in 1869, and soon became the exclusive preserve of the gentry. Even horseracing in its modern form began its variegated life in Newmarket as early as 1600. Then the English are also responsible for inventing lawn tennis, badminton, squash and table tennis. Formula I motor racing effectively got off the ground at Silverstone in 1950, where the first world championship *Grand Prix* was run. What an impressive record this is.

Yet again, there is no nation on the face of the earth that has come up with such ingenuity in devising games that have an enduring appeal. Just think, without the British the world would have no football or rugby or hockey or cricket. We would have to go without tennis, squash, badminton and golf. We couldn't go hunting, shooting or horseracing, or play polo. Yachting and Formula I *Grand Prix* Motor Racing would be definitely out, and we could not even play a game of Monopoly or Scrabble because the British invented those as well. I think it is fair to say that without the British, the world would definitely be a poorer place. The English taught the world to play 'team games', and the emphasis was always on 'fair play', which demanded that you respected your opponent throughout the game. Winning the game wasn't considered essential, but rather playing the game like a gentleman – and above all playing fair – was what really mattered.

When Jacob pronounced his deathbed blessing upon his twelve sons, he came to his son Joseph and he started his blessing to him with the words: *"Joseph is a fruitful bough"*. What an astonishing contribution this little island nation has made to the general good and happiness of mankind. Being a 'fruitful bough' means being productive and fruitful in all areas of life. Is this not a description of the Anglo-Saxon race? It is truly a unique track record never emulated by any other nation or people.

Steam is an Englishman

It is a historical fact that the Industrial Revolution started in Great Britain and grew out of the expanding Atlantic economy of the 18th Century – which might well have been especially designed for Britain. Providence had set the scene once again. Her colonial empire was tailor-made, as it provided a ready market for British manufactured goods. Her own growing population, as it progressively became more prosperous, provided a strong domestic market so essential for success. In an age when it was much cheaper to transport goods by water than by land, no part of England was more than 20 miles from water.

In the 1770s, a great canal-building boom had started, employing mainly Irish labor and linking many of the navigable waterways with canals. This greatly enhanced England's transport network to the major ports, which serviced the Empire. It is not generally recognized to what extent agriculture played a major part in fostering the industrial revolution in England. The plain fact is that British farmers were second only to the Dutch in agricultural productivity in 1700. They were continuously adopting new farming methods and improving their yields. The result, especially before 1760, was a period of record harvests and low food prices. The benign hand of Providence had been at work again. This meant that the average family did not have to spend as much on feeding themselves, giving them the leeway to spend the extra on industrial goods. Thus an eager population was constantly driving up the demand for manufactured goods.

As we have already seen, England had a very sophisticated financial market and, unlike 18th Century France, she had a most effective Central Bank and well-developed credit markets. There was a spirit of enterprise and adventure in the air. The government positively encouraged free trade by imposing few restrictions on the economy. Most British politicians were very strongly committed to the ideal of free trade. Lord Palmerston, who directed British policy for long periods between 1830 and 1865, called free trade one of *"the great standing laws of nature"*. He had a vision of *"commerce...leading civilization with one hand, peace with the other, to render mankind happier, wiser, better... This is the dispensation of Providence..."* *10 Since Britain was likely to be the main beneficiary of free trade agreements, this may look somewhat cynical. Palmerston and his contemporaries did not, however, see anything cynical about equating the interests of Britain with those of humanity and with the will of the Almighty. Palmerston had no doubt that Britain was a force for good in the world and that on occasion the use of violence to bring about improvement could be justified. *11

England was blessed with a large flexible labor market of rural farm workers and cottage workers who were prepared to travel to the new industrial centers tempted by the higher wages on offer. Finally, she was also blessed by having a stable monarchy and government, unlike unhappy France, which had known nothing but revolution and the chaos and mayhem caused by Napoleon's wars. Germany too, after Bismark's Prussian adventures and her war with France in 1870, was in a similar condition. Thus while Britain's two main European competitors were engaged in major political revolutions and war, the most favourable circumstances possible occurred for Britain to rise to supreme industrial hegemony. Providence had arranged to rise up the 'Chief of Nations'.

As early as 1698, Thomas Savery had invented a rather primitive steam engine. Then in 1705, Thomas Newcome produced an engine where the steam in the cylinder was cooled, creating a partial vacuum in the cylinder. This vacuum allowed the pressure of the earth's atmosphere to push the piston in the cylinder down and operate a pump. Come the early 1770s, some of Savery's and many hundreds of Newcome's engines, were working in English coal mines. Then in 1760, a gifted Scottish scientist named James Watt added a separate condenser, which meant that the steam could be cooled without cooling the cylinder.

Just twenty years later the steam engine had become a great commercial success in Britain, and the 'Age of Steam' had arrived. As a 19th Century saying by Ralph, Waldo, Emerson, the American, essayist put it: 'STEAM IS AN ENGLISHMAN!' His actual words were; *"Steam is almost an Englishman!"* *12 He was clearly impressed by the transformational effect the invention of the steam engine had upon British society. This technological development, more than any other, enabled the Industrial Revolution to burst forth at breakneck speed. British engineers and scientists were constantly thinking of new applications for the steam engine. For the first time in recorded history, mankind it seemed had almost unlimited power at its disposal. The steam engine was quickly put to use in many industries within England's industrial heartland. This in turn had a knock-on effect upon coal production, which shot up in direct consequence of ever-rising demand.

Yet another providential Birthright blessing was England's almost unlimited supply of coal and iron ore. The English coal mining industry entered into its glory days. Steam power also promoted important breakthroughs in the English iron industry. Henry Cort developed heavy-duty steam-powered rolling mills, which were capable of spewing out finished iron in every shape and form. Iron had once been scarce and expensive, but Cort's steam driven rolling mills changed all that, so much so that iron became the cheap, basic building block of the modern economy. By way of example, the annual British iron production in 1740 was a mere 17,000 tons, whereas just over a hundred years later it was 3,000,000 tons. In 1848 Britain produced half the pig-iron in the world, and over the next 30 years she managed to treble her output. She had become by far the largest producer in the world, and all of this because 'Steam just happened to be an Englishman!' In this example we have a perfect illustration of the role British inventiveness played in bringing her to her position of global supremacy. This *'latter day'* inventive streak in the British is a gift from God and it forms an intrinsic part of the Birthright blessing Jacob spoke out over the head of Ephraim those 4,000 years ago. Once again, one cannot but marvel at the faithfulness of our God, who can transform the words, spoken over a young boy, into actual reality to this same boy's descendants some 4,000 years later. This is truly inspiring!

A palace made of crystal

Britons had become the titans of technology, and England unquestionably was the laboratory and workshop of the world. Britons began to feel that with their fast evolving technology they could achieve anything. Indeed, Queen Victoria wrote in her diary on April 29, 1851: "We are capable of doing anything." Such was the confidence of the nation, and nothing came to epitomize this positive optimistic spirit more than the building of Crystal Palace for the Great Exhibition of 1851. The Great Exhibition was the brainchild of Prince Albert, the Prince Consort, himself. In many ways it became the prototype of the subsequent modern development of the World Fair and Expo.

Unlike the ill-fated Millennium Dome at Greenwich, Joseph Paxton's Crystal Palace was an astounding success, commonly referred to as one of the 'wonders of the world.' In less than five months, over six million visitors visited the Great Exhibition, and the profits of the show were used to buy 87 acres of land in South Kensington. Upon this same land were built the great museums of the sciences, such as the Natural History Museum, the Victoria and

Albert Museum, the Geological Museum, the Science Museum, as well as the colleges of science, mining, engineering, music and art. What a wonderful legacy to leave behind! In fact the Royal Commission for the 1851 Exhibition still exists, and through the wise administration of its 1851 surplus it has been financing scholarships in the arts and sciences even to the present day.

Queen Victoria opens the Great Exhibition in the Crystal Palace
(courtesy Louis Haghe, Wikimedia)

The amazing fact about the Crystal Palace was that it was a 'prefabricated' building made entirely of glass and iron. The building itself was a revolution in design and construction. It was built not by an architect or an engineer but by a gardener – Joseph Paxton – who was the former head gardener to the Duke of Devonshire. He based the design of his building on the massive greenhouse he had built at Chatsworth to house a rare and gigantic species of lily called *Victoria Regia*, which had come from British Guiana, a far-flung outpost of the

British Empire. Everything about the building was new and daring. 2,200 workmen erected it in just seven months. To save chopping down three beautiful elm trees in Hyde Park, Paxton altered his design by raising the roof of the central cross-isle, thus incorporating them into the building. They served as a beautiful decoration in the glass building, as they truly were 'indoor plants' on a grand scale.

The Crystal Palace was three times as long as St Paul's Cathedral and it had twenty-one acres of interior space; and from the outside it looked like a sparkling jewel set in the luminous greenery of Hyde Park. The interior *décor* was absolutely stunning, a glorious riot of color and light. Queen Victoria and her handsome Prince Albert opened it with great fanfare and pomp. The Prince Consort referred to it as: "The greatest day in our history, the most beautiful and imposing and touching spectacle ever seen". *The Illustrated London News*, glorying in the occasion of the grand opening, lauded Britain as "a state compared with whose power and dominion, the empires of old were but as provinces". *The Times* praised the display of "all that is useful or beautiful in nature or art", as contributing to "an effect so grand and yet so natural, that it hardly seemed to be put together by design, or to be the work of human artificers."

For the few months it stood, the Crystal Palace became the supreme focal point of British pride, as it represented a celebration of everything British technology and ingenuity had achieved. It was also a celebration of 'Empire', and for many it was a time of thanksgiving for all the blessings the Almighty had poured upon Great Britain; for many British people agreed entirely with the sentiment of Prince Albert's personal motto: *We are carrying out the will of the Great and Blessed God!*

America—the new economic juggernaut

After this superlative performance by the British Empire it hardly seems possible that her record could be matched, let alone improved by anyone. Yet, this is exactly what has happened with the American 'star-spangled' economy now dominating the whole world in virtually every sphere. One of the greatest presidents of the United States commenting on America's unique blessings said:

"We find ourselves in the peaceful possession of the fairest portion of the earth, as regards to the fertility of soil, extent of territory, and salubrity of climate . . . We find ourselves the legal inheritors of these fundamental blessings. We toiled not in the acquirement or the establishment of them" (Abraham Lincoln).

Since the dawn of civilization all wealth has been derived from the land. Whether it comes from the crops grown on top of it, or is produced by the mineral wealth stored underneath, land is the ultimate source of all wealth. As Abraham Lincoln put it so eloquently, America has indeed inherited the fairest portion of the earth. The plain fact is that the United States of America is blessed with more productive land than any other nation in the world. From 1803 to 1867, in just sixty-four years, the streams of British, Irish and German immigrants participated in a veritable 'land rush' in which they helped to stake out an enormous continent from the Atlantic to the Pacific Ocean. The federal government assumed jurisdiction over all this newly acquired land. Washington became the repository of more than a billion acres, all virgin territory that was crying out to be developed. It comprised a territory twice the size of Europe. In 1862, at the start of the Civil War, the House of Congress passed the *Homestead Act,* which literally gave the land away to anyone willing to develop it on a small scale. By 1930, there were almost seven million independent small farmers, and they, together with the wheat and cattle barons, railway magnates and mine-owners, developed this rich land that had been lying dormant for multiple centuries, seemingly waiting for the dawn of this very moment in time. Nevertheless, this 'giving away of land' policy led to headlong development that moved at breakneck speed crushing everything in its path. As the Indian tribes fought to preserve their ancestral lands they were literally swept away by this tide of white invaders with their superior weapons. In time it led to the progressive extermination of the indigenous Indian population with hundreds of thousands of Indians perishing through massacres, pestilence and alcohol.

Yet these were the days of the New Frontier, where the danger posed by marauding bands of Indian warriors only added to the excitement of carving out a new territory full of promise. The rich agricultural lands of the Mississippi Valley, the future vast grain fields of the Midwest, the promise of the choice fruit lands of the Pacific coast and Florida, as well as the great forests of the Pacific Northwest, all beckoned to be developed. The United States, since those early pioneering days of the wagon trains, has become the most fertile nation on the earth. Her productive soil has earned her the epithet of being the 'breadbasket' of the world. Her agricultural fruitfulness and abundant crops have become legendary, and in this again we see a perfect fulfilment of the Birthright blessing that was to come upon the descendants of Joseph, as Joseph was to become *"a fruitful bough"* (Genesis 49:22). Just as Joseph, as the Viceroy of Egypt, nearly 4,000 years ago fed the then known world with abundant grain from the great storehouses of Egypt, so America today provides the world with her grain from her vast silos of wheat. For many decades now, whenever the Russians, the Chinese or the Indians have a poor harvest, America has been able to make up their shortfall. In any famine or disaster situation anywhere in the world, American aid is nearly always first to arrive on the scene, usually closely followed by aid from Great Britain and her Commonwealth offspring. In this characteristic too, we see the spirit of Joseph at work in the American people, as Joseph not only saved his brothers from the famine, but he also saved the whole of the then known world with ample grain from Egypt.

The Big country

The Americans have never known what to do with all their food. You only have to visit their restaurants and look at the enormous portions of food you are served. America is the only country in the world where even the poor are fat! The very scale of America is so large that it is hard to conceive if you have not visited the nation and seen it for yourself. The vastness of America has clearly had a huge effect on the consciousness of her people, as they do tend to see it big. In America big is beautiful. The bigger the better! After all, this is the 'Big Country' of the Marlborough cigarette ads. Americans love to drive big cars. It is a place where superlatives and hyperbole abound. America is the land of the 'Big Shot', 'Mr Big', and the famous McDonald's fast food chain became an instant success through her promotion of the Big Mac. The city of New York is affectionately referred to as the 'Big Apple'. This is the place where they really like to 'think big' and build huge tall skyscrapers because they are so impressive and oh so big. Americans especially like making 'big bucks' and 'making it big'.

God's own country!

The Americans have come to refer to their country as 'God's own country'. The expression does appear to hold a grain of truth, as never in the history of man has a country been so singularly blessed. John Winthrop, one of the Puritan founders of the Massachusetts Bay Company in 1630, first coined the phrase of America as a "city on a hill", set apart from other nations. Ever since then this concept has entered the very consciousness of the nation. This sense is also most powerfully conveyed in America's numerous anthems; without a doubt the most rousing song is *America the Beautiful*. Its verses directly acknowledge America's privileged position and her God-given superabundance of material things.

AMERICA THE BEAUTIFUL

O beautiful for spacious skies, for amber waves of grain;
For purple mountain majesties, above the fruited plain!
America! America! God shed His grace on thee,
And crown thy good with brotherhood from sea to shining sea!

O beautiful for pilgrim feet, whose stern impassioned stress,
A thoroughfare for freedom beat, across the wilderness!
America! America! God mend thine every flaw,
Confirm thy soul in self-control, thy liberty in law!

O beautiful heroes proved in liberating strife,
Who more than self their country loved, and mercy more than life!
America! America! May God thy gold refine,
Till all success be nobleness and every grace divine!

O beautiful for patriot dream that sees beyond the years;
Thine alabaster cities gleam, undimmed by human tears!
America! America! God shed His grace on thee,
And crown thy good with brotherhood, from sea to shining sea!

Economically America dominates and calls the tune for the whole world. It is true to say that the world benefits from the success of the American economy, as the Americans are the world's largest direct investors overseas. There is hardly a country on the earth that has not benefited from American investment in their economy, whether through aid or through direct commercial investment. It is a commonly understood that America consumes just over 25 percent of all the energy consumed in the world. This fact is often hurled at the U.S. as a criticism by the environmentalist and anti-globalisation lobbies. Yet these same critics conveniently forget to mention that the U.S. economy today accounts for a staggering 30 percent of the world's total output. A further point to remember is, that since the discovery of shale oil and gas, America has become a net exporter of energy and is set to overtake Saudi Arabia in this regard. The global giants of American industry such as IBM, Microsoft, Oracle, Hewlett Packard, General Motors, Ford, and scores of other big names, have penetrated every nook and cranny of the global market place. Every single one of the world's 'top ten' most valuable brand names are American. Not only are these top ten global brands American-owned, but she also owns a full two-thirds of the top sixty global household names. Most of these such as Intel, Disney, General Electric and Marlborough are so large that their annual turnover is greater than the entire GDP of countries such as Portugal or Greece. In the 1950s the American economy amounted to a phenomenal 50 percent of the total world output. No nation apart from Great Britain before her has ever achieved this level of success.

The U.S. is a country with less than 5 percent of the world population, yet she is in the unassailable position to dictate the economic terms to the other 95 percent! She is able to order her own affairs in her own interest throughout the whole wide world, simply because of her sheer economic and military muscle. The common expression today is that if America sneezes the whole world catches a cold. It is true to say that the whole world does watch the American economy with a great deal of anxiety and interest. Literally thousands of foreign analysts are constantly on the outlook for any signs of a possible recession, as any downturn in the U.S. would directly affect their own economies. The American economy is the only high powered motor that is pulling the world economy along. Without this U.S. high-velocity engine the global economy would barely be able to move forward at all, as apart from China, there simply is no other motor around to do the job. When we examine these extraordinary facts and amazing statistics about America, we are seeing the working out of the 'Birthright' blessing upon the United States of America, and we witness the awesome reality that the God of Abraham has indeed *"SHED HIS GRACE ON THEE!"*

America the 'Inescapable!'

Some years ago *The New York Times* magazine published an article called *America, The Inescapable.* The writer was puzzled by the extraordinary dominance of American culture even in those parts of the world that are known to loathe everything the U.S. stands for. He cited the term *'soft power'*. Joseph Nye, Dean of Government at Harvard University, apparently first coined this expression.

According to his definition 'soft power' is the projection of a nation's interests by subliminal and outwardly benign means. "In the past," he says, *"the preferred method of bringing another country around to your way of thinking was to invade it. Today there is a much bigger pay-off in the exercise of soft power."* No one in the world exercises soft power better than America, as she has seduced the whole world with her goodies from Levi jeans, Nike trainers and Ray-Ban sunglasses on our bodies, to Starbucks, Coca-Cola and McDonalds on our high streets. Walt Disney has delighted and enticed all the children of the world through his cartoon figures such Mickey and Minnie Mouse, Donald Duck, and not forgetting Goofy the dog. More young children than any other films ever made have seen his company's charming films, such as *Snow White and the Seven Dwarfs, Sleeping Beauty, The Lion King,* and *101 Dalmatians.* Their enduring quality is such that every fresh generation of children will enjoy the same stories over and over again. It has all contributed to the projection of America's 'soft power' into the young minds of delighted audiences. Through the prolific Hollywood-based film industry America has projected her influence still further and seduced virtually the whole world to use, to wear and to eat all things American. The 'American Way' has thus become inescapable, as – even though most people may not be aware of it – the whole world has come into her sway. Even so, despite all of this, there has never been a nation in all of history that has amassed so much power and yet used it with, some qualifications, in such a benign way.

Titan of Space technology

Whereas the British had become the 'Titans of Technology' in the 19th Century, driving the world from one technological revolution into another, so America took on this role in the 20th Century. It is almost as if, in this realm too, the baton of leadership was passed from Ephraim, the younger brother, to Manasseh, the elder, that is to say, from Britain to the United States of America. For over two centuries Great Britain had held the accolade of being the most inventive nation in the world. Then with the onset of the 20th Century we see a dramatic change, as suddenly British inventiveness goes into a decline, whilst American inventiveness increases by leaps and bounds.

One of the greatest catalysts was the onset of 'The Space Age' fuelled by the intense rivalry between the two superpowers of the communist Soviet Union and the capitalist United States of America. The space race between these two giants started in earnest in the spring of 1945, when both the Russian and American armies raced towards Peenemunde, the German rocket base. As it happens, the Russians got there first, only to find that the great Werner Von Braun and his top team of engineers had fled to the west into the open arms of American intelligence. The U.S. moved at breakneck speed, shipping the German Peenemunde rocket team together with a hundred V-2 rockets back to America. All Stalin's armies were left with were the smoking ruins of Peenemunde. Despite this major setback for them they were able to play 'catch up' with the Americans, as they managed to get hold of the all-important list of component suppliers, and, as luck would have it, most of these factories were in the Russian-administered zone.

Much to the surprise of the whole world, it was the Russians who scored the first goal in the space race with the spectacular launch of their now legendary *Sputnik* satellite. For maximum effect, they chose an orbit that would bring *Sputnik* directly over the United States, Europe and Asia. It was an enormous *coup* for them, leaving the American Space Agency with egg all over their faces. *Sputnik* had been launched on October 4, 1954, the anniversary of the Russian Revolution, and it came hard on the heels of the Soviet's first H-Bomb test in 1953. Not since Pearl Harbor had Americans felt so vulnerable. Just one month later the Russians sent a much larger *Sputnik* II into orbit, and this time it carried Laika, the first canine astronaut. The dog-loving British soon sprang into action, as the Canine Defence League protested in the strongest possible terms to the Russian Embassy. According to Russian reports at the time, the dog survived his space journey for one full week, duly proving that animal life could survive in space. Thus the Russians had apparently scored yet another spectacular goal in the space race; the score was Russia 2, America 0. More recent information has it that the dog survived only a few hours.

It was not until March of 1958 that the Stars and Stripes made their first appearance into space, as the Americans were able successfully to launch their own Explorer I satellite into orbit around the earth. Then on July 31, 1958, the National Aeronautics and Space Administration (NASA) was created to indicate that America meant business, and that space had become first priority for the nation. A huge investment programme followed the creation of NASA, with the acquisition of the Cape Canaveral test range. Hundreds of millions of dollars were invested in laboratories, test ranges, launch pads and human talent. Before long the talk was of putting a man into space as being the only way to get ahead of the Russians. Then just before the close of the decade the Russians sprang yet another surprise, as they sent an unmanned spacecraft in a 300,000 mile loop around the moon. *Lunik* III also returned a single high quality TV picture of the dark side of the moon. *13

The space race by now was in full swing, and it became clear to the whole world that the Americans were losing the race. The Soviets, having once again demonstrated their technological superiority, took maximum advantage in their propaganda. They milked the psychological and political aspects of their triumphs for all they were worth, and it surely seemed that they were on an unstoppable winning streak. Then on April 12, 1961, the Russians served up another unwelcome surprise for the free world, as the news broke of yet another spectacular space 'first' for the Soviet space programme. The announcement came that Yuri Gagarin, a Russian astronaut, had been the first man in space. Gagarin had orbited around the earth at 18,000 miles an hour and landed safely back home in his *Vostock* spaceship. It was an unprecedented triumph and all of Russia took to the streets to celebrate. The news left many long faces at NASA. America's honour was saved just three weeks later, when Alan Sheppard was shot a hundred miles into space in an arc over the Atlantic Ocean, landing safely 300 miles from the launch pad in Cape Canaveral. The whole flight had lasted barely fifteen minutes, but in those same fifteen minutes Alan Shepard had become an immortal hero of the United States of America. *14

The first man on the moon

Within two weeks of Alan Shepard's successful flight, President J. F. Kennedy had decided to back the Apollo Space Programme that was to send a man to the moon and return him safely to the earth. Thus the President of the United States threw down the gauntlet to the Russians before a packed House of Congress. Kennedy inspired his nation with his 'can do' spirit, as he publicly committed America to achieving this goal before the end of the decade. It seemed then that the only way to regain national pride was to beat the Russians to the moon.

For a time, from here on, the space race between America and Russia became like a game of Ping-Pong, with the ball flying from one court to the other at breakneck speed. Even more spectacular Russian successes were to come, followed by further American successes. The race had the whole world electrified. Space and science had become a huge public relations exercise on both sides of the great divide. The Russians achieved several more stunning 'firsts' in space. They sent Valentina Tereshkova, the world's first female astronaut, into space; and subsequently, Alexei Leonov, one of their astronauts, was the first man to leave his spacecraft and walk in space. It seemed somehow that the Russians were always able to beat the Americans to the punch. The race between the two superpowers had the whole world riveted to their TV sets. The awesome full color pictures being relayed back to earth, showing the glorious beauty of the earth, as seen from space, had the whole world enthralled. 'Man in Space' truly was the biggest story around in those days.

However, wiser minds knew that there was a lot more at stake than just good PR and national prestige. They were aware that the victor in space would end up ruling the world. The race was essentially a race for world dominance. The Communists made no secret of their intentions to bring their communist ideology to the whole world. On the American side the motivation was not so much to achieve world supremacy for the American capitalist system, but rather to stop the Soviet Union from achieving its sinister plan. In truth the communist and capitalist space-titans were engaged in mortal combat in space, and this in front of a global TV audience that was fascinated and excited by this new frontier of exploration for man.

The turning point for America came in 1965, with the launch of the Gemini 4 spacecraft that was positioned atop the mighty Titan II rocket. After a flawless lift-off in front of a live, *via* satellite, global TV audience, and three orbits around the earth, Ed White went for a space-walk that inspired all who saw it. Ed White performed somersaults - body turns with great exuberance and style – all of which were seen live on earth, as his cosmic partner, Jim McDivitt, caught all on camera for the whole world to see. Then came the Apollo 8 mission to the moon at Christmas 1968. The three-crew members of the craft had set up their cameras to film the bleak expanse of craters, dead seas, and mounds of the moon's surface. As the three men raced through space a quarter of a million miles from home, the crew of Apollo 8 had a message for the world:

In the beginning God created the heavens and the earth. The earth was without form and void, and darkness was on the face of the deep . . . Then God said, 'Let there be light'; and there was light. And God saw the light, that it was good . . . .

As the three men each in turn read the first few verses of the Creation account from Genesis chapter one, they could not have foreseen the enormous impact their message would have on the world below. Many who saw and heard it were moved to tears. The effects of this Christmas space odyssey were not easy to calculate, but it certainly proved to be the greatest propaganda *coup* for the

American space programme. Yet, nevertheless, the reading of the first ten verses of the Genesis Creation account had been in stark contrast to the godless atheism of the Communist world. As such it had been a powerful witness sent to the world from beyond the moon. One militant U.S. atheist, protesting at the 'religious broadcast' from the book of Genesis, went so far as to sue NASA for equal time on TV to broadcast his belief that there is no God. What an idiot!

The Eagle has landed!

Then came July 21, 1969, that fateful day when the first moon landing by man would be attempted. The whole world was in suspense, as the three chosen sons of America, Michael Collins, Neil Armstrong and Edwin 'Buzz' Aldrin entered their space capsule atop the giant Saturn 5 rocket. Neil Armstrong had been designated as the first man to walk on the moon, after both he and Buzz Aldrin successfully landed the lunar module on to the surface of the moon. The module was called *Eagle* after that most potent symbol of the United States of America. The *Eagle* was to carry *Ole Glory*, the Stars and Stripes, which was to be planted onto the surface of the moon. The build up to the event was enormous. Over a million people camped out in their tents, caravans, campers and cars around at Cape Kennedy for the blast off. It was the launch of Apollo 11, and with the whole of the world's TV and press present, it seemed like the greatest show on earth was about to begin. The launch went without a hitch and the actual journey to the moon went perfectly according to plan. Neil Armstrong landed the lunar module on a relatively smooth patch of the lunar surface in the Sea of Tranquillity. He immediately reported back to mission control in Houston the famous words: *'THE EAGLE HAS LANDED!'* Then later on came the moment the whole world had been waiting for, as Neil Armstrong stepped onto the surface of the moon and coined the immortal phrase: *"ONE SMALL STEP FOR A MAN – A GIANT LEAP FOR MANKIND."* Most people on the earth agreed with him, as man had indeed entered a new era. It seemed like the Space Age had finally come of age.

Neil Armstrong on the Moon
(courtesy NASA, Wikimedia)

The successful moon landing represented a triumph of technology, with each of the nine million components in the Saturn/Apollo mission working flawlessly. Buzz Aldrin then joined Neil Armstrong on the lunar surface, and their exploits were filmed for the whole world to see. Over a billion people watched the U.S. astronauts on TV and, at the time, it was the largest worldwide audience ever recorded. Space fever had spread throughout the world and everybody was enthralled. After the space heroes had safely splashed down in the Indian Ocean, President Nixon personally went to greet them, and with somewhat ridiculously overblown hyperbole referred to their successful mission and safe return as "the greatest week since Creation!"

It certainly had been an exceptionally good week for America. 'God bless America' has become a somewhat hackneyed phrase; nevertheless God clearly had blessed America in the race to the moon. It had been a very close run. It was clear to the whole world, including their Russian rivals, that America had won the space race. The Stars and Stripes were planted on the lunar surface, and no Russian astronaut has ever landed or walked on the moon. It was a most important victory for America and one of the greatest milestones for her future development into becoming the unquestioned ruler of the world. America's previous victory in the Second World War had been a giant catalyst, which catapulted her into the position of becoming the unquestioned leader of the western world. Her subsequent victory in the space race launched her into a still higher orbit of global dominance. Just think what would have happened to the world if the communist Soviet system had emerged as the victor instead? The American 'Eagle' had indeed landed, and in time it was to lead to a huge spin off in technological products that were to play a major role in America's subsequent economic success.

In naming the lunar module the *Eagle*, the NASA planners had deliberately chosen the very symbol of the United States of America. The 'bald eagle', with its white head and tail, is America's national bird, and it has been designated a protected species. Whereas the 'bald eagle' is without question a symbol that is unique to the United States, it may nevertheless have its origins in a previous age. We have already seen that, according to Yair Davidiy, a specialist researcher into the movements of the 'lost tribes' of Israel, there was a group of Israelites who had a *'bald headed eagle'* as their emblem, at the time the Assyrians were exiling them from the land of Israel. They apparently were from the tribes of Judah and Benjamin, who were forced to join the other ten tribes in their exile and captivity. We also noted that the prophet Micah appears to refer to these people in his writings; this is what he says:

"Enlarge your baldness like an eagle, for they shall go from you into captivity" (Micah 1:16).

Historically, there is in any case a very strong connection between ancient Israel and the eagle symbol, as the eagle was one of the four faces on the chariot described in the book of Ezekiel. Also, around the Camp of Israel in the wilderness, as they journeyed from Egypt to the Promised Land, the emblem for the tribe of Dan was the eagle. Apart from the potent national symbolism encapsulated in the name of the lunar module, 'Eagle' was a brilliant name to choose, as no bird in the world can

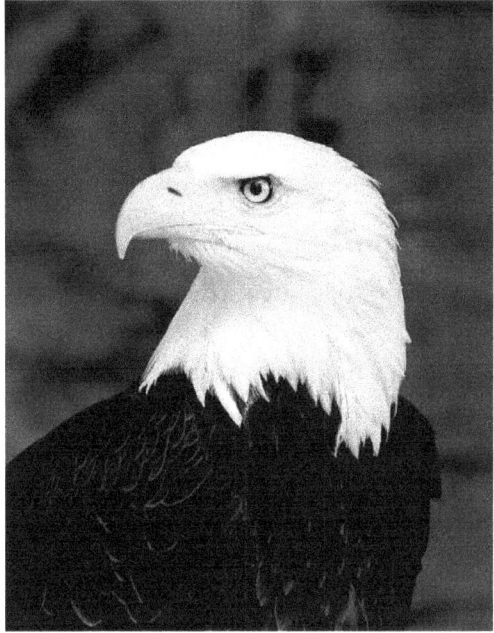

Bald Eagle
(courtesy Saffron Blaze, Wikimedia)

soar like an eagle. Unlike other birds, the eagle is never overcome by a storm. The eagle's primary feathers are tapered at the ends and form slots, which serve as shock absorbers. The lunar module too had been supplied with very sensitive and yet powerful shock absorbers to soften its impact upon the lunar surface. The eagle's primary feathers also increase the wing's efficiency by reducing the drag. When a storm approaches, strong thermal updrafts together with its strong wing construction enable the eagle to be lifted higher than in calm weather. The more violent the storm, the higher the eagle soars. He cleverly makes use of the storm to rise higher and to soar to where he has never gone before. In naming the lunar module 'Eagle', the planners at NASA caused this most potent symbol of

America to soar to a place that was higher than any other place it had been before. The American Eagle had well and truly landed, and God had truly blessed America, the modern day descendants of Manasseh, the son of Joseph. The truth is that America had won the race to the moon because of her Birthright blessing. It was meant to be, as it had all been pre-ordained by a wise and most faithful God, who was simply fulfilling the Covenant he made with his servant Abraham some 4,000 years ago.

Space spin off

With this successful landing on the moon, a new day had dawned and a door had opened that was ultimately to lead to America's now unassailable position as the world's sole superpower. America's historic victory in the race to the moon has subsequently enabled her to lead the world in almost every other area of endeavour. After her moon feat, U.S. spacecraft were the first to Venus, Mars and the Sun, as well as to Jupiter, Mercury, Saturn and Uranus. Her matchless Mariner, Pioneer and Voyager spacecraft are the greatest space-travellers ever sent from earth. What excited the world about man's victory in space was that reality seemed to be catching up with the science fiction writers. These were the days that spawned *Star Trek*, the hugely successful TV series, in which Captain Kirk, Doctor Spock, and 'Beam me up' Scottie became household figures in almost every home. The Steven Spielberg blockbuster *Star Wars* movies followed on to become a global success story, capitalising on the world's fascination with space. It was yet another way, in which America projected its 'soft power' onto the world stage, thereby exercising enormous influence, especially upon the youth of the world.

The need for miniaturisation in space led in turn to tremendous advances being achieved in computer technology and all kinds of electronic equipment, much to the benefit of the electronic giants of American industry. The space programme produced the first satellites, and from this has sprung satellite television, which has become a global industry in its own right. The space satellite also produces the world's first 'Satellite Navigation Positioning System', which has been of enormous benefit to the aircraft, shipping and yachting industries. Robotics is another area of unforeseen development, where today, in the world's most sophisticated car assembly plants; computer-generated robots are assembling cars. Virtually every conceivable type of precision equipment from laser guidance systems to optical instruments have benefited from the technological spin off generated by the American space programme. Solar heating too has been a wonderful and environmentally friendly gift spawned by this programme. The American defence industry has also gained its technological edge over the rest of the world, largely as a result of its victory in the space race. Yet, even the average housewife or homemaker has benefited from the space race, as the non-stick frying pan, through the invention of Teflon, has become a universal gift to millions around the world.

Success breeds success

America has become synonymous with success. She has become a nation of superlatives. The statistics are truly amazing, as the blessings that God has poured upon America, in his faithfulness to His Covenant, are almost beyond belief. America is the biggest consumer of electricity, natural gas and oil in the world. She is not only the top meat-eating country, but also the top chocolate and soft drinks consuming nation in the world *15 The U.S. is also the world's largest car producer and has the longest rail network. The U.S, and the U.K. are the two top airline-using countries in the world, with the U.S. figure for annual passenger miles being approximately six times greater than that of Britain. The United States has a staggering 14,459 airports suitable for jet aircraft. This figure is nearly five times the number of the next nation with the most airports. In fact the U.S, total is greater than the combined figure for the next twelve nations *16

The Bible and the Nobel Prize

One of the most recognized international yardsticks for measuring a nation's excellence is the Nobel Prize. The prize was instituted by order of the last will and testament of Alfred Nobel, the Swedish chemist and philanthropist, who invented dynamite. Alfred Nobel died in 1896, and he endowed his legacy of the Nobel Prize with his huge fortune. The prizes are awarded for outstanding contributions to chemistry, physics, physiology or medicine, literature, economics, and peace and may be awarded annually. It was first established in 1901, and ever since then it has received global recognition as the highest honour that can be awarded for excellence in scholarship and achievement. Although the award of the peace prize at times has been clouded by political chicanery, and has consequently come in for justified criticism, the other awards continue to be seen as the highest possible accolade that this world can offer to the world's greatest inventors, pioneers, writers and scholars.

Having got this far into the book, you won't be surprised to learn that America and Great Britain between them have scooped up a phenomenal *sixty percent* of all Nobel Prizes awarded to the top ten countries since the inception of the prize. The U.S. has won 241 prizes, whereas Britain has won 98, making for a total of 339. The next eight countries in order of achievement are Germany, France, Sweden, Switzerland, USSR/Russia, Netherlands, Italy and Denmark, who between them have only achieved 227 Nobel Prizes. In this context we must not overlook the phenomenal contribution made by the tribe of Judah, as the Jews, who constitute less than one half of one percent of mankind, have won 18 percent of all Nobel Prizes awarded since 1901. The author John Hulley, in his book *Comets, Jews and Christians*, makes some startling claims, based on his research into the causes of man's scientific achievement. He attributes true scientific achievement – using recipients of Nobel Prizes as the criterion – largely to a combination of Israelite ancestry together with relative closeness to biblical truth. Hulley demonstrates that while nearly two-thirds of all award winners have been Protestants, Jews have taken nearly 20 percent. Jews and Protestants between them thus account for 86 percent of the total. Measured on a purely racial basis, the Jews are at the top of the list. *17

John Hulley attributes the relative innovative advantage of Israelite Protestants and Jews to the influence of the Bible upon their societies. He discovered, from the actual prizes awarded, that Catholic and/or atheistic Communist nations had produced hardly any Nobel Prize winners. He also demonstrated that Jewish achievements were greatest when living in Protestant nations dominated by Israelites, such as America and Great Britain. These amazing facts indicate that Bible-based societies clearly are conducive to scientific discovery and technological invention, because they respect the rights of the individual within a framework of God-given laws. The Protestant Reformation was a major turning point for Britain and her budding colonial empire in becoming a world power. The Bible-based societies of the Protestant Reformation attempted to put into practice the practical and ethical commandments of the Hebrew Bible in the economic, political and social sphere. The rate of invention after the Protestant Reformation literally shot up. The fact is that good science flourishes only in a climate that respects and values the individual. It can only prosper in a society that is based upon biblical principles, such as honesty and fair play. It is the adherence to and application of these and many other biblical principles, which have made the British and American societies the most prosperous and powerful the world has ever seen.

Not only have these two sons of Joseph, Ephraim and Manasseh, been awarded sixty percent of all Nobel Prizes since the award began, but they were awarded 112 more prizes than the combined prize total of the next eight nations. Here we see once again the enormous impact of the Birthright blessing that God has bestowed upon America and Great Britain. This catalogue of incredible, exceptional and outstanding achievement for our two brother nations is not simply an accident of history. Sir Winston Churchill's words are worth quoting again, as surely he was on the right track when he said:

"He must indeed have a blind soul who cannot see that some great purpose is being worked out here below."

Is it just an accident of history?

It was no accident of history that Great Britain became the world's first global hegemonic power, with the Royal Navy patrolling the world's sea-lanes. It was no accident that her empire became the biggest in history, and that all of world trade was largely carried in British ships and conducted in Pounds Sterling. It was no accident that Great Britain became the richest and chief creditor nation in the world, earning vast sums from her overseas investments and able to export capital on a giant scale. It was also no accident of history that, with the emergence of the American superpower, history has repeated itself, as Manasseh, the older son of Joseph, took over the baton of world leadership from his younger brother Ephraim. It was all prophesied by their patriarchal father Jacob, as he lay dying on his bed and addressed his two grandsons, the sons of Joseph. It was all meant to happen as he clearly stated in these 'latter days'. *18

It is no accident that the similarities between Britain's global role a century ago, and America's position of global supremacy today are so striking. It is no coincidence that today's global market is designed in America's image and underpinned by American power and interests. It is no accident of history that America's cruise missiles are today's equivalent of the guns of the Royal Navy in previous days. It is also no accident that the U.S. dollar has earned the epithet of the 'almighty' U.S. dollar. It was all meant to be, because it was prophesied to happen. Once those prophecies were uttered, it became inevitable that we should see their perfect fulfilment in these closing days of this age. It has all been written and meticulously recorded in the Bible, that consummate history book of Israel.

CHAPTER FOUR

৵৵

8th Sign
Israel was to have a very large population

"Blessing I will bless you, and multiplying I will multiply your descendants as the stars of the heaven and as the sand which is on the seashore!"

(Genesis 22:17).

Flavius Josephus, the famous Jewish historian who witnessed and recorded the sacking of the Temple and the destruction of Jerusalem by the Roman legions in 70 AD, wrote the following about the 'Lost' Ten Tribes of Israel:

"The Ten Tribes are beyond Euphrates till now, and are an immense multitude!" *1

It was common knowledge to the Jews of those days that the Ten Tribes of Israel dwelt outside the boundaries of the Roman Empire east of the Euphrates River. In fact the reason the Romans were never able to expand to the east was because of the immense strength of the Hebrew-speaking Parthian Empire. These same Parthians were none other than the Israelite descendants of the Ten Tribes of Israel, who had been deported from the Northern Kingdom of Israel by the Assyrians in 721 BC. They were allied to Scythia, another powerful Israelite Empire located to the northwest and northeast of the Caspian Sea. Each Roman attempt to conquer the territory east of the Euphrates had resulted in the most disastrous defeat. Over a period of nearly three centuries they tried to go the way of Alexander the

Great before them, but the Parthians, frequently allied to the Scythians, always stood in their way. *2 The famous 19th Century historian, George Rawlinson, wrote a number of books about the Parthian Empire in an attempt to counter what he called a *"defective"* and *"false"* view of history, which omitted the major role of the Parthian Empire in history. Parthia in every which way was an equal superpower to Rome. The pagan Roman Empire ruled the West, whereas the Israelite Parthian Empire ruled the East, and thus they had divided the world between themselves. As we have seen from the words of Josephus, the Ten Tribes of Israel already were "an immense multitude" in his day, some 1,900 years ago. The question is where did these Israelite multitudes go? The facts of history are that they did not stay where they were, but instead they crossed the Caucasus Mountains into Europe, where most of them eventually settled on the northwest coast of Europe and in the British Isles.

One of the greatest scholars on this subject is Yair Davidiy, who lives just outside Jerusalem. One of his books is entitled *Lost Israelite Identity*, in which he conclusively proves the Hebrew ancestry of the Celtic races. He proves that tribes of Israelite descent migrated by various paths to the west and became assimilated by Celtic civilization. He brings evidence from the Bible, *Talmud*, archaeology, mythology, linguistics, Greek and Roman authors, and general history. His whole emphasis is on scholastically orientated sources of information, and he substantiates all the important points in his book by supplying references from academically acceptable works. Yair Davidiy has also published eight additional works on this subject; some of these are *The Tribes, Role to Rule, Bible Truth*, and *Origin*.

Another author of great scholarship on the migrations of the tribes of Israel is Steven M. Collins, an American, who as mentioned earlier has written a benchmark book entitled *The 'Lost' Ten Tribes of Israel . . . Found!* This most fascinating work is a thrilling read, yet at the same time a work that is very well researched and documented. He has recently published several other works, which are based upon his original book: these are respectively, *The Origins and Empire of Ancient Israel*, and *Israel's Lost Empires*. There is no need to go over ground that has already been covered by other authors. Anyone wishing to discover more about the migratory paths followed by the so-called 'Lost' Ten Tribes need only look at the books listed in the Recommended Reading List.

Where is this 'great multitude?'

The reason for this chapter is to emphasise a pivotal part of the Covenant that God made with Abraham. One of the most prominent promises contained in the 'Birthright blessing' was that the descendants of Abraham would be very numerous. *Israel's History Book* puts it in beautifully poetic language:

"Blessing I will bless you, and multiplying I will multiply your descendants as the stars of the heaven and as the sand which is on the seashore!" (Genesis 22:17)

At first sight it would appear that this promise has not been kept, because where on earth are all of these Israelites? People today, when they think about Israel, immediately associate it with a teeny-weeny little country in the Middle East, surrounded by hostile Arab nations. Only some six-and-a-half million Jews live in Israel, and the other Jews in the world number no more than around ten million. So, at the most, there are some seventeen million Jews in the world, who can actually be identified as such. Where then are these innumerable multitudes promised to Abraham's descendants through his son Isaac? Surely a population of only seventeen million cannot count as being *"descendants as the stars in heaven and as the sand which is on the seashore"*. Even allowing for the use of metaphor, hyperbole, and a degree of poetic licence, these expressions lead one to think of many more than just seventeen million! Let's face it; this hardly describes a great multitude, does it? The truth is that if you go out from the premise that the Jewish State of Israel, together with all the other Jews in the Diaspora, constitutes **'all'** of Israel, the promise God made to Abraham makes no sense in that it clearly has not been fulfilled. However, when we examine the historical facts and recall that the ten northern tribes of Israel split away from the kingdom in 975 BC to set up their own separate kingdom to the north of Judah, it then all starts to make sense. When we then go on to discover that this promise of the 'Birthright' was not in fact made to Judah, the ancestor of the Jews, but to the two sons of Joseph instead, things really start to fall into place.

The Prophecy of Moses

The 'Birthright' promise of an innumerable multitude descending from Abraham through his son Isaac and grandson Jacob has most certainly come true when you take into account the combined populations of the world's nations of Israelite descent today. The promise has come true, as it is truly staggering to see the populations that have sprung from the British Isles. Just look at the former British colonies today. Look at Australia and Canada, as well as New Zealand. Notice also all of the British expatriate communities in South Africa, Kenya, Zimbabwe, Saudi Arabia, the Gulf States, as well as all of those in the Far East. The Birthright promises of the Abrahamic Covenant were given to Ephraim and Manasseh, the two sons of Joseph. The other tribes of Israel, although also greatly blessed, would not inherit the actual Birthright blessing. Ephraim and Manasseh were to become the most populous tribes of Israel. This means they would also need the largest territory for their populations. Ephraim and Manasseh, between them carved up the whole continent of North America. Ephraim alone established yet another continent, Australia, as exclusive territory for its expanding island population.

For those who are aware of the identity of the nations who represent the twelve tribes of Israel in the West today, it is relatively easy to calculate the approximate numbers involved. If we count the current population of the United States of America, Great Britain plus her kith and kin in the Commonwealth countries, the nations of north-western Europe, plus the Jews and all the Israelite expatriate populations worldwide, the total estimated population descended from the patriarch Jacob, comes to at least 600 million people. Notice, this refers to those descendants of the Twelve Tribes of Israel who came out of Egypt with Moses in that great Exodus! Yes, believe it or not, there are today at the very minimum around 600 million descendants of Jacob on the earth, and remember, Jacob's name was changed to Israel! Incredible as it may seem, even the Scriptures confirm this fact, as Moses himself prophesied that the children of Israel would become *'a thousand times more numerous'* than they were in his time. Read all about it in Israel's amazing history book.

Moses made a most astonishing prophecy! Moses himself prophesied that the descendants of those Israelites who came out of Egypt would one-day number six hundred million! Can you believe that? In the Book of Exodus it records that there were some 600,000 Israelite males in the Exodus, besides women and children. Scholars are agreed that these 600,000 males represented men of a military age, who were able to bear arms. Estimates of the total number making the Exodus vary from two to three and a half million people (Exodus 12:37). In the Book of Deuteronomy Moses addresses those same six hundred thousand Israelite men that came out on foot in that great Exodus from Egypt by prophesying the following words over them:

"The Lord your God has multiplied you, and here you are today, as the stars of heaven in multitude" (Deuteronomy 1:10).

We know that any scientific book about the cosmos will tell you that there are billions and billions of stars in the universe. So what is Moses saying here when he compares mere 600,000 men as being equal to "the stars of heaven in multitude"? Is the Bible per chance contradicting science here? Well, no, because according to modern science, the approximate number of stars that can be perceived by the naked eye in the darkness of the desert is around 600,000, including those stars that make up the Milky Way. Having compared the 600,000 Israelite males (besides women and children) who came out of Egypt, to the number of stars that can be observed by the naked eye, Moses goes on to prophesy over those same 600,000:

"May the Lord God of your father's make you A THOUSAND TIMES MORE NUMEROUS than you are, and bless you as He has promised you!" (Deuteronomy 1:11, emphasis added).

A thousand times more numerous than 600,000 = 600,000,000 (six hundred million), and thus once again we see a prophecy spoken out around three and a half thousand years ago, fulfilled in our time! Six hundred million is far more than the 14 to 18 million Jews reckoned to be in the world today, but then the Jewish people of today form only part of the picture, as they constitute only one of the twelve tribes of Israel. In considering today's recognized Jewish population of the world, we need to also take into account the multiple millions of Lost Jews that are around. Most of them, much like their brothers from the Ten Tribes, have no idea of their Jewish roots. When King Ferdinand and Queen Isabella of Spain issued their Royal edict on March 30, 1492, all the Jews of Spain were given just four months to either convert to Roman Catholicism, or suffer being expelled from the country. Then on July 30th of 1492, just three days prior to the ominous 9th of Av in the Hebrew calendar, the entire Jewish community, some, 200,000 people were being expelled from the country.

There were four kinds of Jews who were being vomited out of Spain and Portugal in those days.

- *Conversos,* who outwardly converted to the Roman Church scenario but were never really trusted by non-Jews of the community.

- *Crypto-Jews,* who were forcibly pressured into a "conversion." Yet all the while they maintained their biblical Torah background in secret, though never without intense surveillance and fear of persecution.

- *Maranos,* the term for swine or pigs in early Spanish, who outright refused baptism. They were also known as *Anuisim,* or *"unwilling,"* and as refugees ran for their lives whenever and wherever they could. *3

Tens of thousands of refugees died while trying to reach for safety. In some instances, Spanish ship captains charged Jewish passengers exorbitant sums, and then dumped them overboard in the middle of the ocean. In the last days before the expulsion, rumours spread throughout Spain that the fleeing refugees had swallowed gold and diamonds, and many Jews were knifed to death by brigands hoping to find treasures in their stomachs. *4

Most of these Jews found refuge in the Netherlands and the Americas, and over time they have become 'hidden' from the world. There have been many studies done on the hidden Jews of South America, including by Jews in Israel. The majority of Hidden Jews are found in Brazil and Mexico, an estimated ten to fifteen million in Brazil, and five million in Mexico. The official figures given for registered Jews in both countries are only 100,000 and 40,000 respectively. For other countries like Chile, the information is hard to come by. *5 Considering that most nations harbor hidden Jews, who have lost the knowledge of their origins, my personal estimation is that the total numbers may well be in excess of 35 million. As the tribe of Judah was very much part of the Exodus together with the other tribal sons of Jacob, this figure would be included with the 600 million indicated by the prophecy of Moses.

Not all Israel came out with Moses!

However, there are one or two problems with the above calculation! When Moses gave his prophecy about the Israelites becoming *"a thousand times more numerous,"* he was addressing those 600,000 men of military age. The fact is that, only fighting men between twenty and fifty years old, were being counted, leaving aside the women, the young and the older generation. This is the reason why scholars variously estimate the number who came out of Egypt to be around two and a half to three million souls.

David Rohl, the Egyptologist and historian, says that archaeological finds indicate a high proportion of females to males (3 to 1) in the land of Goshen amongst the 'Apiru' (Hebrews) just before their Exodus from Egypt, which is consistent with the Egyptians having attempted to kill off all male Hebrews in their infancy. *6 This changes the picture quite dramatically, as with women outnumbering the men of military age by a factor three to one, the total figure of those coming through the Exodus needs to be revised upwards. A more correct estimate therefore would be that around five to six million leaving Egypt under the leadership of Moses. Then, in addition we need to also consider *"the mixed Multitude"* of Egyptians and other foreigners who, according to the Scriptures went with them. However, we have no way of even estimating how many of these had attached themselves to Israel in this great Exodus. What is clear is that the numbers commonly accepted by the mainstream scholars is a massive under estimation of the actual people who made this most epic of all journeys.

Remember, in chapter two we emphasized the little known fact that **'not all of Israel came out with Moses!'** The great sages of Israel understood this fact, as well as the modern rabbinic scholarship, which variously estimate that 80 percent of the Israelite nation had already left Egypt prior to the Exodus. We then saw how Balaam the prophet looked down on the vast post-Exodus encampment of the Israel nation from on high and spoke out the following words:

"Who can count the dust of Jacob, or number 'ONE FOURTH' of Israel? (Numbers 23:8-10.)

Note that YHVH, the Holy Most Righteous God of Israel, inspired Balaam when he uttered those prophetic words. In this we are given a definitive answer, only 25 percent of the Hebrew nation came out of Egypt with Moses in the great Exodus. This indicates that the rest of the nation, amounting to 75 percent of the total population, had previously departed from the land of Egypt. Thus if the six million Israelites that left Egypt in the Exodus, only represented 25 percent of the total, then the whole nation must have numbered 4 x 6, bringing the total to a staggering 24 million Israelites. Apply the multiplication formula of Moses' prophecy, e.g. 24 x 1,000 = 2.4 billion. This means that the descendants of Jacob/Israel number around one third of mankind! This should by no means surprise us, as it is a superb fulfilment of God's Covenant with Abraham. This promise was repeated to Abraham's grandson, Jacob, at Bethel, when God reiterated the covenant as follows:

"Also your descendants shall be AS THE DUST OF THE EARTH; you shall spread abroad to the west and the east, to the north and the south; and in you and in your seed all the families of the earth shall be blessed." (Genesis 28: 14, emphasis added).

The faithfulness of our Creator knows no bounds, and you may be sure to find hundreds of millions of Israel's descendants in Asia, Asia-Minor, the Middle East, in Europe and Africa, as well as in both North, and South America. At the moment they are still hidden from view and largely out of sight. Soon the day will come when the veil which God has placed over their faces will be removed at His command, and then the whole world will stand in utter astonishment at the global extent of Israel's descendants – as many as the dust of the earth!

Chapter Five

❧

9th Sign
Israel was to be a royal kingdom

"When your days are fulfilled and you rest with your fathers, I will set up your seed after you, who will come from your body, and I will establish his kingdom. He shall build a house for My name, and I will establish the throne of his kingdom forever . . . And your house and your kingdom shall be established forever before you. Your throne shall be established forever" (2 Samuel 7:12-13 & 16).

"For thus says the LORD: 'David shall never lack a man to sit on the throne of the house of Israel'" (Jeremiah 33:17).

Sarah—the mother of nations

One especially important feature of the Abrahamic covenant is that there is to be a royal or kingly line, whose offspring are destined to become the rulers over Abraham's descendants. For the Lord not only promised Abraham that kings should come out of his loins, but he reiterated the promises of his Covenant to Sarah, the barren wife of Abraham. He said:

"I will bless her and also give you a son by her; then I will bless her, and she shall be a mother of nations; kings of peoples shall be from her" (Genesis 17:16).

Notice the promise that Sarah is to become a "mother of nations". The record shows that Sarah had only one son, namely

Isaac, and therefore it is only through the direct descendants of Isaac that these 'nations' could come into being.

Where are Sarah's nations?

What do you mean, "Where are Sarah's nations?" Surely, everybody knows that the Jews alone are the descendants of Sarah through her son Isaac. Yet the Scripture account in the book of Genesis clearly speaks about more than one nation. The question is: Where are Sarah's nations today? Notice she is not to become "a mother of 'a' nation", but that she is to become "a mother of nations". The commonly held theory that the Jews constitute all of Israel hereby stands exposed as a lie and a sham, as the inspired word of God clearly states that the matriarch Sarah is to become "a mother of nations", clearly inferring 'many nations'. It is only when one understands the reality that Israel split into two separate kingdoms with each going their separate way in the world that this prophecy can possibly make any sense. One part of the original kingdom of Israel was to lose the knowledge of her origins, whilst the other (Judah) retained it through her adherence to her religion. It is amongst that 'Lost House of Israel' that most of Sarah's nations are to be found! The promise has been fulfilled, as Sarah in her role as the matriarchal mother of the Celts, Khumry, Goths, Vandals, Alans, Anglo-Saxons, Friesians, Jutes, Vikings and Normans, has indeed become the "mother of nations". She is the mother of all the Semite Caucasians, who, from around 500 BC, for hundreds of years moved from the shores of the Caspian and Black Seas to their new homelands in Western Europe and the British Isles. Thus Sarah, the wife of Abraham has become 'mother' of America, Great Britain, Canada, Australia and New Zealand, as well as Ireland. She is also the 'mother' of those Israelite, mainly coastal nations of north-western Europe, such as Norway, Sweden, Finland, Iceland and Denmark, as well as the Netherlands, Belgium, Luxembourg, France and Switzerland. Apart from these, she is also the mother of all the Israelites scattered throughout the world, all those hundreds of millions in the north, south, east and western parts of the earth.

Above all she is also the matriarchal 'mother' of the State of Israel itself. Thus the prophecy has been fulfilled to the letter, as in counting these modern Israelite nations we can specifically identify as such; we discover that Sarah has become the 'mother' of not less than seventeen nations. As it happens the number seventeen is highly significant in the Hebrew alphabet, in that this number seventeen appears to be associated with deliverance and 'redemption' throughout the Scriptures. For instance Noah's ark came to a rest on the mountains of Ararat on the 17th day of the seventh month; the Israelites in their Exodus from Egypt crossed the Red Sea on the 17th day of Nisan; Esther fasted for three days, and on 17th Nisan, and she then told King Ahasuerus of Haman's plot to kill all the Jews in the whole of the Persian Empire. This association with the number seventeen is no accident, as the very heart of God's Covenant with his chosen people Israel is that he has promised to redeem her (Jeremiah 31:31-35).

The Seventeen Flags of Sarah's Nations
(courtesy Wikimedia)

Sarah—the mother of kings

"I will bless her and also give you a son by her; then I will bless her, and she shall be a mother of nations; kings of peoples shall be from her" (Genesis 17:16).

At the same time that these glorious promises were made God changed her name from Sarai to Sarah. The Hebrew meaning of this new name is 'Princess', and thus the name would be in harmony with her new identity and destiny, as only a princess can be a   mother of kings. The question is: Where are these royal descendants of Sarah, the wife of Abraham today?

The phrase *"kings of peoples shall be from her"* denotes that there were to be several kings ruling over different Israelite nations at one and the same time. Is this not exactly what we see in the world today? The fact is that most nations of Israelite descent have a hereditary monarch at their head. The only exceptions are the republican states of the USA, Finland, Iceland, France, Switzerland, Ireland and Israel. The rest like Britain, Canada, Australia, New Zealand, Norway, Sweden, Denmark, Netherlands, Belgium and Luxembourg are all kingdoms ruled by hereditary kings and queens. It is common knowledge that all the royal houses of Europe are related to each other. In view of the promises given to king David of Israel, as well as to Abraham, Sarah and Jacob, you can be sure that these same royal families are all descended from King David himself, and thus even today in these European royal houses his dynasty lives on.

The Lion of Judah in the Coat-of-Arms of Jerusalem (courtesy Wikimedia)

The Coats-of-Arms of Europe
(courtesy Wikimedia)

The Scepter of Judah

When Jacob, Abraham's grandson, was on his deathbed he spoke a prophetic individual blessing over all of his twelve sons and when he came to address his son Judah, he said the following: *"The sceptre shall not depart from Judah, nor a lawgiver from between his feet, until Shiloh comes"* (Gen. 49:10). 'Shiloh' was a reference to the Messiah, a direct descendant from King David. This same Shiloh is a reference to the Messiah, the Divine Deliverer, who would come to deliver and rule over a restored Israel in the end times. This same Shiloh is the hope of Israel even to this day. Ask any religiously observant Jew and he will tell you the same thing. And it is absolutely true to say that modern-day Celtic or

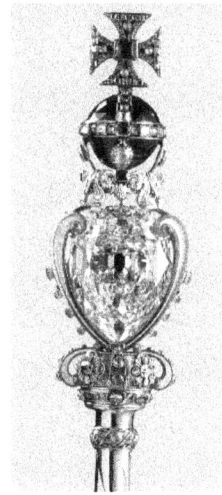

The Royal Scepter

91

Anglo-Saxon descendants of the Lost House of Israel are entitled to have that same hope! Furthermore, it is also true for those two billion plus Hebrew descendants of Abraham and Sarah, even though they are as yet totally unaware of the fact.

Moreover, we should not overlook God's absolutely unconditional promise that the Royal Sceptre would never depart from Judah, together with the immutable promise of the everlasting continuance of the Royal House and Throne of David. The prophet Nathan comes to King David of Israel and, speaking of his son Solomon, he utters the most amazing prophecy about the future of David's throne:

"When your days are fulfilled and you rest with your fathers, I will set up your seed after you, who will come from your body, and I will establish his kingdom. He shall build a house for My name, and I will establish the throne of his kingdom forever. . . And your house and your kingdom shall be established forever before you. Your throne shall be established forever." (2 Samuel 7:12-13,16).

The psalmist confirms this promise and reinforces its absolute certainty once again:

"I have made a covenant with My chosen, I have sworn to My servant David: 'Your seed I will establish forever, and build up your throne to all generations.'" (Psalm 89:3-4).

Your seed, your throne and your kingdom will be established forever and to all generations! What could be clearer than that! 'Forever' does mean 'forever', and 'all generations' does mean 'all generations' that will ever live on this planet. There is a considerable mystery about these prophecies, as on the face of it they have not ever been fulfilled. History records that this Royal Sceptre of the Royal House of David has not reigned over the kingdom of Judah since the nation went into captivity to Babylon. The fact is that ever since that time the Jewish people have been under Gentile dominion. They have had to wait 2,500 years before they were restored to full independent nationhood, when in 1948 the independent Jewish State was established in the Holy Land. The irony is that this independent Jewish State is a 'Republic' and not a Kingdom! This begs the question: Where are the royal descendants of King David and over which kingdom or kingdoms do they reign?

Seven witnesses to a Royal Covenant

The prophecy is that "the sceptre shall not depart from Judah" and that King David's throne is to be established forever, to all generations. Yet, the plain facts of history do not appear to show that these prophecies have been fulfilled. This is true if we look for this royal line in Judah. It is obvious that we need to look in another direction if we are to find this royal Davidic dynasty actually ruling over a territory and subjects today. Where do we find such a Royal lineage in the world? Let us examine and see if we can find any indication in the history book of Israel as to what kind of people these royal descendants of King David would actually rule over? The prophet Jeremiah gives us the answer to this mystery:

"FOR THUS SAYS THE LORD: 'DAVID SHALL NEVER LACK A MAN TO SIT ON THE THRONE OF THE HOUSE OF ISRAEL' " (Jeremiah 33:17).

Notice what the prophecy does **not** say! It does **not** say that a descendant of King David, who was from the tribe of Judah, would always sit on the throne of Judah! The Prophet Jeremiah makes it clear beyond all doubt that DAVID WOULD NEVER LACK A MAN TO SIT ON THE THRONE OF THE HOUSE OF **ISRAEL**!

The record of history itself confirms that the Jewish people have not had a Jewish King ruling over them since they returned from their captivity in Babylon! The Hasmonean princes, who occupied the throne of Judah, were of the tribe of Levi. Even the infamous King Herod the Great, who greatly restored, extended and beautified the Second Temple in Jerusalem, just prior to the birth of Christ, was not a descendant of Judah, let alone of King David. This King Herod was not even an Israelite. He was an Idumean, a people who in turn were descended from Esau, and he was a Roman stooge ruling over the then Roman province of Judea. He was a foreign king and a cruel despot, much despised by the Jews at the time.

After the Romans sacked Jerusalem in 70 AD and burned their most glorious Temple, the Jewish people became dispersed throughout the world, and in all that time they have never had their own kingdom. Even now with the return of the Jews and the re-establishment of the nation of Israel in the Land of Promise in 1948, they are being ruled over by a President, not a King. Yet the Bible, that great prophetic history book of Israel, makes it abundantly clear that descendants of King David will always rule over Israel. God actually calls in seven witnesses from nature itself to establish, underline and confirm his covenant with King David of Israel:

"Thus says the Lord: 'If you can break My covenant with the DAY and My covenant with the NIGHT, so that there will not be day and night in their season, then My covenant may also be broken with David My servant, so that he shall not have a son to reign on his throne, and with the Levites, the priests, My ministers. As the HOST of HEAVEN cannot be numbered, nor the SAND of the SEA measured, so will I multiply the descendants of David My servant and the Levites who minister to me'" (Jeremiah 33:20-22, emphasis added).

In verse 25 the prophet also mentions THE EARTH as one of God's witnesses to his covenant with King David. The seven witnesses in order are DAY, NIGHT, THE HOST (of heaven), HEAVEN, THE SAND, THE SEA, and THE EARTH.

God is saying that as long as there is a day and a night, and as long as there are the hosts of heaven, that is the suns, the moons, the planets, the stars and galaxies, there will always be a descendant of David sitting on the throne of Israel. As long as the earth continues to revolve around its own axis there will always be a member of this Judeo-Davidic family wielding the sceptre over a kingdom OF ISRAELITES on this earth. As long as there is sand and sea, and as long as there is an earth, there will always be a son of David sitting on the throne of Israel.

Could anything be stated in more absolute terms than these? The Christian churches, in their ignorance of the true meaning, are inclined to spiritualize these absolute prophecies away, by saying that God is speaking of a spiritual throne, a spiritual sceptre and a heavenly kingdom. Yet the prophecy is clearly speaking of a literal throne, an earthly kingdom and the lineal royal descendants of King David, and emphatically states that all of these are to endure forever and ever. As the saying goes: *'The proof of the pudding is in the eating!'* This is precisely the case in the issue of King David's descendants ruling over Israel, even to this very day! The plain fact is that it can be proved beyond any shadow of doubt to those who have the open mindedness of spirit to recognize the huge amount of evidence that exists for all of us to see.

Where is the Royal Throne of David today?

We have already seen that God has decreed that a descendant of David will always rule over Israel. Thus if we want to find the 'Lost House of Israel' today we will need to look for a most prominent and most ancient Royal Throne and Kingdom. *It is a matter of: "Find the throne of David and you will find the Lost House of Israel", or: "Find the Lost House of Israel and you have found the Throne of David!" These two go together like a horse and carriage.* This means all republics are automatically disqualified; we need to look for a kingdom! There are very few of them left in the world today. Consider the royal houses of Sweden, Norway, Denmark, Netherlands, Belgium, Luxembourg, Spain, Jordan and Saudi Arabia, as well as the United Kingdom of Great Britain and Northern Ireland. Then there are some more minor potentates amongst the oil rich Gulf States, and some in Africa and also in Asia. Amongst all of these kingdoms the Kingdom of Great Britain is without question the greatest and most prominent of them all. After all it is the British Queen that rules over Canada, Australia and New Zealand plus some other territories as well. It would be wise therefore for us to begin our search for the true identity and descent of the lineage of King David with the House of Windsor!

Where are the descendants of King David now?

The British Royal family can legitimately claim descent from King David of Israel in 1100 BC. It is possible to trace the ancestry of Queen Elizabeth II through the kings of Scotland and Ireland back to King David. The College of Heralds in London has traced the ancestry of the present Queen and established that she is the 144th direct descendant of King David. This means the British Royal family has existed for over three thousand years as the Davidic Dynasty ruling over the Tribes of Israel. This also means that the Queen herself is from the tribe of Judah, much like King David himself. This in direct fulfilment of prophecy, as through his prophet Jeremiah, God Himself decreed that:

"DAVID SHALL NEVER LACK A MAN TO SIT ON THE THRONE OF THE HOUSE OF ISRAEL" (Jeremiah 33:17).

We find the fulfilment of this most certain prophecy exemplified in that most inspired speech by John O' Gaunt in Shakespeare's Richard II:

> This royal throne of kings, this scepter'd isle
> This earth of majesty, this seat of Mars,
> This other Eden, demi-paradise;
> This fortress built by Nature for herself
> Against infection and the hand of war;
> This happy breed of men, this little world;
> This precious stone set in the silver sea,
> Which serves it in the office of a wall,
> Or as a moat defensive to a house,
> Against the envy of less happier lands;
> This blessed plot, this earth, this realm, this England.

The very fact that a direct descendant of King David of Israel reigns over Great Britain, Australia, Canada and New Zealand clearly indicates that these nations are of Israelite descent. God gave King David the following most amazing promise:

"Once I have sworn by My holiness; I will not lie to David: his seed shall endure forever, and his throne as the sun before Me; it shall be established forever like the moon, even like the faithful witness in the sky" (Psalm 89:35-37).

A Temporary Custody of the Crown

The Queen of Great Britain holds the crown by a divine stewardship. She is merely the present day custodian of God's promise to King David, as she possesses both the Sceptre and the Crown *"until He comes whose right it is"*. Whoever inherits the crown after Queen Elizabeth II, whether it is Prince Charles or his son Prince William, they will only have temporary custody of the crown, as ultimately this same Throne, Sceptre and Crown are earmarked for the promised Messiah of Israel. The prophet Ezekiel refers to this in Ezekiel 21:25-27. He prophesies the removal of the crown from Zedekiah, who was the last king to rule over the Kingdom of Judah. This same Zedekiah rebelled against the King of Babylon (2 Chronicles 36:11-13), and as a direct result Nebuchadnezzar, the King of Babylon, killed all the sons of Zedekiah before his very eyes. He then gouged out the eyes of Zedekiah and took him in chains to Babylon, where he languished in prison until his death. *1 To the pagan King of Babylon, it was clear that the Throne of David was destroyed the moment when all the male heirs were killed. This is Ezekiel's most important prophecy on the subject:

*"And thou, profane wicked prince of Israel, whose day is come, when iniquity shall have an end, Thus saith the Lord GOD, Remove the diadem, and take off the crown; this shall not be the same: exalt him that is low, and abase him that is high. I WILL OVERTURN, OVERTURN, OVERTURN IT; AND IT SHALL BE NO MORE, **UNTIL HE COME WHOSE***

RIGHT IT IS; AND I WILL GIVE IT HIM" (Ezekiel 21:25-27 KJV - emphasis added).

The Jewish interpretation

The Jewish sages and scholars interpret the phrase, "until he comes whose right it is", to mean that their promised Messiah will come to claim his right to the Throne of David, as 'he alone is the one whose right it is'! They base their belief on numerous scriptures such as those found in Zechariah 14 and 12; as well as in Jeremiah 31, Joel 3 and Isaiah 24, to mention just a few. The key scripture for Judaism and the religiously observant Jew is mentioned in Genesis, the first of the five books of *Torah*, where Moses records Jacob's last words to Judah, whilst on his deathbed: *"The sceptre shall not depart from Judah, nor a lawgiver* (margin, ruler's staff) *from between his feet, until SHILOH come; and unto him shall the gathering of the people be"* (Genesis 49:10 KJV – emphasis added). 'SHILOH' in Hebrew literally means 'THAT IS TO HIM' or it can also mean 'THAT IS HIS'. It is the Throne of David 'that is to Him' or 'that belongs to Him'. It is the Throne of David 'that is coming to Him' or 'that is destined to come to Him'. It is the Throne of David 'that is His'. This same 'SHILOH' is the Jewish Messiah, who is to come to re-gather, unite and restore Israel, and He is the one whose ultimate right it is to sit upon the Throne of David.

The Christian interpretation

Evangelical Christian scholars on the other hand interpret the phrase differently, as they say that Jesus will come again as King of kings and Lord of lords to sit on the Throne of David. These scholars do not necessarily contradict the Jewish interpretation; rather their application, as they understand it, spells out New Testament enlightenment, as to the identity of this 'Shiloh' or Messiah that is to come. Jesus was not only born a Jew but he was also a direct descendant of King David of Israel. His mother Mary was of royal stock, being of the house and lineage of David. Mary was descended from Nathan, King Solomon's brother, whereas her husband Joseph was descended from King Solomon through Coniah. Joseph, like Mary, was of royal stock, having Judah, Pharez, David and Solomon for ancestors. Being of the house and lineage of David, as stated in Luke 2:4, he took his wife Mary with him to Bethlehem, the city of David, to be taxed there. Christian scholars thus base their belief on Old Testament, as well as on New Testament prophecies of a great Deliverer and Saviour, who is to return to the earth to bring peace, deliverance and restoration to the world. One of the most well known Scriptures they cite each year, as a prelude to the nativity of Christ, is the account of the angel Gabriel visiting the Virgin Mary:

"The angel said to her, 'Do not be afraid, Mary, for you have found favour with God. And behold, you will conceive in your womb and bring forth a Son, and shall call His name JESUS. He will be great, and will be called the Son of the Highest; and the **LORD GOD WILL GIVE HIM THE THRONE OF HIS FATHER DAVID.** *And He will reign over the house of Jacob forever, and of His kingdom there will be no end'"* (Luke 1:30-33, emphasis added).

They then quite naturally connect this with a prophetic utterance by the prophet Isaiah in the Old Testament, made famous by Handel's *Messiah*:

"For unto us a Child is born, unto us a Son is given; and the government will be upon his shoulder. And His name will be called Wonderful Counsellor, Mighty God, Everlasting Father, Prince of Peace. Of the increase of His government and peace there will be no end, upon **THE THRONE OF DAVID AND OVER HIS KINGDOM***, to order it and establish it with judgement and justice from that time forward, even forever. The zeal of the LORD of hosts will perform this."* (Isaiah 9: 6-7, emphasis added)

The irony is that Jesus most certainly was not a Christian! The undeniable fact of history is that Jesus was a Jew, born of Jewish parents in Bethlehem, the city of David. The New Testament Scriptures make it unmistakably clear that Jesus was a *Torah*-observant Jew. In all of his teaching he encouraged his followers to observe the commandments of *Torah*. Not only was he born a Jew, but also as he commenced his official ministry at age thirty he became an important Rabbi who gained a considerable following amongst his fellow Jews. Another important fact to remember is that all of his twelve disciples were also *Torah*-observant Jews. Thus the double irony is that the Apostles like their Master were not what you would call Christians either! In addition we also need to bear in mind that the Christian religion we see in the world today in all of its multifarious forms, as well as its tens of thousands denominations, bears almost no resemblance to the original teachings of Jesus, or his Apostles. Instead it was the Celtic form of Christianity that found such ready acceptance in the British Isles, which in its early days most closely resembled the original teaching of Jesus. These Celtic Christians, like Jesus himself and his twelve Apostles, were *Torah*-observant in that they kept the seventh day Sabbath, as their day of rest; they kept the Passover, and observed the *kosher* food laws of the Old Testament. Unlike the Christian church that was to emerge several centuries later on, these early Celtic Christians remained faithful to the original Hebrew roots of their faith. The particular Nazarene sect of Judaism, which Jesus did establish bears no comparison with the Christianity that emerged from the embrace of the pagan Roman Empire several centuries later on. Nevertheless, some think it is possible that the Jewish *Shiloh*, or Messiah, and the Christian Jesus, as King of kings and Lord of lords, may well be one and the same person, as, after all, they are both destined to rule on the throne of David in the Messianic age to come. In this context it can well be said that Queen Elizabeth II and her successors are merely the temporary custodians of that illustrious throne of David, until *"He comes whose right it is"*! The understanding that the royal throne of Great Britain is a present day continuation of the ancient Throne of King David of Israel, in direct fulfilment of prophecy, does add a very special dimension to the British royal family.

Is this the end of the Davidic dynasty?

The Bible, that superb history book of Israel records a line of kings, each of them a descendant of David in a continuous dynasty, down to King Zedekiah. As we have already seen, the armies of King Nebuchadnezzar of Babylon captured this king, his eyes were put out, and he was then taken to Babylon where he died in a dungeon. Just prior to his deportation all his sons were slain before his very eyes. The Babylonian invaders also killed all the nobles of Judah, who were not already imprisoned or enslaved at that time, so that none could remain to sit on the throne of David! The Chaldean armies of Babylon destroyed Jerusalem and burned Solomon's glorious Temple, as well as the king's palace, and took the Jews as a captive slave people to Babylon. From that day there is no record of any king of the line of David ruling over Judah. On the face of it, and judging by the evidence available at the time, the royal dynasty that King David founded had come to an inglorious end. Had the sceptre departed from Judah? Had the throne of David ceased? If this were true the prophetic word of God would stand completely discredited. There has to be another answer! What then is the answer to the puzzle?

If the throne of David ceased with Zedekiah, then it does not exist today! And if it does not exist, how will Shiloh – who depending upon your view is either the Jewish Messiah Ben David, or Jesus Christ, as Christians call their Saviour, *'whose right it is'* – sit upon a throne that does not exist? It does no good for the Christian church to 'spiritualize' this throne away, and in doing so they are contradicting their own sacred book, the Bible. We read in 1 Chronicles 29:23, *"Then Solomon **sat on the throne of the LORD** as king instead of David"*. This is quite clearly speaking about a literal physical throne with a literal physical monarch that is described here as *"the throne of the LORD"*. This disproves the unscriptural line of thought in many churches today that the throne has somehow been transferred to heaven for Christ to reign upon spiritually.

We have already seen how God swore by His own holiness that the seed of David would endure forever and that his throne as the sun before Him would be established forever (Psalm 89:35-37). By definition therefore it cannot be true that the Davidic lineage ceased when the sons of Zedekiah were being slaughtered by the Babylonians in 585 BC, as God does not lie! There has to be another explanation! The prophet Jeremiah affirms that the glorious Messiah is coming to sit on an *'existing'* throne! This is why the present British royal family can only be the temporary custodians, tenants or stewards of that throne, as they are simply holding it for someone else *'whose right it is!'*

Royal affirmations from England and Scotland

The first monarch of the United Kingdom, King James I of England and VI of Scotland, in 1618 rebuilt the dilapidated Alders Gate in the city of London. On the north side he decorated the center of the arch with a figure of himself on horseback flanked by two niches in which he placed the figures of two of the foremost prophets of Israel – Samuel and Jeremiah. Under the carved image of Jeremiah was quoted the text of Jeremiah 17:25. This text is highly revealing, as it gives a most remarkable insight into the mind of King James. This is what it says: ***"Then shall enter the gates of this city kings and princes sitting on the throne of David, riding on chariots and horses, they and their princes accompanied by the men of Judah and the inhabitants of Jerusalem; and this city shall remain forever."*** Is it not remarkable that this king, whose very name is derived from Jacob, saw himself as the heir and descendant of King David of Israel? King James, by this monument carved in stone, clearly demonstrated that he saw himself as being seated upon the throne of David. Furthermore, King James claimed that the Lord had made him "King over Israel". He also had a gold coin struck called *'the Jacobus'*, named after himself, and upon it he had inscribed in Latin the prophecy of Ezekiel 37:22, which stated: ***"I will make of them one nation in the land on the mountains of Israel; and one king shall be king over them all; they shall no longer be two nations, nor shall they ever be*** *divided into two kingdoms again"* (Ezekiel 37:22). Thus he saw the coming together of the kingdoms of Scotland and England under his crown as a forerunner and partial fulfilment of Ezekiel's prophecy about the ultimate reunification of the two Houses of Israel. As it happens, it does have the ring of truth about it, as Judah might well be called the ruling tribe of the Scottish nation, whereas, Ephraim most certainly is the ruling tribe of the English.

Gold Coin of King James I of England and VI of Scotland
(courtesy Classical Numismatic Group, Inc., Wikimedia)

Long before James I, King Edward IV (1461-1470; 1471-1483) had published his family tree in which he emphatically claims his direct descent from Jehoshaphat, a most noble and righteous King of Judah. This same Jehoshaphat (872-848 BC) was the fifth direct descendant of King David, who, unlike his great ancestors David and Solomon, merely ruled over the kingdom of Judah. Edward IV's ancestral pedigree was published on an 18-foot long scroll, which even today is kept at the Lancashire Records Office at Lancaster.

Queen Victoria reputedly spent one million Pounds researching the genealogy of her family and was able to trace her ancestry all the way back to king David of Israel. It was a truly astonishing sum for her time. No doubt her heralds were greatly assisted by the meticulous research carried out by her royal ancestor King Edward IV. Even then, it was no new discovery, as some 1,400 years before Victoria's reign; the Saxon kings traced themselves back to Odin, who in turn traced back his descent to David. Proof of this exists in very ancient manuscripts held in the Heralds' College, London. Sharon Turner also refers to this fact in his standard work. *2

His Royal Highness, Prince Michael of Albany, head of the Royal House of Stewart, in his recent eye-opening work, *The Forgotten Monarchy of Scotland*, actually claims descent from the ancient Royal House of Judah. He writes:

"Scotland's royal heritage is the oldest in Europe, and it can be traced back well into the BC era. The legacy of the Scots kings was hewn on the Stone of Destiny, the venerated relic of the Beth-el Covenant. (See: Genesis 28:18-22.)

"The Royal House of Dalriada, through which all kings of the Scots traced their succession from the biblical Kings of Judah, from the Princes of Greater Scythia . . . many regarded the Stewarts as their biblical kings. Prior to becoming High Stewards of Scotland, the Stewarts' maternal forebears were Seneschals in Brittany, and they were of the same ancestral stock as the earlier Merovingian Kings of the Franks, in descent from the ancient Royal House of Judah." *3

From the authoritative statements made above, we can deduce that the Scottish royal house of Stewart traces its descent all the way back to King David of Israel, through both the male and the female lines. It is because God decreed that David's throne would endure forever, that throughout history, kings of the royal line of David have held to the concept of the "Divine Right of Kings". A very good example of this is Charles I, of the royal house of Stewart, who in his struggle with Oliver Cromwell and the British parliament maintained his divine right to rule, right up to the moment of his execution on January 30, 1649.

The sitting tenants of the Throne of David

Queen Elizabeth II of Great Britain and the British Commonwealth currently has the honour of being the 'sitting tenant' of King David's throne. The point to remember is that the throne is not hers, as it belongs to 'Him whose right it is'! Whoever sits on this throne, at the time when Messiah returns to establish His rule upon the earth will simply have to hand the sceptre, the crown and the throne over to Him. It can therefore be said that the current British royal family are merely keeping the throne of David warm for the prophesied great King yet to come! Is this not a most remarkable revelation!

Jeremiah's special Commission

The Prophet Jeremiah was still a minor, a teenager just seventeen years old, when he received his calling as a Prophet to the nations. He gives the details of his commission in the first chapter of his own book detailing his prophesies. He records the account of his special commission as follows:

"Then the word of the LORD came to me, saying: Before I formed you in the womb I knew you, Before you were born I sanctified you; I ordained you a prophet to the nations." (Jeremiah 1: 4-5).

Jeremiah is ordained a "Prophet to the Nations!" What nations might this be referring to? Is Jeremiah sent to all the nations in the world, or is he sent to a particular group of nations? The word translated as "nations" in the text is the same word used when the LORD said to Abraham, *"I have made you a father of many nations;"* *4a and when he said to Rebekah, the wife of Isaac, *"Two nations are in your womb."* *4b Clearly Jeremiah's calling is to the *"two nations,"* *the two houses – Israel and Judah;* the inheritors of the "Birthright" and the "Sceptre." His commission is to the offspring of Jacob only, and not to all the nations of the earth. Jeremiah then records the essence of his divine commission, as follows:

Then the LORD put forth His hand and touched my mouth, and the LORD said to me: "Behold, I have put My words in your mouth. See I have this day set you over the nations and over the kingdoms, TO ROOT OUT and to PULL DOWN, TO DESTROY and to THROW DOWN, TO BUILD and TO PLANT." (Jeremiah 1: 9-10, emphasis added).

Jeremiah's most painful commission is to *"root out, to pull down and to destroy the Davidic kingdom* then ruling over the kingdom of Judah. His task was to *"throw down the throne of David, and root out that branch of the royal family that occupied the throne at that time.* This cannot possibly mean that God's promises to King David have become null and void – *"For God gave the kingdom to David forever and his sons by a covenant of Salt."* *5

Notice, Jeremiah's task after he had 'rooted out' and 'pulled down' and destroyed the royal family occupying the throne of David ruling over the kingdom of Judah, was to BUILD AND TO PLANT IT ELSEWHERE! This had to be accomplished before Jeremiah's death. Where and how did Jeremiah build and plant the throne? Judah was no more, as she had gone into captivity in Babylon. Jerusalem lay in ruins and the Temple of Solomon was burned down. The only place where the throne could be replanted was in Israel. The only problem is that the Northern Kingdom of Israel was no more, as the ferocious warrior Empire of Assyria had taken the entire nation into captivity over 130 years previously. Even the Assyrian Empire did not exist anymore, as the Persians had defeated then at the battle Carchemish, and who knows where all those Israelites had gone. On top of all of this all the male descendants of Zedekiah, the last king of Judah were dead, having been killed by Nebuchadnezzar, the king of Babylon. What was Jeremiah to do? Where could he go?

The Triple overthrow of a Royal Throne

The king of Babylon was convinced that he had rooted out and destroyed the throne of David for all time. With all the male heirs to the throne of David slain, was God's promise to King David broken?

Was there no one left to inherit that throne? King Nebuchadnezzar of Babylon would not have been aware of the laws of Israel, which in certain circumstances allowed for female succession and inheritance. The very thought would have been utterly inconceivable to him, as females of the royal lineage of Babylon would never be considered for rulership or government. The very idea of female succession was reprehensible to all of the male dominated pagan societies surrounding the land of Israel at the time. Nevertheless, in the book of Numbers Moses was given a very specific instruction by God. *"If a man die, and have no son, then ye shall cause his inheritance to pass unto his daughter"* (Numbers 27:8 KJV). This divine ruling has become known as the law of Zelophehad, whereby a woman may inherit a throne in the absence of a male heir. This is in direct contrast to the 'Salic Law' operating on the European mainland such as France and Germany. This code of laws of the Salian Franks and other Germanic tribes specifically excludes women from royal succession. It is no coincidence that in Great Britain, as well as in the Netherlands and the Scandinavian countries, the ancient law of Israel applies, as in all these kingdoms a queen may reign in her own right. Some of Britain's greatest monarchs have been queens.

The big question now is did Zedekiah, the last king of Judah, have any daughters? The answer is found in the book of Jeremiah, where the prophet speaks about the aftermath of the calamity that has come upon the kingdom of Judah through the Babylonian invasion. In Jeremiah 43:6, we see mention of *"the king's daughters"*, and the prophet here relates how he and Baruch, his scribe *cum* secretary, were travelling with them.

W.H. Bennett, FRGS, the great genealogist, speaking of one of these daughters of King Zedekiah in his authoritative document states the following:

*"Genealogical records kept through the ages show the descent of our Royal Family through the kings of Scotland from the ancient kings of Ireland. Further, these records, as well as the most ancient Irish ones, show the descent of the Irish kings from Tea Tephi (Tamar), elder daughter and heir of Zedekiah, last king of Judah. As the Royal family of the kingdom of Judah was the House of David, it follows that in its descent from Tea Tephi, our Royal House is the continuation from the House of David, and consequently, the British Throne is the Throne of David." *6*

Ancient Irish records speak of a Hebrew Princess, who arrived in Ireland with a Prophet and his Scribe, and of how she married the Chief King of Ireland. From this same union can be traced the descent of the Irish and Scottish kings, of which the Royal House of Windsor is the present day continuation.

The prophet Ezekiel prophesied that the throne of David would be overthrown no less than three times. He gave his prophecy in Ezekiel 21: 25-27, where it says the following:

*"And thou, profane and wicked prince of Israel, whose day is come, when iniquity shall have an end, Thus saith the Lord GOD, **Remove the diadem, and take off the crown; this shall not be the same: exalt him that is low, and abase him that is high. I WILL OVERTURN, OVERTURN, OVERTURN IT;** and it shall be no more, until he come whose right it is; and I will give it him"* (KJV – emphasis added).

We need carefully to dissect this prophetic statement so that we may understand its true meaning:

"Remove the diadem, and take off the crown." King Zedekiah of Judah had the crown – it was removed and taken from him. He subsequently died a prisoner in a Babylonian dungeon after he had witnessed the slaughter of all his sons and male heirs.

"This shall not be the same." This means that the diadem is not to cease, but instead a change is to take place. The throne is to be overturned and another is to wear the crown. God's promise to David is not to go by default!

"Exalt him that is low, and abase him that is high." Who is the one that is "high"? King Zedekiah of Judah! Now he is to be abased and he is to lose that crown. The kingdom of Judah itself has been "high", while Israel, after her forcible removal into captivity by the war-like Assyrians, has been low these many years without a king (Hosea 3:4). Judah is to be abased, as history itself testifies to the fact that from hereon she has ceased to be ruled by the lineal descendants of David. Thus it is Israel that is to be exalted! Henceforth it is Israel that will be ruled by the royal descendants of David.

"I will overturn, overturn, overturn it; and it shall be no more, until he comes whose right it is." What was to be overturned? What is the subject here anyway? It is 'the diadem, the crown, the throne' that is to be overturned . . . not just once – it is to be overturned three times!

Throne of David moves from Judah to Ireland

The first overturn occurs soon after the death of King Zedekiah, when Jeremiah, together with his scribe Baruch, took the king's daughter to Ireland to replant David's dynasty there amongst the tribes of Israel, who had earlier migrated to the Emerald Isle. Jeremiah was the grandfather of these Hebrew princesses, and Baruch, his faithful scribe, was also of the blood royal, as he was their uncle.

An important point to consider is that the Babylonian invaders let Jeremiah go free. He travelled west with a group of Jewish fugitives to Egypt accompanied by his scribe Baruch and the daughters of Zedekiah, Judah's last king (Jeremiah 43:1-7). The *"king's daughters"* were of the royal dynastic line of King David. The Bible duly records that the party arrived at Tahpanhes where the then Pharaoh of Egypt had a palace fortress (Jeremiah 43:1-7). *7 The great Victorian archaeologist and Egyptologist, Sir Flinders Petrie (1853-1942), carried out many excavations throughout Egypt. One of his excavations took place at Tahpanhes, situated in the present day town of Tell Defneh. He found the remains of a great fortress palace that even today goes by the name of 'Qasr Bint el Jehud', meaning, 'Palace of the Jewish Princesses'. Thus, here we find independent archaeological evidence, as well as independent oral evidence, both of which confirm the account given in *Israel's History Book*. We find confirmation that princesses of the royal house of Judah at one time stayed in this remote outpost of the Egyptian empire.

The Bible does not tell us what happened to Jeremiah and the daughters of Zedekiah after their arrival at Tahpanhes in Egypt. However, God told the prophet that it would not be   safe for him to remain in Egypt (Jeremiah 42:13-22). It is certain, therefore, that he did not stay in Egypt. The question is: Where did he go? There was no way back to Judah, as the kingdom had fallen. There was also no way back to Israel, as the northern kingdom had ceased to exist after the Assyrian invaders had taken its entire population into captivity well over a century previously. The prophet was aware, though, of the whereabouts of other Israelite settlements, colonies and even royal kingdoms in the western isles of the sea. In Jeremiah 25:22, he wrote about Tyre and Sidon *"and the kings of the isles which are beyond the sea"* (KJV). He could not go to the cities of either Tyre of Sidon on the coast of Lebanon because they were in the territory ruled by the Babylonians. He had to take the daughters of Zedekiah to a place of safety in the west, well beyond the reach of Israel's enemies. There was thus really only one place to go, and his comment that the isles were beyond the seas confirms that he was well aware that those islands were beyond the Mediterranean Sea. Hence Jeremiah and his royal party set out for Hibernia (Ireland), and this is where he duly arrived and settled, as confirmed by many legends in Irish folklore. *8

No other nation on earth has this folklore or legendary tradition of an ancient prophet such as Jeremiah visiting them. Jeremiah's visit with the royal princesses is at the center of all of Ireland's legendary tradition. Only one place on earth claims to have the grave of the prophet Jeremiah. Only one country's history speaks of a great prophet and lawgiver, with his scribe Baruch bringing a king's daughters from Egypt. Only one country claims the Harp of King David for its own. That country is Ireland, also known as 'the Emerald Isle', a veritable jewel in the sea.

The first settlers of Ireland

The historians are unanimous about the first settlers of Ireland being the Tuatha de Danaan, or literally the Tribe of Dan, one of the Twelve Tribes of Israel. The Greeks referred to them as the Danaoi, in Latin they were called Danaus. In Hebrew, the word Dan means *judge*. It is therefore no coincidence that the word Dunn in the Irish language means just what Dan means in Hebrew, *i.e.* a judge. In Genesis 49:17, the patriarch Jacob, whose name was changed to Israel, foretells on his deathbed what would befall each of his twelve sons, and of Dan he says: **"Dan shall be a serpent by the way"**. Another translation direct from the original Hebrew is: **"Dan shall be a serpent's trail"**.

It is a fact of history that the tribe of Dan named every place where they went, after Dan, the father of their tribe. In the book of Judges 18:29, it is recorded how a company of some 600 Danite soldiers captured the city of Laish, and *"they called the name of the city Dan, after the name of Dan their father"*. Remember, in Hebrew, vowels were not written. The sound of the vowel had to be supplied by the speaking. Thus, the word 'Dan' in its English equivalent would be spelt simply 'Dn'. It might be pronounced as 'Dan, Den, Din, Don, or Dun', and still represent the original Hebrew name. Just before Moses died, he too gave a prophecy about each tribe of Israel, and of Dan he said: **"Dan is a lion's whelp; he shall leap from Bashan."** Bashan was an area of 'Palestine' territory incorporating also the coastal areas of Southern Lebanon; hence Dan is to leap from Bashan in 'Palestine'. These Danites were amongst the foremost seafarers of the ancient world and were closely allied to the Phoenicians. That Dan's leap landed him in Ireland is very clear, as we find his name everywhere on the place names of Ireland. We find it in Lon-don-derry, Dungarven, Dun-dalke, Don-negal, Dans-lough, Dan-sower,

Dan-monism, Dun-drum, Duns-more, Din-gle, Danesfort, Donohill, Doneraile, Donaghadee, Dunabrattin, Dunhill, Duneen, Dunlavin, Duncormick, Dunmanway, Dunmanus, and many more.

The word 'Hebrew' is derived from the name 'Eber', who was the great-great-great-great-grandfather of Abraham. 'Eber' is the root of the word 'Hebrew' meaning 'Colonizer' or 'Colonist, whilst another meaning is; *'he who crosses over.'* Spain was a major Israelite colony, and we can denote the name 'Eber' in her name, as the ancient name for Spain was 'IBERIA'. She was also referred to as the IBERIAN PENINSULA, and the most famous river in Spain is the 'RIVER EBRO'. An ancient name for Ireland was IBHERIU or IBERIU, and ancient Gaelic histories record that the ancestors of the Gaelic settlers of Ireland came from IBERIA (Israelite Spain). Ancient Ireland was also called 'HIBERNIA', a name that preserves the Hebrew root word 'Eber'. Note how closely the words 'IBHERIU' and 'IBERIU' coincide phonetically with the pronunciation of the word 'HEBREW'.

According to the Encyclopaedia Britannica, the Greeks listed the 'DANAANS' or 'DANUANA' as a distinct seafaring people as early as 1200 BC. These 'Danaans' were part of a seafaring alliance of peoples known as the 'SEA PEOPLES', who raided and settled in Mediterranean coastlands at the time. The Israelite tribe of Dan, whose territory included a strip of land on the Mediterranean shore, had a nautical identity, *e.g.* Judges 5:17, refers to Dan remaining *"in ships"*! When studying the ancient history of Ireland, we find that prior to 1000 BC, a strong colony called *'Tuatha de Danann,'* [tribe of Dan], arrived in ships and drove out the other tribes and settled there. *9

The ancient breach is healed

Later on, in the days of King David of Israel, a colony of the line of Zarah arrived in Ireland from the Near East. These Danite colonizers of Ireland were being ruled over by a prince of the Zarah branch of the royal family of Judah. Then in 569 BC, according to the ancient oral history of Ireland, as recorded and meticulously written down for posterity centuries later in the various annals and chronicles of Ireland, an elderly, white-haired patriarch, sometimes referred to as a saint, came to Ireland. With him was the princess, daughter of an eastern king, and Simon Brach, which in different accounts is spelt 'Breck, Berech, Brach, Brug, Bruch or Berach' – who accompanied him. *10

At this point it is interesting to note that 'Baruch' was the Hebrew name of Jeremiah's scribe or secretary. Notice how closely this Hebrew name, which means 'blessed' resembles the names given by the writers of the early Irish annals. Could this be just another coincidence? Surely not! Remember that in those early days between 500 and 600 years BC, the Book of Jeremiah would not have been written, let alone been available in Ireland. So how then could these records, written by the ancient bards and historians of Ireland, come up with this name Baruch that is so intimately associated with the prophet Jeremiah?

The name of the princess was Tea Tephi, and she was none other than the daughter of king Zedekiah of Judah, who had come to such an unfortunate end at the hands of the king of Babylon. This royal party included the son of the king of Ireland, who had been in Jerusalem at the time of the siege. There he had, according to Irish legendary tradition, become acquainted with Tea Tephi. He married her shortly after 585 BC, after the city had fallen. Then in 583 BC, Eochaidh the Heremon was crowned High King of Ireland after his marriage to Tea Tephi, the daughter of Zedekiah, the king of Judah. Heremon Eochaidh I is said to have been able to orally recount his ancestry back to the patriarch Judah through his son Zerah, the twin brother of Pharez. *11 Eochaidh and Tea Tephi, according to these extraordinary Irish legends, thus fulfilled the command of Jacob that Judah should rule over the house of Israel.

To summarize, Eochaidh was descended from the royal Zerah line of the patriarch Judah, whereas Tea Tephi was descended from the royal Pharez line of Judah, which had produced the royal House of King David. Thus the two royal lineages were brought together in their union exactly as prophesied (Genesis 38:27-30 and Ezekiel 21:25-27). According to this unique legendary tradition, most if not all the royal families of northwestern Europe have in turn descended from this marriage.

The harp of David — an Irish symbol

Besides the royal family, Jeremiah brought some unique artefacts from Israel, such as a harp, a large chest, and a wonderful stone called 'lia-fail' or 'stone of destiny'. The harp of Irish heraldry bears testimony to the fact that 'The Harp of King David' had become the Royal symbol of the Irish kings for over a thousand years. It is still one of the most potent symbols of Ireland today. Order a pint of Irish Guinness beer and you will find the golden Harp of King David prominently displayed on the bottle. Ryanair, the famous short haul Irish airline, also prominently displays the Harp of David symbol on its aircraft tailfins as part of its corporate image. The question is: Why should a country like Ireland use this uniquely Davidic symbol if there is no connection? Why should the Harp of King David have played such a prominent role in over two and a half thousand years of Irish history?

Another interesting fact is that the crown worn by the kings of the line of Heremon and the other sovereigns of ancient Ireland had twelve points. With all the evidence of the Israelite origins of the Irish people, the twelve points of the royal Irish crown could be none other than yet another reference to the Twelve Tribes of Israel. The twelve points on the crown were in effect declaring that it was the crown of Israel that these Irish kings wore.

The Stone of Destiny

An aged guardian, whom the Irish historians referred to as Ollam Fodhla, accompanied Tea Tephi, the Hebrew princess. Ollam Fodhla in Hebrew has the connotation of 'revealer' or 'sage'. The name of Erin's capital was changed from the Celtic Cathair Crofin to

Tara, which is a Hebrew word derived from *Torah*, meaning, 'precept, law, teaching or instruction'. Jeremiah would have been 58 years old when he left Jerusalem for Tahpanhes in Egypt. This can be determined from his age at the time of his calling as a prophet. Jeremiah was still a minor, a mere youth, only seventeen years old, when he received his call as the "Prophet to the Nations," in the thirteenth year of Josiah the son of Amon, king of Judah. By utilising these two key details it is possible to work out his age at the time of his departure from Jerusalem with the *"kings' daughters."* The Scripture account does not tell us how long he remained in Tahpanhes, or indeed the duration of his subsequent stay in Israelite Spain, or the time it took to sail to Ulster in Northern Ireland. It is probable therefore that he reached his destination at around age sixty. This explains why the Irish records refer to him as *"an aged Guardian."* Nevertheless, this same Ollam Fodhla, meaning *"revealer"* or *"prophet,"* established an educational and political establishment in Tara, in ancient Ireland, and he dominated the affairs of the ancient kingdom for forty years. His influence caused a national reformation, as he re-established the Mosaic code of law of Israel. The famous Four Courts of Georgian Dublin were decorated with large medallions of the world's greatest lawgivers. They included King Alfred, King Solomon, Confucius, Moses and Ollam Fodhla.

Jeremiah's Grave is located in Ireland

Jeremiah would thus have been a hundred years old when he died. There is a place in Ireland called Ollam Fodhla's, that is to say, Jeremiah's Cairn, which is the proudly named spot of the burial place of the great ancient prophet of Israel. It is situated on the most elevated spot of the entire range of hills, 904 feet above sea level. His tomb is situated in Schiabhla-Cailliche near Oldcastle, County Meath, in Ireland, not far from Tara, in the ancient royal cemetery of the kings of Ireland. A huge cairn of stones marks the spot, and a large carved stone in the shape of a great megalithic stone chair is still pointed out as Jeremiah's judgement seat. Whereas, the graves of most of the prophets of the Bible may be found in either Israel or present day Jordan, there is no record of Jeremiah's grave in all of the Middle East. *12 Most of the locations of the graves of the Patriarchs, Matriarchs and Prophets of Israel are well known, and are well cared for even in Muslim countries. Nevertheless, Islamic extremists recently blew up the shrine traditionally regarded to be the burial place of the Prophet Jonas in Iraq's second largest city Mosul. The Islamic State militants, who overran the city in June 2014, and imposed their harsh interpretation of Islamic law, apparently first ordered everyone out of the Mosque of the Prophet Younis, or Jonah, before blowing it up, claiming it had become a place for apostasy not prayer. *13 There is not a single country other than Ireland that claims to have the grave of the Prophet Jeremiah on its soil.

Jeremiah and his party brought with them a pillar stone, which has ever since been used as the coronation stone for the Irish royal descendants of King David. According to the *Annals of Ireland by the Four Masters* - 'Inis Fail', signifying the 'Island of Destiny', was the name given by the Tuatha di-Dannans, from a remarkable stone they brought into Ireland, which was called Lia Fail, or Stone of Destiny. A remarkable coincidence about the name 'LIA-FAIL' is that, whereas Hebrew reads from right to left and English reads from left to right, you can read this name either way, and it still is 'lia-fail.' Even in this remarkable fact, and wholly apart from the many legends associated with it, we have yet another indication of the Hebrew origin of this Stone of Destiny. Could this too be just another coincidence? It was upon this self-same highly revered stone that all the Irish kings were crowned in a most solemn ceremony.

The extraordinary fact is that *Israel's History Book* confirms that the ancient kings of Israel were also crowned on or by a most sacred stone. Thus the Irish kings were adopting an exclusive Israelite custom in their coronation ceremonies. The question again is: Why? Why would these ancient Irish kings adopt a custom that previously had only been practiced in ancient Israel? Why would they do this if there really were no connection? Confirmation that Jacob's pillar stone did indeed feature in the coronation of the kings of ancient

Israel can be found in *Israel's History Book* in 2 Kings 11:14 and 2 Kings 23:3.

Remember also that Jacob set up this pillar stone for a *'witness'*, and as such any coronation, any covenant, any oath or vow made upon, by, or near this stone would carry special significance, as the stone itself represented the House of God.

In Irish 'Lia' is stone and 'Fail' means fate, hence the name given to it as the *'stone of fate', or the 'stone of destiny'.* But it is the 'stone of destiny', only because it is Jacob's Pillar Stone, which he used as a pillow at Bethel. Remember, the explanation given in chapter five that Bethel in the Hebrew language means the 'House of God'. We find an amazing connection here in the fact that Tea Tephi was called 'The Daughter of God's House'. In reality she was thus called the *'Daughter of Bethel'.* 'Lug' is Celtic for God, and 'Aidh' means a house; hence the word 'Lughaidh' means 'God's House', or Bethel in Hebrew. Amergin, the Chief Druidic Bard to King Dermot, monarch of Ireland in the 6th Century, in the notes of the *Annals of the Four Masters*, refers to Tea Tephi as follows:

> *'A rampart was raised around her house*
> *For Teah, the daughter of Lughaidh,*
> *She was buried outside in her mound,*
> *And from it was named Tea-mur.*

Further background on Jacob's pillar stone

The shape and size of the Stone of Destiny makes sense of the account given in Genesis chapter 28, which is if you really believe it is the same stone Jacob used as a pillow stone all those years ago. First, it is in fact about the size of a big pillow, being about 26x16x10 inches. By definition, because of its precise rectangular shape, it must already have been a stone that had been cut into a building block shape when Jacob found it. The original stonecutters had probably rejected the stone because it had a crack in it, and thus it had been discarded before being finished.

117

There is also a tradition that when it came to the building of Solomon's Temple that this Pillar Stone of Jacob, which was called the House of God, should be included in the building. However, the builders rejected it because of the large crack in it. There seemed to be no way it could be used as the cornerstone of the Temple. If the Stone of Destiny really is Jacob's pillar stone then it is easy to see how he could stand it upon its end to be a 'pillar'. Even so it would still have been difficult because it weighs over 300 pounds.

When we check the original Hebrew meaning of the word translated as 'pillar', we see that it means a 'stone marker', which often were large stone pillars. **Most likely Jacob set it up as a pillar or stone marker so that he could find the exact location when he returned.** I dare say he never thought it would take him 21 years before he would come back to the same spot. It was a highly significant and most unusual act for Jacob to anoint the 'pillar stone' with oil. The question is: Why did he do it? He did it simply because he was inspired to do it! In ancient Israel the anointing with oil was only ever reserved for the inauguration of a high priest or the coronation of a king. Thus by anointing this stone that he had already formally named as 'God's House', Jacob was adding to the stone the symbols of a High Priest and a King. Thus by this anointing the stone came to signify a Royal Priesthood attached to God's House. The anointing of the stone was in fact a prophetic act signifying that the stone or 'rock' represented the promised Messiah of Israel (Psalm 95:1).

According to the Scriptures, this Bethel Stone is the only one that has ever been anointed; hence among stones it is pre-eminently *'the Anointed One'*. One can imagine that from hence forward this 'pillar stone' became one of the most potent sacred symbols in all of Israel. Remember the anointing of this stone occurred hundreds of years prior to the birth of Moses and the giving of the Mosaic Law. Thus this pillar stone of Bethel predated the sacred Ark of the Covenant, and all the descendants of Jacob would have held it in the highest regard. They most certainly would not have left it lying around in the desert.

Jacob returns to his stone marker

Twenty-one years, two wives, two concubines and a dozen children later, Jacob was commanded to return to Bethel. Once there he built and anointed a more permanent altar (Genesis 35:1-15). This was almost certainly the time when Jacob decided to bring the original pillar stone with him, as he had replaced the stone with a proper altar to the God of Israel. It was whilst he was at this place that his name was changed to Israel, as God Almighty once again appeared to him saying: *"Be fruitful and multiply; a nation and a company of nations shall proceed from you, and kings shall come from your body"*. Notice that the announcement that kings would descend from him occurred there at Bethel. Although the account does not specifically say so, the inference is that Jacob was also informed about the future relationship that this pillar stone might have to those kings that would come from his body.

The Shepherd Stone of Israel

If we now once again move on to the end of Jacob's life when he blesses his twelve sons on his deathbed, we see that he blesses each one in turn in the order of their birth. We already know that these blessings actually were prophetic pronouncements that would have a special relevance for Jacob's offspring *'in the last days'*. When he finally came to son number eleven, he addressed Joseph, and pronounces the fabulous 'Birthright' blessing over him. Suddenly he stopped midway to say: ***"From 'thence' is the shepherd, the stone of Israel"*** (Genesis 49:24 KJV – emphasis added). Please note, Jacob's name was changed to Israel, and the **'stone of Israel'** is none other than Jacob's pillar stone! The phrase *'from thence'* means 'out of there', or 'out of that place'; Bethel was the place of the stone and this surely proves that that it came *from thence, i.e. Bethel.* It follows that if Jacob referred to this stone on his deathbed as having come *from thence,* therefore it must have been with them there in Egypt. By mentioning the 'Shepherd Stone of Israel' right in the middle of his prophetic blessing over Joseph, Jacob is formally committing the safekeeping of this sacred stone to the House of Joseph. As it happens the little town of Bethel was situated in the territory that later on was to be allocated to the tribe of Ephraim, the younger son of Joseph.

A Shepherd has to go with his flock

It is interesting to note how Jacob refers to the Stone of Israel as the **"Shepherd."** Why is this significant? **What does a shepherd do**? By calling the stone the 'Shepherd of Israel' the patriarch Jacob is expressing the character of the stone, as a shepherd must always go with his flock. When we consider the characteristics of a shepherd it becomes obvious that **this pillar stone should be with Israel in all their wanderings.** The reason this is important is because what we see here is the establishment of a permanent pattern for all time. Remember that this sacred 'Shepherd Stone' of Israel not only represents the House of God, but it also represents that future High Priest and King – the Messiah of Israel.

Once we understand this principle of the shepherd going with his flock, it should not surprise us to see this stone turn up wherever the children of Israel have made their home.

Stone of Destiny Replica
(courtesy Bubobubo2, Wikimedia)

A much traveled Shepherd Stone

Now this Shepherd Stone, alias the Stone of Destiny, or Jacob's Pillar Stone has two iron rings that have clearly been used for transporting it by sliding a pole through both rings. Thus four strong men without too much effort could carry it. There is a groove worn between the two rings, which testify of having been gradually eroded by transport for an extended period. The stone would have been taken to Egypt when Jacob and his entire household moved there to join Joseph. It also would have left Egypt when Moses led the children of Israel in that great Exodus, and it would have accompanied them throughout their wanderings through the wilderness. It would have gone with them as they crossed the river Jordan to enter their Promised Land. Most certainly it would have stayed in Jerusalem from the time of King David until the fall of the city in 585 BC. From there it would have travelled with Jeremiah back to Tahpanhes in Egypt and from there by ship to an Israelite colony in Spain and then onwards again by ship to Ireland.

Thus the 'Shepherd Stone of Israel,' that the great patriarch Jacob had referred to on his deathbed, had come back to join the flock of the 'Lost House of Israel'. History has confirmed that from this time forth, every king or queen who has reigned in Ireland, Scotland or England has been crowned upon that self-same pillar or coronation stone. Queen Mary Tudor, who became known as bloody Mary, was the only (and perhaps not insignificant) exception, as she refused to be crowned upon it. Queen Victoria herself was crowned twice upon that stone, the first time, as the Queen of Great Britain, and the second as Empress of India. It is most significant that no other nation or kingdom, apart from the ancient Kingdom of Israel, has ever had this unique custom. This raises again the question: Why? Why should first the kings of Ireland, closely followed by the kings of Scotland, and these then to be closely followed by the kings of England and Great Britain, observe this extraordinary custom of crowning their kings upon an ancient stone? Why would the Irish,

Scottish, and English royal dynasties all in turn adopt this uniquely Israelite custom if there really were no connection?

When you pause to consider that all of this is simply a continuation of the ancient coronation customs of ancient Israel, it becomes almost too wonderful for words to express. Just think of it, ever since King David of Israel was crowned upon this 'Stone of Destiny', all his royal descendants and successors have been crowned upon this same stone in an unbroken tradition that has lasted for 3,000 years. What a marvelous testimony and *'witness'* this pillar stone of Jacob truly is!

Throne of David moves from Ireland to Scotland

The first of these overturns, we have already traced from Judea in 'Palestine' to the islands to the 'northwest' of Jerusalem, which are in the 'great waters'. History confirms that the next two of the 'overturns' forecast occurred in these same islands. To put it in another way, we can rightfully say that the three overturns landed the scepter and throne *seriatim* in Ireland, Scotland and England. Notice, even after the third overturn, the royal throne of David is still, as the word of God declares, *'in the isles afar off'*, and *'in the sea'* (Isaiah 49:1 and Jeremiah 25:22 KJV).

The second overturn occurs when in 506 AD King Fergus crosses to Scotland to be crowned 'King of the Scots' in Iona Abbey. He brought with him the 'LIA FAIL', now called 'THE STONE OF DESTINY, or 'JACOB'S PILLAR STONE', from Tara in Ireland for his coronation. The Scots also referred to the stone as the Stone Regal, as it was used for only one purpose, namely the coronation of a new king.

According to a certain Dr. Poole, who after careful examination commented upon the stone as follows: This stone is dull reddish or purplish sandstone, with a few small-embedded pebbles; one of these is quartz and the other two of a dark substance. The rock is calcareous and is not of the kind which masons call freestone. Chisel marks are visible on one or more of its sides. There is no rock of this kind in England, Ireland or Scotland.

Professor Odlum, an eminent geologist and Professor of Theology at Ontario University, discovered a stratum of sandstone high up near a cliff in Bethel that was geologically the same as the Coronation Stone. He took a sample and was able to carry out microscopic tests, from which he concluded that it was a perfect match. He wanted to get a pea-sized chip of the 'pillar' stone in Westminster Abbey and he asked for formal permission – to which the Archbishop of Canterbury replied that it would take an Act of Parliament, signed by the King, and even then he would not provide it! The Archbishop was right, of course, as it surely would have been sacrilege to tamper with this sacred stone.

King Fergus also brought with him, in AD 506, his Royal Standard, the 'Lion Rampant', which is the Royal Emblem of Scotland to this day. This 'Lion Rampant' was not his invention, as it had always been the Royal Emblem of Judah, frequently referred to as 'The Lion of Judah!' From this same King Fergus there sprang a long line of Scottish kings, which preserved the lineage of King David for a further 1,100 years until the year AD 1603.

Lion Rampant of Scotland
(courtesy Wikimedia)

Coat-of-Arms of
Jerusalem
(courtesy
Wikimedia)

Throne of David moves from Scotland to England

The third overturn occurs when King James VI of Scotland became James 1 of the United Kingdom of Scotland and England. Thus the three 'overturns' or transfers of King David's throne have been completed exactly as prophesied by Ezekiel. Our present Queen Elizabeth II is a direct descendant of King David of Israel. Thus genetically speaking she is descended from the tribe of Judah, as was King David before her. As she wields the ruling 'Scepter of Judah' over her British subjects, she rules over God's own 'Birthright' people Israel! She too, like her ancestors before her, was crowned upon the same stone which the English call Jacob's Pillow.

At one time Joshua took a stone, set it up, and said to all Israel: *"Behold, this stone shall be a witness to us, for it has heard all the words of the LORD which He spoke to us. It shall therefore be a witness to you, lest you deny your God"* (Joshua 24:27).

Thus we see that a stone may indeed be a witness, and what a witness it has been! The historians of these Sceptered Isles, either wittingly or unwittingly, have made Lia Fail (sometime spelt Leag Phail), a witness to an unbroken line of sovereigns, for it has been the throne upon which their rulers have been crowned, ever since it was landed in Ireland. The Coronation Chair of England has been in constant use to crown the monarchs of England ever since AD 1296, when Edward I had it constructed for his coronation. The chair had

been built specifically to house the coronation stone, or the Stone Regal, which Edward brought from Scotland. Therefore it is this coronation stone that provides yet another proof of Britain's Israelite ancestry. Believe it or not, the 'BRIT-ISH,' the Covenant People, are indeed Israel.

Coronation Chair with Jacob's Stone of Destiny

The Stone's secret hiding place during World War II

To give some indication as to what importance the British authorities attach to this 'pillar stone' of Jacob, you need only hear the account of how they ensured its safekeeping during the Second World War. As the dark storm clouds of war ominously gathered apace all over Europe, the British government made the decision to pack most of her art treasures from the National Gallery and the British Museum and move them to safety in carefully prepared caverns in the Welsh mountains.

So what did they do with Jacob's Pillar Stone? The British government buried the 300 lb. stone deep under the floor of Westminster Abbey, whilst a plan of its exact geographic location was sent to the Prime Minister of Canada. Thus throughout the blitz, as German bombs rained on London, Jacob's Pillar Stone, otherwise called the 'Shepherd of Israel', remained with her flock quite safe buried deep underground in Westminster Abbey in London.

The question here is: Why did the British government go to these extraordinary lengths to protect and safeguard this 'Pillar Stone'? We are talking here about an event that actually occurred in the twentieth century! Why would a modern twentieth century government take these measures over what, to all accounts, is merely a piece of sandstone rock? Why would they bother to inform the head of another government of the secret location where they had hidden this stone? Surely there can be only one explanation. The British government of the time actually believed that its own destiny was in some mysterious way bound up with this sacred Stone of Destiny. This is why they took such pains in protecting and hiding it, and this is also the reason why they resolved that the precious stone remain behind in the beleaguered London of 1940.

Then on the November 30, 1996, on St Andrews Day, exactly 700 years after Edward I of England removed the Stone from the Abbey of Scone in Scotland, the Stone was returned to Scotland. Even since the 1950s there had been mounting clamor for this in Scotland. With Scottish devolution in prospect, the British government led by the then Prime Minister John Major, agreed after first seeking the advice of H.M. the Queen, to return the Stone to Scotland. In reality the decision was an act of appeasement and political expediency, and intended as a sop to the Scottish nationalists who sought devolution. Others affirm that there was a much deeper reason for the sudden removal of the Coronation Stone from Westminster Abbey. The reason being that the Dean and Chapter of Westminster Abbey, had introduced *"multi-faith"* services in the Abbey. It was felt that the anointed Bethel Stone, which the Patriarch Jacob anointed as *"the House of God"* could not bear to be in the presence of those who practice pagan religion. Hence there was a pressing spiritual reason why the Stone had to depart so suddenly from the place where it had rested for seven hundred years.

There had been no hint of what was to come when the Prime Minister rose to his feet in the House of Commons on July 3, 1996, to make a statement about the Stone of Destiny:

"The Stone of Destiny is the most ancient symbol of Scottish kingship. It was used in the coronation of Scottish Kings until the end of the 13th century. Exactly 700 years ago, in 1296, King Edward I brought it from Scotland and housed it at Westminster Abbey. The Stone remains the property of the Crown. I wish to inform the House that, on the advice of Her Majesty's Ministers, The Queen has agreed that the Stone should be returned to Scotland. The Stone will, of course, be taken to Westminster Abbey to play its traditional role in the coronation ceremonies of future sovereigns of the United Kingdom. The Stone of Destiny holds a special place in the hearts of the Scots. On this the 700th anniversary of its removal from Scotland, it is appropriate to return it to its historic homeland. I am sure that the House would wish to be assured that the Stone will be placed in an appropriate setting in Scotland. The government will be consulting Scottish and Church opinion about that. The Stone might be displayed in Edinburgh Castle alongside the Honors of Scotland, Europe's oldest crown jewels."

Subsequently, on the November 3, 1996, with great pomp and circumstance the Stone of Destiny was taken in solemn procession to Edinburgh Castle to be installed in the "Crown Room" in the castle fortress.

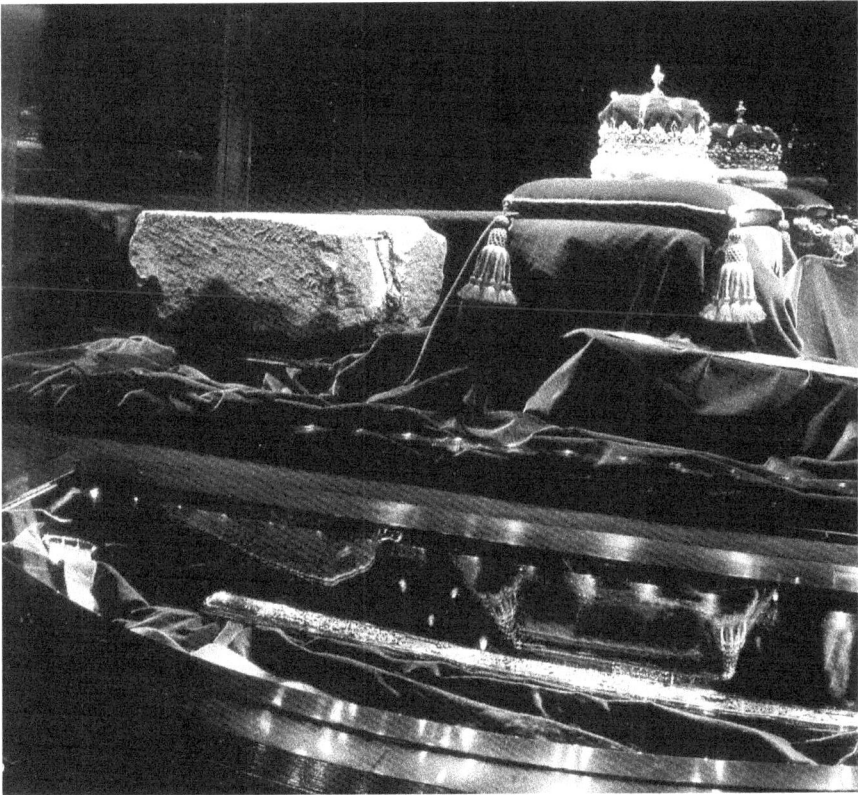

Crown Room of Edingurgh Castle with Stone of Destiny

More royal descendants of King David!

Apart from King Zedekiah of Judah there was another king of the House of David who had ended up in a Babylonian dungeon. His name was Jehoiachin, the immediate predecessor to Zedekiah. At age eighteen he had been taken prisoner together with his wives on a previous incursion into the territory of Judah by king Nebuchadnezzar of Babylon (2 Kings 24:8-15). The Bible records that after thirty-seven years of imprisonment he was released at age 55 by Evil Merodach, a later king of Babylon, who appointed him as his royal vassal with authority over all the other vassal kings of the Babylonian Empire (2 Kings 25: 27-30). This same Jehoiachin was survived by his son Jeconiah, who in turn was blessed with five sons, all of them lineal descendants of King David. *14 As the territory of the empire comprised many Israelite tribal population groups taken into captivity by the previous Assyrian Empire, it is likely that this direct descendant of King David and his successors ruled over Israelites within the boundaries of Babylon's vast empire. After the demise of the Babylonian and Persian Empires the successors of these Davidic kings became the kings of independent Israelite nations and empires in Asia. It is clear from the biblical account in the book of Chronicles chapters three and four that the royal house of David did not die out after the fall of Jerusalem. His numerous descendants were vassal kings first to the Babylonians, then to the Medo-Persians, and from there they went on to become independent kings over the various Israelite Parthian, Scythian, Cimmerian, and Saka empires. In the waning years of those empires their Israelite populations moved west into mainland Europe in a great migratory movement that lasted for many centuries. Clearly, as the various tribes and clans migrated west into mainland Europe on route to its coastlands and the British Isles, their kings and royal princes from the House of David would have led the way.

Ultimate reunification

There now only remains for the final part of Ezekiel's prophecy to be fulfilled, when Messiah, whom the Jews refer to as 'The Lion of Judah', comes to take the throne, as He is the one WHOSE RIGHT IT IS! This means that this Shepherd Stone of Israel is going to travel again. The final destiny of this stone that represents Messiah's Royal Priesthood is to be moved back to Jerusalem. That is the much-prophesied moment when this 'Rock of Israel' will serve as the physical seat of Messiah's Royal Throne. It is the time when the promised Messiah, the King, is going to rule over the Twelve Tribes of Israel. In the book of Ezekiel, Chapter 37, we read the following most astonishing prophecy regarding the future re-unification of the Kingdom of Judah with the Kingdom of Israel:

"As for you, son of man, take a stick for yourself and write on it: 'For Judah and for the children of Israel, his companions.' Then take another stick and write on it, 'For Joseph, the stick of Ephraim, and for all the house of Israel, his companions.' Then join them one to another for yourself into one stick, and they will become one in your hand. And when the children of your people speak to you saying, 'Will you not show us what you mean by these?' – say to them, 'Thus says the Lord GOD: "Surely I will take the stick of Joseph, which is in the hand of Ephraim, and the tribes of Israel, his companions; and I will join them with it, with the stick of Judah, and make them one stick, and they will be one in My hand." '

"And the sticks on which you write will be in your hand before their eyes. Then say to them, 'Thus says the Lord GOD: Surely I will take the children of Israel from among the nations, wherever they have gone, and will gather them from every side and bring them into their own land; and I will make them one nation in the land, on the mountains of Israel; and one king shall be king over them all; THEY SHALL NO LONGER BE TWO NATIONS, NOR SHALL THEY EVER BE DIVIDED INTO TWO KINGDOMS AGAIN'" (Ezekiel 37:16-22 – emphasis added).

Thus it is written in the Scriptures that the Kingdom of Judah (the Jewish people, and their companions), and the Kingdom of Israel (the British, her Commonwealth offspring, the United States of America, plus the nations of North-western Europe, and all of their myriads of companions scattered in the four corners of the earth), will be re-united into ONE KINGDOM again. Nothing in heaven and earth can possibly prevent this from happening, as the word of prophecy has never failed. It is the Word of God Himself and therefore by definition it cannot fail. What an awesome destiny lies in store for our nations! It is only the realization of our true origins that will begin to enable us to enter into the matchless fullness of our ultimate destiny. It is only this knowledge of our 'hidden' ancestry that has the power to change our perceptions of everything around us in the most meaningful way. As Israelite nations our need has never been more urgent, as more than ever before, we need to recapture the vision of our God-given destiny.

CHAPTER SIX

⊱⊰

10th Sign
The Lion and the Unicorn

"Judah is a lion's whelp; from the prey, my son, you have gone up. He bows down, he lies down as a lion; and as a lion, who shall rouse him?"

(Genesis 49:9)

"His glory is like the firstling of his bullock, and his horns are like the horns of unicorns; with them he shall push the people together to the ends of the earth: and they are the ten thousands of Ephraim, and they are the thousands of Manasseh" (Deuteronomy 33:17 KJV – emphasis added).

"God brought him forth out of Egypt; he hath as it were the strength of a unicorn; he shall eat up the nations his enemies, and shall break their bones, and pierce them through with his arrows. He crouched, he lay down as a lion, and as a great lion: who shall stir him up? Blessed is he that blesseth thee, and cursed is he that curseth thee"

(Numbers 24:8-9 KJV – emphasis added).

The purpose of heraldry is to identify

Almost from the very dawn of civilization, man has sought to identify himself with emblems and signs to explain his existence, his identity, beliefs, culture and affiliations. This was especially true of those who exercised power and dominion, as the emblem or sign came to represent a potent symbol of their power. We are all familiar

131

with the emblems of the Pharaohs of ancient Egypt. The spectacular blue and gold headgear of the Pharaoh Tutankhamen received worldwide fame through the discovery of his tomb. On his forehead we see the golden cobra, which was thought to protect the king by spitting fire at his enemies. The royal emblem of the cobra was designed to strike fear into the heart of his subjects. Other symbols of Pharaoh's sacred kingship and royal power were the crook and the flail. Archaeologists have established that, apart from Egypt, the 'double-headed eagle' was the emblem of the monarchs of the ancient Hittite Empire around 2000 BC. The same emblem was later adopted by subsequent cultures, the most recent of which are Czarist Russia, as well as the Austro-Hungarian Empire and the Hapsburg dynasty.

In the days of the Roman Empire the Eagle came to represent 'imperial power'. The military standards of the Roman legions were decorated with eagles. Men renowned for their bravery carried the standards, and where the 'eagles' led, the soldiers were bound to follow. Later on, after the fall of Rome, Emperor Charlemagne, having been crowned king of the Romans, revived the use of the Eagle, which was to remain the symbol of the Holy Roman Empire. Napoleon Bonaparte, one of the more recent emperors of the Holy Roman Empire also selected the eagle as the emblem for Imperial France.

In the legends and works of art in ancient Greece, there is a record of the emblems used by both sides in the Trojan War. In Israel's biblical history book we find that each of the Twelve Tribes of Israel had an emblem or standard, and that by God's command these were in regular use during the forty years of wandering after their Exodus from Egypt. This is clearly stated in Numbers 2:2, where we read: *"Every one of the children of Israel shall camp by his own standard, beside the emblems of his father's house; they shall camp some distance from the tabernacle".*

Thus these emblems and symbols that had started out mainly as a badge of power progressively became a means of identification, as their primary purpose was to identify. On a crowded battlefield the issue of who was who became increasingly important, as in the mad *mêlée* of battle confusion it was essential that one should be able to distinguish between friend and foe. The Crusaders fought under the banner of a red cross. More recently, in the Second World War, the Nazis fought under the sign of the Swastika, whereas the British fought under their Union Jack, and the Americans fought under the Stars and Stripes. The primary purpose of each of these was to identify the group.

Heraldry—a most accurate science

Remember: the paramount purpose of heraldry is to identify! From the most ancient times, families, clans, tribes, cities and nations have used emblems and symbols as a means of identification. In the course of time the world of heraldry evolved with banners, badges, shields and colors, not to forget Coats of Arms, all designed to promote particular identity and affiliation. Dr Samuel Johnson said that, *"Heraldry is the science of fools!"* With all due respect, little did he know that heraldry is not only one of the most ancient, but also one of the most accurate, sciences in the world. Thus we have family crests, coats of arms, clan and tribal emblems, tartans, national emblems and flags, religious symbols, church emblems, corporate logos and even football club emblems. They are all designed as badges of identity. The right to use these emblems invariably was jealously guarded, as it passed from generation to generation; and rarely, if ever, was the emblem of one family, tribe or city adopted by another. Because of this our courts have long since recognized the importance of emblems in tracing heirs and in identifying the ancestral roots of families. It is most strange therefore that our historians, and especially the ethnologists among them, have not deigned to use this knowledge to record the history and movements of the peoples of these British Isles and north-western Europe. Had they turned to heraldic emblems, as a source of knowledge, our history books would most certainly tell a very different tale. At the very least we would all have been aware of our Israelite origins and ancestry.

This brings us to the Royal Arms used today by Her Majesty Queen Elizabeth II. According to Pitkin's Guide on Coats of Arms, the Royal Coat of Arms of the Queen of Great Britain has evolved over 900 years. In actual fact the origin of the British Royal Coat of Arms goes back at least three thousand years. The most striking features of the royal arms are, without question, its supporters, *i.e.* 'the Lion and the Unicorn'. The unicorn formerly was a badge of the kings of Scotland. Before James VI of Scotland became, additionally, James I of England, two silver unicorns with golden horns, manes and hooves supported his arms. To signify the fact that he united two crowns, he incorporated the arms of the lion of Scotland into the arms of Great Britain. King James kept the English lion 'supporter' but banished the red dragon (of Wales) 'supporter' in favour of one of his Scottish unicorns. The lion and the unicorn have been the 'royal supporters' of the Royal Coat of Arms ever since then. Students of heraldry recognize by common consent that the unicorn belongs to Mediterranean and Eastern mythology.

Scottish Royal Coat of Arms (courtesy Sodacan, Wikimedia)

By now it should come as no surprise to the reader to find that both the lion and the unicorn of Britain's Royal Coat of Arms are of Israelite origin. In fact the basic heraldic emblems of Britain, Ireland, the United States, Norway, Sweden, Denmark, Iceland, the Netherlands and several other kindred nations are IDENTICAL with those of ancient Israel. Further, in the case of Britain and the United States, incredible as it may seem, we actually have no others, as ALL of our heraldic emblems are of Israelite origin! For, with the exception of the Welsh dragon, every national emblem of Britain and the United States is an authentic Israel emblem. *1

Christian doubts

Christians have argued in the past, and no doubt will argue in the future, that these emblems must have been adopted from the Bible after our Celtic and Saxon ancestors became Christians. This theory really does not hold water because the Bible simply was not available to them, because the Roman Catholic Church, fearing that their own deviations from the Holy Writ would be exposed, deliberately denied access to the Scriptures of the Bible. For well over a thousand years Christendom was kept in almost total darkness, as the Bible was shut away in Roman Catholic libraries and monasteries. During these dark ages the masses of the people were being kept in total ignorance of its contents.

Change did not come until William Tyndale became imbued with a burning conviction to see that a copy of the Bible should be placed in the hands of every man, woman and child in England, and in a language they could understand. He spent most of his life translating into English, first the books of the New Testament, and then those of the Old Testament. Before he could finish his mammoth undertaking he was seized, accused of heresy, imprisoned and finally executed. Just before they put him to death in AD 1536, he uttered this heart rending prayer: *"O God, open the king of England's eyes"*. His prayer was obviously heard and answered, as it is a fact of history that within one year of his death, in 1537, King Henry VIII of England commanded that a Geneva Bible be chained to the lectern of every church in his realm. Then some seventy-four years later in

1611, King James I, had his Authorised King James Version of the Bible published. It is clear that as our forefathers did not have access to the Bible, they therefore could not possibly have adopted Israelite heraldic emblems from this source. In fact it is quite a sobering thought that the Bible, this most ancient of sacred books, has only been generally available for ordinary people for some four hundred years!

The second reason this Christian theory holds no water is simply the fact that these Israelite emblems were in use by our Celtic and Saxon ancestors centuries before the Christian era even began. Others may try to rubbish the heraldic evidence of our Israelite origins by putting it all down to coincidence. Let us remind ourselves of that maxim on coincidences: 'If something happens only once it is probably an accident, if it happens twice it may only be a coincidence, but if it occurs three times or more, then it has meaning'. The startling fact is that there are more than THIRTY of Israel's emblems represented in the heraldry of Great Britain and the United States of America alone – far too many to be a coincidence! It is just not possible that this could be a mere coincidence. It simply must have meaning.

The King 'Jacob' Bible

Another most interesting point is that the names James, Jacobus, Jacob, Jack and even Yankee, are all equivalents. Once again this makes for yet more fascinating conclusions. The first British king to unite England and Scotland (both are the Israelite people of Jacob) into one kingdom was King James I, (King Jacob). His very name means Jacob in English. Could this be mere coincidence too?

Also this same King James I formally authorised the translation of the Bible into English in order to make it widely available to the population at large, and it has become known as the King James Bible. The King James – Jacob – became the 'Authorised Version' of the Bible. The version owed much to William Tyndale and indeed it became his greatest testament. This same version has for centuries been used as the main Bible for the English-speaking people around the world. The King James Version has since with good reason been termed "the noblest monument of English prose". Its revisers in 1881 expressed admiration for "its simplicity, its dignity, its power, its happy turns of expression – the music of its cadences, and the felicities of its rhythm". Like no other book before or since, it has shaped the foundations and the character of all of the major public institutions of the English-speaking peoples worldwide. Is it not curious that this book, which more than any other gave the British people the confidence and the zeal to build their great empire, was 'authorised' by a king whose very name James, was a reminder of Jacob, that great patriarch and founding father of Israel? Remember also that Jacob is another name for the patriarch Israel, as Jacob's name was changed to Israel. Thus the King James Bible could also rightly be called the King Jacob Bible or even the King Israel Bible! The main point to consider is that the KJV of the Bible – for hundreds of years the main Bible of the English-speaking people – bears the very name Jacob (Israel) through its English equivalent name, 'James'. Is it not stretching credulity too far to believe that this is also a mere coincidence?

Royal Coat of Arms of
King James I
(courtesy Sodacan,
Wikimedia)

The origin of Israelite emblems and symbols

It is interesting to note that most of the symbols and emblems denoting the tribes of Israel, *i.e.* the descendants of Jacob, are derived from the blessings and prophecies he pronounced on them, as recorded in Genesis 49. For example, when Jacob came to bless his youngest son, Benjamin, he said: *"Benjamin is a ravenous wolf; in the morning he shall devour the prey, and at night he shall divide the spoil"* (Genesis 49:27). It follows from this that the 'wolf' had become the symbol for the tribe of Benjamin. When reading Jacob's prophecy, the Vikings immediately spring to mind, as their roaming seafaring warrior bands had a fearsome reputation for brutality. The prows of their sleek ships frequently were adorned with either a wolf's head or with the head of a dragon. The word 'ravin' comes from the Hebrew root word 'taraph,' pronounced as 'tawraf' meaning to pluck off or to pull to pieces. This ferocious wolf-like characteristic was epitomised by the Vikings who, like wolves, liked to hunt in packs. These Viking warriors for three centuries struck sheer terror into the hearts of all the communities of northwestern Europe through their destructive power.

It so happens that the wolf's head is one of the key national symbols of Norway. Viking   religion and mythology is littered with references to the wolf. Their god Odin was Lord of the Hall of the Slain, to which came all brave men who had died in battle. Odin lived there with his 'wolves' and 'ravens' and drank wine. Odin, Vili and Ve, the first gods of the Viking pantheon, were believed to have created the sun and the moon to hasten unceasingly before the 'wolves' that ceaselessly pursued them. Their mythology also speaks of the end of the age, which is preceded by a time of untold depravity when all ties and restraints would vanish with fratricide and incest reigning unchecked. Then there would come a time of war and discord, after which an Axe age, a Sword age, a Storm age and finally a WOLF age, would lead to the overthrow of the earth. Then the 'wolf' Fenrir, whose jaws stretch from heaven to earth, breaks his fetters, and the 'wolf' swallows Odin. It surely doesn't sound like a happy ending! However, beyond this destruction, Viking mythology speaks of a green and verdant Paradise, so perhaps it is not so bad after all!

Once you understand that the heraldic emblems are the keys to unlocking the identity of the tribes, it becomes a great deal easier to follow the path that the tribes of Israel took, after they freed themselves from their captivity in the lands of the Assyrian empire. As the symbol of Benjamin was a wolf, we can trace this tribe to Dacia, in present day Romania, where they used the wolf symbol. From there they subsequently travelled *via* northern Germany, only to move on into Denmark and Norway. It is from this Scandinavian base that they then invaded the coasts of England and northwestern Europe. The Vikings frequently settled permanently in the lands they invaded, and perhaps their largest permanent settlement was in Normandy in France, as the Normans are predominantly of Viking blood. The very name Normandy gives away the origin of the people, as it is derived from 'Norsemen', which is how the Viking invaders were referred to in their day.

Benjamin is likened to a wolf, which characteristically was also the symbol of the Normans. William the Conqueror himself used the wolf as his symbol, and it is depicted on the famous Bayeux Tapestry, which his beautiful wife, Matilda of Flanders, wove in honour of his great victory. Thus, when the Normans led by William the Conqueror invaded England in AD 1066, it was really the tribe of Benjamin establishing her rule over her fellow Israelites. It would be relatively easy to write a book about the identity of the tribe of Benjamin, because once you are prepared to accept the link with the Vikings and start to investigate from that vantage point, the evidence is truly significant and most convincing. Proof of Benjamin's warlike nature can be found in the biblical account of Gibeah (Judges Chapters 19-20). Other Benjaminites mentioned in the Bible are Ehud, one of the great judges and deliverers of Israel, also King Saul, the first King of Israel, and Jonathan, his son, as well as Abner, the commander of his armies. Mordecai too was from the tribe of

Benjamin, and even the apostle Paul, all of these men shared the same characteristic, in that without exception, they were men of great courage. A famous present day Israeli politician, Benjamin Netanyahu also claims descent from the tribe of Benjamin.

Names such as Wolf, Wolfe, Wolff, Woolf, or Woolfson are thought to be Jewish, yet strictly speaking their name is a badge of another of the tribes of Israel, as it portrays their descent from Benjamin. Remember, when the Ten Tribes of Israel rebelled against the son of Solomon, they set up their own kingdom in their tribal territory to the north of Jerusalem. The only tribe to stay loyal to the king was the tribe of Benjamin, and their territory was in Jerusalem and its surrounding area. In the biblical sense the Jews today are primarily composed of the tribes of Judah, Benjamin and Levi, as these are the remnant of the tribes that returned from their captivity in Babylon. These three tribes are specifically listed in the census records of the Books of Ezra and Nehemiah. Nevertheless, like Benjamin Netanyahu, there are quite a few Jews in the world today who know their descent is from Benjamin. However, strictly speaking, even though they are of Israel, they cannot 'genetically' be true Jews, as a Jew in the 'genetic' sense by definition has to be descended from the tribe of Judah. By way of comparison the same applies in these British Isles, as it is just as true to say that a Welshman can never be an Englishman and an Englishman can never be a Scot, yet they can all rightly claim to be British citizens.

The reason for using the example of Benjamin is merely to illustrate the principle that the emblems and symbols of the tribes of Israel are derived primarily from the blessings that the patriarch Jacob pronounced over his twelve sons while on his deathbed. Those blessings contained not only an awesome prophetic self-fulfilling power, but they also provide us with the most vital keys to the identity and whereabouts of the tribes of Israel in our day. Moses too addressed the Twelve Tribes as he gave his final blessing to Israel just prior to his death, and his words are recorded in Deuteronomy 33. Some of the characteristics Moses mentioned also became tribal emblems, with the result that a number of the tribes ended up with a secondary as well as a primary emblem. Thus those prophetic deathbed blessings, first of all by Jacob, and secondly by Moses, as recorded in the inspired history book of Israel, are the key to unlocking not only the individual characteristics of each tribe, they also convey their precise individual identity. Furthermore, they present us with the key to their heraldic emblems. This in turn confirms that the origin of heraldry goes back close to 4,000 years to the very foundation of Israel and the time of the patriarchs. It also reveals that historians and scholars should not view heraldry as something that is merely subjective, but that it is a most important research tool in its own right, which has sadly been overlooked in the past.

The Royal Arms of Great Britain

Going back to the Royal Coat of Arms of Great Britain we find that in the two 'supporters' of the Coat of Arms we recognize the Lion of Judah and the Unicorn of Israel. Judah's primary symbols are a single lion and/or three lions. These may be in a resting or in a rampant position. The emblem or symbol of Judah is based upon the words Jacob spoke over the head of his son Judah. As he was dying he spoke the following words:

"Judah is a lion's whelp; from the prey, my son, you have gone up. He bows down, he lies down as a lion; and as a lion, who shall rouse him?" (Genesis 49:9).

This is where the term "The Lion of Judah" has its origin. The patriarch Jacob went on to say: *"The sceptre shall not depart from Judah, nor a lawgiver from between his feet, until Shiloh comes"*. The lion since time immemorial has been considered the king of the beasts; hence it is easy to see the connection between the sceptre, the supreme symbol of royal power, and the lion, which also is a symbol of royalty. Jacob therefore prophesies that a kingly line or royal dynasty will come from Judah, which eventually is to produce Shiloh or Messiah. Thus the lion 'supporter' of Britain's Royal Coat of Arms is a Jewish heraldic symbol that originates with the tribe of Judah. The lion was the emblem that symbolised the ancient kingdom of Judah.

Now, when we come to the sons of Joseph, we find that Moses, as he blesses the Twelve Tribes just prior to his death, gives us the key to the emblem that signifies Israel. Let us read his words in *Israel's History Book*:

"His glory is like the firstling of his bullock, and his horns are like the 'horns' of unicorns; with them he shall push the people together to the ends of the earth: and they are the ten thousands of Ephraim, and they are the thousands of Manasseh"* (Deuteronomy 33:17 KJV – emphasis added).

Joseph here is being likened to an ox or a bullock, and also to a unicorn. Notice too the double emphasis placed upon the word *'horns'*. Here then, we see that Joseph is likened to an ox/bullock, a unicorn and a horn. When we add these symbols to those blessings mentioned by his father Jacob, we see that Joseph is likened to: an Olive Branch, some Arrows, an Ox, a Unicorn and a Horn. These emblems were then adopted by and divided between the two sons of Joseph, Ephraim and Manasseh. The Ox, the Unicorn and the Horn became the emblems of the tribe of Ephraim, whereas the Olive branch and the bundle of Arrows became the emblems of the tribe of Manasseh. As Ephraim was the leading tribe of Israel, the unicorn became the emblem that symbolised the ancient kingdom of Israel. Thus the lion of Judah and the unicorn of Israel have become the two main pillars that support the Royal Coat of Arms of Great Britain. How could this be mere coincidence! *2

The Hebrew word for 'unicorn' as used in *Israel's History Book* is "RE'EM." This beast has been identified as an oryx, a type of straight horned deer, and as a kind of auroch or wild bull now extinct. Jewish *Midrashic* sources apply the term 'RE'EM' (Feliks p.9) to both the deer and the bull. This could explain why the heraldic representation of a unicorn looks more akin to a horse-like deer than a bull. In profile the oryx

Royal Coat of Arms of Great Britain (courtesy Sodacan, Wikimedia)

appears as if it had only one horn. Ancient Assyrian illustrations apply the term 'rimu' to the wild ox and thus the Hebrew word 'RE'EM' in the Bible may be considered equivalent to 'bull'. In the book of Numbers (24:8) where the text speaks of the *"strength of the unicorn"* the written Hebrew contains a hint that the expression of strength (*toyafot*), meaning perhaps the horns which are normally plural, in this case have become ONE (*toyafat*). The idea of a "one-horned" or unicorn is recalled in the Jewish writings of the *Talmud* (Hulin ch.3) where it is said that the first man Adam, sacrificed one. A number of Jewish Sages such as Sadia, Ibn Ezra and Menasseh ben Israel also confirmed the 'RE'EM' to be a unicorn, and Kaplan in *The Living Torah* discusses this subject. In the Greek Septuagint translation of the Bible the Hebrew word 'RE'EM' was translated as 'one-horned' or unicorn. Unicorns were depicted on Egyptian walls in the Biblical Era and were also popular themes in Assyrian heraldry. It is of interest to note that the descendants of Joseph spent much time as a captive people both in Egypt and also in Assyria. In heraldic terms the meaning of the 'unicorn' is virtue and courage. *3)

Again we find in *Israel's History Book* the account of the king of Moab, who ruled over a territory in present day Jordan, trying to hire a prophet to curse Israel. The name of the prophet in question was Balaam, and he was only too willing to oblige, as he was the sort of person who would do anything for money. When Balak, the king of Moab, hired Balaam to curse Israel, Balaam could not do it, as God forced him to **bless** Israel instead. These are the prophetic words the God of Israel compelled him to speak:

*"God brought him forth out of Egypt; he hath as it were **the strength of a unicorn;** he shall eat up the nations his enemies, and shall break their bones, and pierce them through with his arrows. He couched, he lay down **as a lion, and as a great lion**: who shall stir him up? Blessed is he that blesseth thee, and cursed is he that curseth thee"* (Numbers 24:8-9 KJV).

Is it not a most remarkable coincidence that two of these prophetic emblems, the lion and the unicorn, which were given to Israel with that compulsory blessing, are today to be found in the Coat of Arms of Great Britain?

Royal Throne in Queen's Robing Room

Royal Throne in House of Lords

The Chained Unicorn

When you look upon the British Royal Coat of Arms, notice that there is something very strange and distinctive about the unicorn! The lion representing Judah is portrayed as freestanding and unattached, whereas the unicorn representing Israel wears a golden chain and is tied down. This chain symbolises the captivity of Israel, as when the House of Israel rebelled and started worshipping gods other than the God of Israel, she was by way of punishment taken into captivity by the Assyrians. The whole population was transported somewhere to the southeast and the southwest of the Caspian Sea. The prophets prophesied that in time they would move away from the place where their Assyrian captors had taken them and be established in a new island home to the northwest of Jerusalem. To date they have not left their new home to return to their own ancestral land from which they were taken some 2,700 years ago. Thus technically the House of Israel, as represented by the unicorn, is still considered to be in captivity, and this is what the chain signifies.

Chained Unicorn

Notice that in the Coat of Arms the lion representing Judah is **not** chained down. This is owing to the historical fact that, while the House of Judah also sinned and suffered the consequences by being taken into captivity by the Babylonians, nevertheless they, unlike their kinsmen from the House of Israel, returned after seventy years of captivity. The House of Judah rebuilt the Temple at Jerusalem and their descendants dwelt there until Roman times, when Titus destroyed their second Temple and the Jews were once again dispersed from their land. Nevertheless, generation after generation of small Jewish communities have ever since maintained their presence in the Holy Land. Then, after nearly 1,900 years of wandering, the Jews finally regained their independent statehood in

1948, and even to this very day, the Jews are returning to their ancestral land, the Land of Promise. In reality these are only the advance guard, as in due course of time, according to the hundreds of prophecies spoken by the prophets, the other tribes will also return. It is then that the Unicorn of Israel can finally take off her chains, as all the tribes of Israel will once again be united in **'their'** Land of Promise.

The lion also represents the royal line of King David ruling over the House of Israel, exactly as was prophesied. When you put all of these things together, it all fits perfectly the premise that the Brit-ish people, *'the people of the Covenant'*, are indeed Israel.

King David's Royal Emblem

Any royal house or throne requires emblems and symbols for personal identification and for official use on documents and property. In order for these symbols and emblems to be recognized both nationally and internationally, they would have to continue without any fundamental change from generation to generation. What then were the emblems of the Royal House and Throne of King David of Israel? As a member of the Tribe of Judah, David would have used the emblem of that tribe which, as we saw previously, was

a *couchant* Lion. Yet, because David and his descendants were now being separated from the tribe of Judah to become the Royal House of the whole nation, some change was necessary to show this distinction. Otherwise how would anyone be able to distinguish between the emblem of the Royal House and that of any other part of the Tribe of Judah? Thus, to establish the distinction, the Lion's posture was changed from *couchant* to *passant* and a Crown was added.

Crowned Passant Lion on top of Crown

146

While a Crown may not be the oldest symbol of a throne or a royal house, it is nevertheless very old, and to this day it is universally recognized as a symbol of a kingdom or monarchy. By adding a Crown to the *passant* Lion, a Crowned *Passant* Lion became the emblem of the Royal House and Throne of David. Consequently, in view of God's promise that the House of David is to continue as the Royal House of Israel forever, it must still be in existence today. Where then do we find a Royal House and Throne today whose official emblem is a Crowned *Passant* Lion? You guessed it! We do not have to look very far, as in the official emblem of Great Britain (the Royal Coat of Arms) we see facing us on the left a Crowned Rampant Lion, the emblem of the House and Kingdom of Judah, and on the right a Rampant Unicorn, the emblem of the House and Kingdom of Israel. These two symbols now united are upholding a large Crown, the emblem of a Throne, which is in possession of a Crowned *Passant* Lion, the emblem of the Royal House of David. What clearer proof could there be? *4

The Harp of King David

Even before he came to the throne of Israel, David had his own emblem. Ancient Israel was renowned for its music and musicians. The Levites were famous for their cantors or vocalists, and the Levitical choral music that accompanied the services around the Tabernacle was of the most excellent quality. Israel in those days had become a major power and the royal court of ancient Israel was a place of excellence where the finest musicians would entertain the king, the princes, nobles and foreign ambassadors. Among the greatest of these musicians was David. As a

*King David Playing the Harp
by Gerard van Honthorst
(courtesy Wikimedia)*

147

young man he was chosen out of the whole nation to be the Chief Musician at the court of his predecessor, King Saul. (1 Samuel 16:14-23.) David's favourite instrument was the harp, on which he became the most celebrated performer of the ancient world. Inevitably, the harp became his personal emblem. As such, it was inherited by the reigning branch of his descendants and so became the personal emblem of the reigning head of the House of David. Where then do we find a Royal House whose reigning head has a personal emblem that contains a harp? Perhaps by now you will know the answer? *5

The Royal Scepter

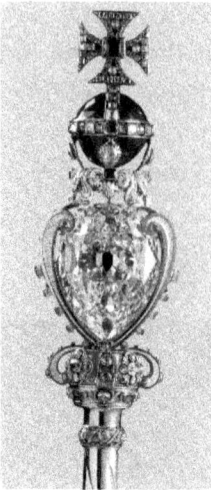

The Royal Scepter

There are a number of other emblems that point to the Davidic origins of the Royal House and Throne of Great Britain. In the record of Jacob's blessing of his sons, there is the promise that from among the descendants of his fourth son, from Judah would descend the future Royal Family of the nation of Israel. The promise goes: *"The sceptre shall not depart from Judah"* (Genesis 49:10). While we have been unable to find any evidence that the Tribe of Judah ever used a sceptre as an emblem in ancient Israel, nevertheless, the promise would most certainly be remembered. David, prior to his designation as the future king of Israel, had been a shepherd. He was to become the shepherd king of Israel and he never forgot his early days as a shepherd. According to the *Midrash*, King David minted a coin that featured a staff and a shepherd's pouch on one side and a tower on the other. *6

The two most important tools of a shepherd are his rod and his staff. It is interesting to note that the Hebrew words for both can be variously translated as rod, staff, crook, stave, club and even sceptre. The rod and the staff are symbols of the shepherd's authority over the sheep. The fact that the same word can also be translated as sceptre, which conveys the authority of a king is remarkable. Even in ancient Egypt we see this connection between the shepherd's crook and the royal authority of her Pharaohs, as the Pharaoh's symbols of authority were the crook and the flail. When David of the Tribe of Judah ascended the Throne of Israel, it was recognized that the prophetic promise had been fulfilled. For the first time in their history, a Prince of the Tribe of Judah wielded the sceptre, the symbol of royal authority as King of the Israel nation. Consequently, the sceptre too became an emblem of King David and his royal descendants. It should therefore come as no surprise to find that in Britain's ancient Coronation ceremony the Sceptre plays a most important role. Students of the ceremony have noticed that the Sceptre holds a place of importance in the Coronation service almost equal to that of the Crown itself. Once again, we find that a symbol of the House and Throne of David is identical to a symbol of the British Royal House and Throne. *7

As we have briefly considered an aspect of the Coronation service, we need to consider that the service involves three other associated items which are given to the Sovereign and which have an Israelite origin. They are the Signet (ring), the Bracelets and the Rod (staff). These three were part of the pledge given by the patriarch Judah to his daughter-in-law Tamar, before she conceived by him and as a result bore his twin sons Pharez and Zarah, as recorded in Genesis 38:12-25 KJV. In the use of the Ring, the Bracelets, and the Rod we see yet further evidence pointing to Britain's Royal House being descended from Judah. *8

*The Coronation of Her Majesty Queen Elizabeth II
pictured wearing the Imprerial State Crown and holding the Royal Scepter
and the Sovereign's Orb*

Dieu et mon Droit

Have you ever wondered about these words? *Dieu et mon Droit* - literally means *'God and my Right'*. It used to be understood from ancient times that kings rule by God's grace, or indeed by divine right. Most of us have heard of the 'Divine Right of Kings'. The king that most clearly comes to mind is King Charles I, who rigorously maintained his faith in the prerogative of the Divine Right of the Lord's

Royal Coat of Arms of Great Britain (courtesy Sodacan, Wikimedia)

Anointed. He died at the scaffold where with great dignity he paid the ultimate price for this very principle. It could be that the famous motto *Dieu et mon Droit* simply is a reference to the Divine Right of the Lord's Anointed for which King Charles I died. King Henry V first introduced the motto to the Royal Coat of Arms, although some of his royal successors have used different mottoes. For instance Queen Elizabeth I and Queen Anne used *Semper Eadem,* which means *'always the same'*. Mary I, also known as Bloody Mary, used the motto *Veritas Temporis Filia*, or *'Truth is the daughter of time'*. King James I, who introduced the King James Bible, sometimes used *Beati Pacific* (*'Blessed are the peacemakers'*) as his motto. Dutch-born William IIIs motto was *Je Maintiendrai, 'I shall maintain'*, which is still the motto of the Dutch royal family to this day.

Although the royal motto 'God and my Right' may well be a reference to the divine right of kings, it almost certainly has a dual

151

meaning. Having come this far in the book, we must surely by now be aware of the 'Birthright' that the patriarch Israel/Jacob conferred upon the sons of Joseph. As every single aspect of the Royal Coat of Arms is either an Israelite or a Davidic symbol, it follows that the motto too must be a reference to the same origins. We only have to add one word to the motto to see the most amazing connection: "God and my 'BIRTH' Right". In fact, in the French language *Dieu et mon Droit* clearly implies, "God and my Birthright"! Thus it would appear that even this royal motto is yet another reference to the covenant God made with Britain's ancestral fathers Abraham, Isaac and Jacob.

Honi soit qui mal y pense

'Evil to him who evil thinks' is the meaning of the legend that is on the blue and gold garter that surrounds the shield of the Royal Coat of Arms. This blue and gold garter around the shield signifies that the bearer is a knight of the Most Noble Order of the Garter, founded by King Edward III in about 1348. The garter is part of the insignia with which a knight is invested. Since the reign of King Henry VIII, the Sovereign and the Knights Companion of the Order have encircled their arms with this garter. What could the meaning of this legend be? To what do the words *'Evil to him who evil thinks'* refer?

Order of the Garter (courtesy Sodacan, Wikimedia)

The answer lies in the blessing Balaam was compelled to speak over Israel, when he said: *"Blessed is he that blesseth thee, and cursed is he that curseth thee"* (Num. 24:9 KJV). Can we see the connection? On one hand we have, *"Evil to him who evil thinks"*, and on the other we find, *"Blessed is he who blesses you and cursed is he who curses you"*! Thus we see that even the very legend, *Honi soit qui mal y pense*, is a direct reference to a prophetic utterance that can only apply to Israel. The collar of the Order is the oldest form of personal decoration in the world. Legend has it that the collar of this most noble Order has its origin in ancient Egypt, recalling the moment when Pharaoh put the chain of authority around Joseph's neck. *9

The Star of David

The six-pointed star commonly known as the Star of David is a unique Israelite symbol which, as the name implies, has royal connections with King David of Israel. Its correct name is 'The Shield of David' or, in the Hebrew language, *'Magen David'*. This symbol has its roots in the Ancient Paleo Hebrew alphabet, which was the predecessor of the present Hebrew alphabet. In this old alphabet the equivalent of the English letter 'D', *i.e.* the Hebrew letter *Dalet*, was shaped like a triangle. Thus this ancient triangular shaped

Star of David (courtesy Wikimedia)

Dalet was used at both the beginning and the end of the name 'DAVID'. We need to bear in mind that vowels are not used in either ancient or modern Hebrew. King David was the great warrior king of Israel, and the Israelite armies that were led by him bore the Star of David – two interlaced *Dalets* to signify the first and last letters of their King's name. In this we can see the origins of the term the 'Shield of David' or in the Hebrew language the *'Magen David'*.

Used as a Royal Seal

This Shield of David is also sometimes referred to as the Seal of Solomon. King David in all probability used it as the symbol of his royal authority, rather than by King Solomon. A royal seal is the 'mark' that signifies the king's authority on documents, and it would also be used to identify those servants of the king, who are carrying out a commission under the authority of the Crown. The six-pointed star comprising an upright and an inverted pyramid may be considered symbolic of the union of the divine with the earthly.

Today we would instantly recognize it as the official flag of the State of Israel. Ironically, the Jews are not really entitled to the national name 'Israel', as has already been covered in previous chapters; this name was formally given to the two sons of Joseph by the patriarch Jacob. The Jews, who are from the tribe of Judah, would more accurately proclaim their true identity by flying a flag containing the emblem of the Lion of Judah. They are descendants of the House of Judah, not of the House of Israel. Nevertheless, their use of the Shield of David on their national flag and on their synagogues and their rabbinical courts is very significant. It is a clear indication that they look upon it as a mark of Israelite identity and as a support for their claim of descent from the people over whom the House of David reigned. We can see that this emblem has been, and still is, used as evidence of a claimed relationship to ancient Israel and the Throne of David. *9

This raises a stark question . . . .

If the Israeli State uses it as evidence in support of a claimed continuity of the nation and people over which the House of David ruled, then "WHY DOES BRITAIN USE IT?"

Star of David on swords of Commissioned Officers owing allegiance to the British Crown

"What do you mean, "Why does Britain use it?" You may well ask, as incredible though it may sound, Britain does use the Shield of David all the time! Remember, that a 'royal seal' is the mark of 'royal authority' that has since time immemorial been used to identify those who are carrying out a commission under the authority of the crown.

In Great Britain's armed forces all officers receive their commission and their authority from the Sovereign. They are in effect an instrument and an extension of the Sovereign's authority. The curious thing is that in Great Britain the symbol of that authority is the Shield of David. This emblem appears near the hilt on the sword of all commissioned officers owing allegiance to the British Crown. At one time it also appeared on sleeves of the uniforms of certain ranks of the Royal Naval Reserve. Why on earth should this be? Surely, the only viable explanation is that our Royal House and Throne are in fact the continuation of the House and Throne of David. *10

U. S. Marine Corps Sword

In the United States however, the officers of the U.S. military derive their authority from the President, who is the head of all three branches of the armed forces. In the U.K. all officers are awarded a sword, as a symbol of their commission, whereas in the U.S. only the members of Marine Corps receive this distinction. U.S Marine Corps recruiting advertisements usually display a fearsome Marine in full dress uniform carrying a beautiful sword. If you carefully look, you can clearly see the "Star of David," just below the hilt of the sword. If in doubt, ask any Marine! Is it not curious that both America and Great Britain use this Davidic symbol in their armed forces as a symbol of their authority? *11

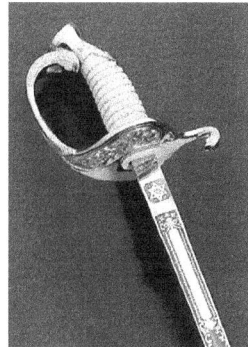

Star of David on U. S. Marine Corps sword

A secret from the Royal Robing Room

Another most remarkable sign of Britain's royal connections with the Shield of David is found in the Royal Robing Room in the Palace of Westminster in the House of Lords. The Queen's Robing Room is a private room over which the sovereign has complete authority. The room is the Queen's private chamber that she uses but once a year for the purpose of being robed in her royal robes for the opening of Parliament. The room contains a magnificent throne situated on a dais three steps above the floor. The wooden parquet floor surrounding the red carpet of the steps and the dais is of the finest quality and within its borders it contains the most magnificent marquetry using different colored woods. The border is divided into squares and each square contains the Shield of David! If this is not amazing in and of itself, it does not end there, as each Star of David emblem contains a further uniquely Israelite emblem at its center. These alternating emblems refer respectively to the 'Rose of Sharon' and a version of the 'Breastplate of the High Priest.' The 'Rose of Sharon' portrayed within the Shield of David has twelve petals symbolising the Twelve Tribes of Israel. In this we have the most astounding visual evidence that this royal throne does indeed represent the Royal Throne of King David of Israel. Just let us pause for a moment and consider the question: "Why would the British Royal House of Windsor in all of their heraldic emblems proclaim their connection with Israel and the Royal House of David? Why would they do it if it were not true?

Shield of David in parquet flooring in the Royal Robing Room

Apparently the practice of marking officers' swords with the Shield of David is comparatively modern, having begun in 1830. However, the use of this Davidic emblem in the British Isles goes back many centuries before 1830, as many old Scottish regiments used it well before this date. The Shield of David also appears in the Arms of several of the old Scottish noble families, such as those of the Duke of Buccleuch and Lord Napier for instance. There is also a most ancient cup belonging to the Chief of the Clan MacLeod that confirms the connection between our Royal House and the House of David. This family heirloom of the Kings of Ulster was given to the Chief of the Clan MacLeod sometime in the eighth century. Thus it is over thirteen hundred years old, yet the central decoration is the Shield of David. This becomes very significant when we remember that our Royal Family is descended through the kings of Scotland from the kings of Ulster. Even today, the central shield of the Arms of Northern Ireland carries King David's six-pointed star. *12

Star of David in Royal Arms of Northern Ireland (courtesy Tom Lemmens, Wikipedia)

Thus, at least as far back as a thousand years ago in Britain, and long before that in Ulster, the Shield of David was in use as a heraldic emblem by the ancestors of our Royal House. Having seen this veritable mountain of evidence, how can anyone possibly doubt that the British Royal Throne can be anything other than the continuation of the House and Throne of King David of Israel? Did not the prophets say that his House and his Throne would endure to all generations? Well, we have the fulfilment of those prophecies before our very eyes in the House of Windsor.

The St. Edward's Crown represents the Camp of Israel

St. Edward's Crown

There are hidden symbols in the St Edward's Crown, of which almost no one is aware. These symbols are of a deep spiritual nature, and once we understand their true significance, it should leave us in a state of complete awe. It should by now not come as any surprise that in order for us to understand these amazing revelations we have to go back to ancient Israel. Having come this far let us carry on, as we are going on the most incredible journey of discovery. Do try and keep an open mind and prepare yourself to be surprised and amazed.

The four brigades of the Camp of Israel

"For My house shall be called a house of prayer for all nations." Isaiah 56:7

THE TEMPLE INSTITUTE

After the Exodus from Egypt, which occurred around 1449 BC*, the twelve tribes camped around the Tabernacle, which was situated right in the center of the camp. The four-sided camp was organized into four brigades – one brigade on each side – with each brigade comprising three tribes. A leading tribe led each brigade, and each brigade came under the standard of their leading tribe. Thus the Tribe of Judah led the Brigade of Judah, which incorporated the tribes of Zebulun and Issachar. The Judah Brigade camped on the East of the Tabernacle under its tribal standard, 'The Lion of Judah'. The tribe of Ephraim was the brigade head placed over the tribes of Benjamin and Manasseh; and this Ephraim Brigade camped to the West of the Tabernacle under its tribal standard of an 'Ox' or 'Bull'.

The tribe of Dan was appointed as the brigade head over the tribes of Naphtali and Asher; and the Dan Brigade was situated on the north side of the Tabernacle and marched under its standard of an 'Eagle'. The tribe of Reuben was head over the tribes of Simeon and Gad; and this Reuben Brigade camped on the Southside of the Tabernacle under its tribal standard of 'The Face of a Man'. *13

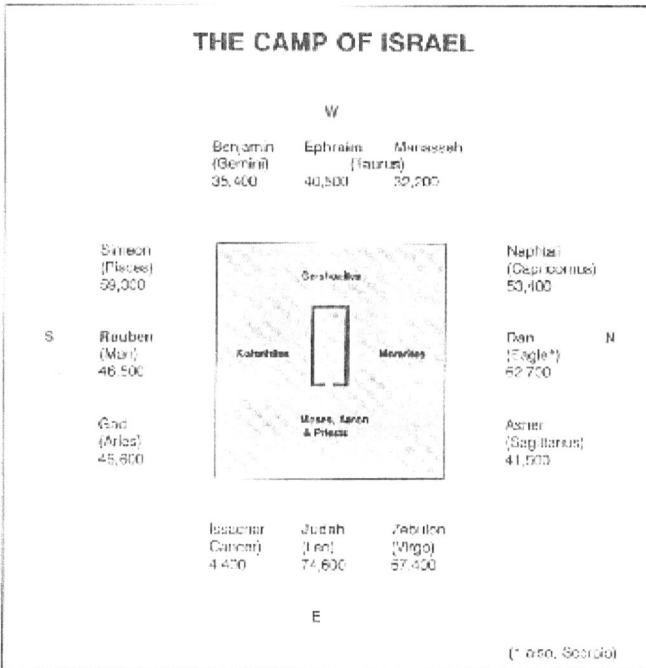

The Camp of Israel showing the Four Brigades
(courtesy Chuck Missler)

Each Tribe had its own standard

As we have already seen, heraldry is not an invention of the Middle Ages; rather its origins go back to ancient Egypt. The Twelve Tribes of Israel used their tribal standards as a continuing form of identification ever since their Exodus from Egypt. We have Israel's own biblical history book to confirm this fact in the Book of Numbers 2:2, where it states: *"Every man of the children of Israel shall pitch by his own standard, with the ensign of their father's house"* (KJV). So much for our heraldic experts who pronounce that heraldry originates in the Middle Ages, with the advent of the knights and their armour. Here we have clear evidence that these Israelite tribes stood by their tribal standards and their fathers' ensigns some three and a half thousand years ago.

To sum up the heraldic emblems of the Four Brigades: the standard of the Brigade of Judah was a Lion, the standard of the Brigade of Ephraim was an Ox, the standard of the Brigade of Dan was an Eagle, and the standard of the Brigade of Reuben was the Face of a Man. This is obviously most important as we find several references in the Bible to these four emblems. One of the most intriguing of these is found in the Book of Ezekiel 1:10: *"As for the likeness of their faces, each had the face of a man; each of the four had the face of a lion on the right side, each of the four had the face of an ox on the left side, and each of the four had the face of an eagle".*

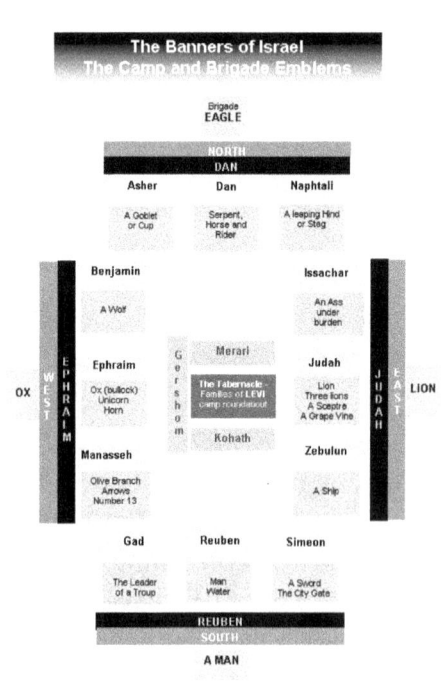

The Four Banners of Israel (courtesy Ron Wallace)

Isn't this a most remarkable discovery? You may well say: "What on earth has all of this got to do with the St Edward's Crown? As we will soon discover, "It has **everything** to do with the St Edward's Crown!"

Another biblical reference to the Four Brigade Standards of the Camp of Israel we find in the New Testament Book of Revelation 4:7-8.

160

"The first living creature was like a lion, the second living creature like a calf, the third living creature had a face like a man, and the fourth living creature was like a flying eagle. The four living creatures, each having six wings, were full of eyes around and within. And they do not rest day or night, saying: 'Holy, holy, holy, Lord God Almighty, who was and is and is to come!'"

The Four Faces of Israel
(courtesy
http://jahtruth.net/bkofke.htm)

The very fact that these four Tribal Brigade Standards are referred to in both the prophetic Books of Ezekiel and Revelation indicates the great significance of these four leading tribal emblems. We could speculate as what these four tribal symbols might possibly mean. However, our purpose is only to emphasise the importance of these four tribal brigade standards in the context of the St Edward's Crown.

Each Tribe of Israel had its own jewel

Not only did each of the Twelve Tribes have its own tribal emblem or emblems, but another most remarkable fact is that each tribe also had its own birthstone. This is a most fascinating discovery, as each tribe had its own jewel! This jewel too was a badge of identification for the tribe! We find the authority for this in Israel's biblical history book in the Book of Exodus 39:10-14, where Moses gives the precise instructions for the 'Breastplate of the High Priest': *"And they set in it four rows of stones: a row with a sardius, a topaz, and an emerald was the first row; the second row, a turquoise, a sapphire, and a diamond; the third row, a jacinth, an agate, and an amethyst; the fourth row, a beryl, an onyx, and a jasper. They were enclosed in settings of gold in their mountings. **There were twelve stones according to the names of the** *sons of Israel: according to their names, engraved like a signet, each one with its own name according to the twelve tribes"* (emphasis added).

Replica of High Priest's Breastplate
(courtesy Dr. Avishai Teicher, Wikipedia))

Can we now begin to see the connection with the bejewelled St Edward's Crown, with which British monarchs have been crowned for at least a thousand years? Despite the fact that the original Crown of St Edward was destroyed in Cromwell's time, the present crown is an exact copy made in 1661. The fact that Cromwell destroyed the original crown does not affect its significance as a symbol, for even a flag wears out and is replaced by a new one. The astonishing reality is that this unique Coronation Crown in every respect follows the design of the Camp of Israel! There is not a crown like it in the whole world! A crown too serves as a badge of identity and as a heraldic device. Once you start to study these things you will soon discover that no two crowns are alike. Each nation has its own design, for just as flags and coats of arms are emblematic of nations and peoples, so also are crowns. Thus each crown tells its own fascinating story, and there is no crown in the entire world that can match the St Edward's Crown for the depth of its symbolism.

Around the golden base of the Crown of St Edward we find twelve precious stones, which are identical, at least in kind, with the jewels affixed to the breastplate of the High Priest of Israel.

Major-General H.D.W. Sitwell, CB MC, Keeper of the Jewel House in the Tower of London, in an authoritative work entitled *The Crown Jewels*, confirms that there are twelve jewels around the base of the Crown of St Edward. In describing the Crown he says: "*The band is set with twelve precious or semi-precious stones*". This is also true of the original St Edward's Crown, for he quotes Sir John Ferne who, in *The Glory of Generosity*, printed in 1586, not only states that there were *twelve* jewels but also gives us their names. No less than six of these names are identical to the names listed in Exodus 28, as being on the breastplate of the High Priest. That the other six names are not the same is readily understandable when we consider the fact that in ancient times the names of jewels and precious stones were merely a description of their appearance. However, today in our time, as any jeweller will tell you, jewels are classified and named according to their chemical composition and crystallisation. It follows from this that many jewels and precious stones of today do not have the same names that they had in ancient times. Thus the fact that there are some differences between the modern names of the jewels on the base of the Crown and the biblical names of those on the breastplate of the High Priest does not prove they are different jewels. *14

At this point it is appropriate to use the analogy of the probability of coincidence once again. If only one of the named jewels was the same, as those mentioned on the breastplate of the High Priest, it could be considered an accident. If there were two jewels named that were the same, it could be considered mere coincidence! If there were as many as three named jewels the same in the Crown and the Breastplate, then it must have meaning! In this case we have no less than six jewels with identical names and this surely constitutes evidence of proof.

The present Crown, as rebuilt in 1661, was as far as possible an exact replica of the original one. All the available evidence indicates that the jewels taken from the old Crown were used on the new. Thus we have every reason to believe that the '*twelve jewels*' around the base of the present Crown are identical, at least in kind, to the '*twelve jewels*' that were such a prominent feature on the breastplate of the High Priest of Israel.

Thus we face the amazing fact that for well over a thousand years British sovereigns have been crowned with a Crown bearing '*twelve jewelled symbols*', each identifying one of the Twelve Tribes of Israel. Is this not the most astonishing indication of the ancient origins of the kingdom and people of Great Britain? Surely, we have here yet further positive evidence of their Israelite identity! *15

St. Edward's Crown

When we view the Crown as a whole, we can see that in form and structure it is a model or replica of the Camp of Israel, as it was arranged during their forty years wandering through the wilderness after the Exodus from Egypt. The layout of the Camp is clearly described, as consisting of the Twelve Tribes in four groups or Brigades encamped around a perimeter of an open space. At the center of the open space was the Tabernacle and above it was that luminous Pillar of Cloud denoting the presence of the God of Israel. These three features are clearly symbolised in the structural features of the Crown of St Edward. Just as the Twelve Tribes were encamped around an open space, so also the twelve jewels, symbolising these same Twelve Tribes, are set around the base of the hollow Crown. Just as the Twelve Tribes are arranged in four groups of three tribes each, so also four upright bars delineate four groups, each comprised of three jewelled emblems located on the base of the Crown.

The Camp Of Israel

The Four Brigades of Israel (courtesy http://www.british-israel.us/29.html)

Notice also how the four Brigade Standards of Judah, Ephraim, Reuben and Dan are represented on the Crown These Brigade Standards would have been raised higher than the individual tribal emblems of the tribes.

So, also on the Crown, we find above its base with the twelve jewels signifying the twelve tribes, four upright bands containing four larger jewels in the same relative position to the four Brigade leaders of the Camp of Israel.

The Camp of Israel represents the Kingdom of God

Ancient Israel in the days of Moses was a Theocracy, and the Camp of Israel was a representation of the Kingdom of God, with Twelve Tribes, in four divisions, living in the Presence and under the Rule of their King. Their Divine King, the God of Israel, was at the same time the Sovereign Creator of the Universe. The Pillar of Cloud above the Tabernacle at the center of the Camp denoted the Presence of the God of Israel. So also the Cross, at the center of the Crown, is, according to Christian theology, the emblem of that same God, even though his name is Jesus in the English language. In His language, that is to say in the Hebrew tongue, His name is Yeshua, which means 'Salvation'! According to the Protestant Evangelical wing of the Christian church, He is that Shiloh *'whose right it is to wear that Crown'.*

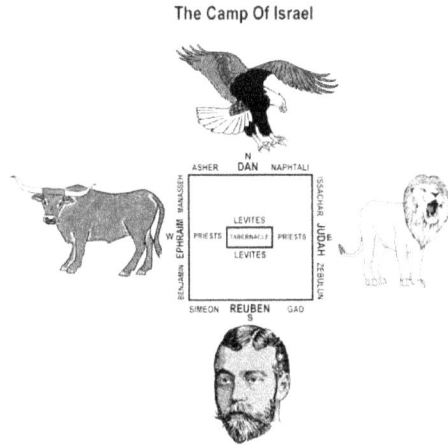

165

According to the tenets of Judaism the wait is for Messiah Ben David, the promised Deliverer and King of Israel, as in due course of time it is the destiny of Israel to become a Theocracy once again. The Crown of St Edward is a representation and a prophetic symbol of that Messianic Kingdom, which alone is capable of bringing peace, happiness, and perfect fulfilment to all the people of this most unhappy world. As such, the St Edward's crown is a spiritual emblem of the highest significance. Notice that the golden cross is standing on top of a golden orb symbolising the world, and this indicates that the *Shiloh who is to come, and whose right it is to wear that Crown and sit on that Throne, will rule the whole world through His 'chosen' nation Israel.* This essentially wraps up and summarizes the Gospel of the Kingdom that was first announced by John the Baptist, and subsequently preached by Jesus Christ and his twelve Apostles, including later on by the Apostle Paul.

St. Edward's Crown
A model of the Camp of Israel

166

The Fleur-de-Lis

No doubt you have noticed the beautiful diamond encrusted golden Fleurs-de-Lis positioned on the four corners of the St Edward's Crown. Many heraldic experts and historians over the ages have puzzled over the origins of this most royal of royal emblems. Most experts consider the Fleur-de-Lis to be a purely French royal symbol, and yet it appears amongst the royal paraphernalia of England's ancient Saxon kings. The earliest appearance of the Fleur-de-Lis in England was featured on the crown of Aethelred I, who reigned from 866 to 871 as King of Wessex. He was the fourth son of King Egbert, whose reign in 802 started out as King of Wessex and ended 37 years later as King of the English and overlord of Wales. It is fair to assume that if the son wore the royal mark of the Fleur-de-Lis; his father would have done so before him. If this is the case then the Fleur-de-Lis has played an important part in the royal insignia of Great Britain for no less than 1,200 years. Alfred the Great, too, would have been familiar with this most special of all royal emblems, and yet none of these Anglo-Saxon kings had any involvement or connection with France.

Countless origins have been suggested – far too many to cover in this brief outline – but one thing all the scholars are agreed on is that the Fleur-de-Lis is deeply intertwined with France. In the days prior to the French Revolution it was generally looked upon as the definitive emblem of the kings of France. Even today, over two hundred years later, most people when they see this most gracious lily emblem still automatically associate it with France. The French connection seems to go back a long time, as on a coin of the Roman Emperor Hadrian, Gaul (*i.e.* France) is depicted as a female figure holding a lily. As Hadrian commenced his rule in AD 117, we thus have historical confirmation, going back nearly 1,900 years, which associates the lily with France. The obvious questions are: "How did the French come by this emblem? How did they acquire it? How did it come to be associated with royalty? Why was it associated with royalty? How do we explain the mystery of the early Anglo-Saxon kings of England also using this most royal of all heraldic symbols, and this despite the fact that they had no connection with France?" The truth is that once you research this subject you find that most of the royal houses of Europe at some time or other used the Fleur-de-Lis in their regalia. It is a mystery that has baffled and confounded even the greatest scholars in heraldry and antiquity. Nevertheless, just because the experts do not know the answer, does not mean there is no answer! Logic alone tells us there must be an answer to this puzzle. What could the answer be?

Might it be possible that the reason the experts in heraldry have not been able to understand the origins of the Fleur–de-Lis is because they have overlooked the only source of research material that could give them the answer?

The Fleur-de-Lis has been adopted as the ultimate emblem of royalty. Its use in the royal dynasties of Europe goes back well over a thousand years, and in the case of France it goes back nearly 2,000 years. The emblem must have come from somewhere! The answer to this mystery is to be found in the Bible, that superb history book of Israel. It is the one textbook all the heraldic researchers have overlooked, presumably thinking that the answer could not possibly be found there. Yet, when we examine the pages of this book, we discover that the emblem of this noble lily originated with King Solomon, the wisest, greatest, richest and most glorious king who ever lived. There are many references in the Bible that associate the lily with King Solomon. The lily is first mentioned in connection with the building of Solomon's Temple. The front entrance of Solomon's Temple was adorned with two giant bronze pillars, one on each side. These huge pillars were thirty-nine feet in height and twenty feet in circumference. Now notice how these pillars were decorated:

*"The capitals which were on top of the pillars in the hall were in the shape of **lilies**"* (1 Kings 7:19 – emphasis added).

The bronze altar for burnt offerings stood in the inner court in front of the porch of the Temple, and between the altar and the porch there was a huge bronze laver holding no less than 22,000 litres of water for ritual washing. This laver or bath rested upon twelve bronze oxen, representing the twelve tribes of Israel, arranged in four groups of three oxen, each group facing one of the four points of the compass. Let us notice how the rim of this giant ritual bath was decorated:

*"It was a handbreadth thick; and its brim was shaped like the brim of a cup, like a **lily** blossom. It contained three thousand baths"* (2 Chronicles 4:5 – emphasis added).

In King Solomon's own book, *Song of Songs*, the lily is featured no less than eight times. His chapter two starts with: *"I am the rose of Sharon, and the **lily** of the valleys. Like a **lily** among thorns, so is my love among the daughters."* (Song of Songs 2:1-2 emphasis added). Solomon here mentioned the lily in connection with the rose of Sharon, which is an emblem of Israel. In fact he sees himself as the embodiment of not only of the lily, but also of the rose of Sharon. The prophet Hosea, when speaking about the final restoration of Israel, conveys the very heart of God as he speaks the following words of comfort: *"I will be like the dew to Israel; he shall grow like the **lily**, and lengthen his roots like Lebanon"* (Hosea 14:5 – emphasis added).

Even the New Testament makes the most amazing connection between the lily and Solomon. Jesus in his famous Sermon on the Mount mentions lilies and Solomon in the same breath:

*"So why do you worry about clothing? Consider the **lilies** of the field, how they grow: they neither toil nor spin; and yet I say to you that even Solomon in all his glory was not arrayed like one of these"* (Matthew 6:28-29 – editor's emphasis).

All together there are some fifteen references to lilies in the Bible, and of these no less than fourteen are connected either directly or indirectly to King Solomon, whereas the other is a direct reference to a yet future, restored Israel. This surely represents overwhelming evidence that the Fleur-de-Lis originates with King Solomon of Israel. This most simple of all royal emblems is also the most distinguished, as it was the personal emblem of the most distinguished and wisest king who ever lived.

The Tudor Rose

In the fifteenth century, England was troubled by a ferocious civil war that lasted for the best part of thirty-five years. It became known as the 'War of the Roses' that had resulted from the rivalry between the royal pretenders of the Houses of York and Lancaster. Each side had its own emblem. A white rose represented York, whilst the House of Lancaster was symbolised by a red rose – hence the term 'War of the Roses'. At the end of the war Henry Tudor united the Red Rose of Lancaster with the White Rose of York through his marriage to Elizabeth, the daughter of Edward IV. He chose as his

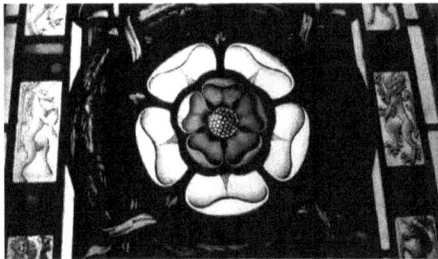

Tudor Rose Stained Glass
(courtesy The Museum of the Order of
St. John, Clerkerwell, London)

symbol a rose with both red and white petals, i.e. a large white rose with a smaller red rose superimposed on top of it, and with five green leaves around it. Paintings from the Elizabethan period show that there was a real variety of rose in existence in those days that looked very much like the Tudor Rose of Henry VII. It is rather interesting to think on the possibility that the royal horticulturists of Henry Tudor's day worked hard to develop a rose just like it. The astonishing fact is that the Tudor Rose, presumably unbeknown to Henry Tudor himself, in reality was THE SYMBOL OF ISRAEL.

The Assemblage of Israel

The ancient Jewish writings of the Zohar speak of a rose of alternate red and white petals, which symbolises Israel. In the beginning of the 'Zohar' it says (emphasis added):

" *'As the rose among the thorns, so is my love among the maidens.'* "

"What is the rose? It is the Assemblage of Israel, the Community of Israel. For there is a rose above and a rose below. Just as the rose which is among the thorns has red and white, so does the Assemblage of Israel have justice and mercy. Just as the rose has thirteen petals, so does the Assemblage of Israel have thirteen measures of compassion encompassing it on all sides. Five strong leaves surround the rose."

Adin Steinsaltz wrote a book about Jewish mysticism entitled *The Thirteen Petalled Rose,* and he based his title on the above passage in the Zohar.

Is it not extraordinary that an ancient symbol signifying both the Assemblage, as well as the Community of Israel, should after an interval of over 2,000 years resurface as a Royal Emblem of England? The red and white 'Tudor Rose' with its ten petals becomes the symbol of all subsequent English monarchs, and as such it has become a symbol of England itself. To this day, it still is an official symbol of Great Britain. It is a symbol that like so many of Britain's' other royal emblems, cries out to reveal her ancient Israelite origins. The Tudor Rose with its ten petals is a most unique emblem that represents Great Britain, aka – Israel!

Why does the Tudor Rose have only ten petals?

Notice, the Tudor Rose admittedly has only ten petals, whereas the *"Rose of Israel"* described in the Zohar has thirteen. To some this may seem like a discrepancy, yet the very opposite is the case, as it only provides further confirmation and proof of Britain's descent from the Ten Tribes. The ancient kingdom of Israel, as ruled by King David and his son King Solomon consisted of thirteen tribes.

Remember how the patriarch Jacob sired twelve sons who subsequently grew into the Twelve Tribes of Israel. Yet, on his deathbed Jacob adopted the two sons of Joseph, Ephraim and Manasseh, to whom he gave the blessing of the Birthright. He placed Ephraim the younger son of Joseph above Manasseh, his elder brother, and thus Manasseh became the Thirteenth Tribe of Israel. The *'Rose of Israel'* refers to the whole Assemblage and Community of Israel, *i.e.* all thirteen tribes.

The Tudor Rose on the other hand with its 'Ten Petals' symbolises those 'Ten Tribes' that rebelled over taxation. These Ten Tribes split away from the kingdom in the reign of Rehoboam, the son of Solomon, to set up their own independent kingdom to the north of Jerusalem, and they called their kingdom 'Israel'. Thus it can be seen that the 'Ten Petals' of the Tudor Rose clearly represent that same kingdom and those same 'Ten Tribes of Israel'.

Another interesting aspect is that the giant bronze doors of the Eastern Gate of the Temple of Solomon were decorated with the symbol of the 'Rose of Israel'. According to authoritative rabbinical sources there was a beautiful rose garden within the precinct of the Holy Temple in Jerusalem. It was situated between the present Western ('Wailing') Wall and the actual Temple itself. *16

The amazing motto of the Tudor Rose

Not many people are aware that the Tudor Rose has its own motto. Henry Tudor, being fully aware of the origins of the symbolism of the red and white rose, almost certainly devised the text himself. The words were considered to be of such significance that it was subsequently adopted as the royal motto of the Tudor family. It conveys a powerful allusion to the throne of David in ancient Israel. Like all mottos of that time it was phrased in Latin – the text reads – *"Hac Rosa Virtutis de Celo Missa Cereno Eturnu(m) Florens (Fulgens) Regia Sceptra Feret"* and in modern English this reads:

"This rose of virtue sent us from on high shall shine in sceptered state eternally."

Hac Rosa Virtutis de Celo Missa Cereno
Eturnu(m) Florens (Fulgens) Regia Sceptra Feret

This rose of virtue sent us from on high shall shine
in sceptred state eternally

Notice it speaks of a *rose of virtue,* e.g. (the rose of Israel) *sent to us from on high,* e.g. (by the God of Israel) *shall shine in sceptered state eternally* – meaning it shall rule for all of eternity. This text can only be a reference to the throne of King David of Israel, as it alone was ever established for all of eternity. The patriarch Jacob was the first to prophesy of this sceptered throne on his deathbed when he addressed his son Judah, saying, *"The sceptre shall not depart from Judah, nor a lawgiver from between his feet, until Shiloh comes."* (Gen. 49:10). As mentioned earlier, 'Shiloh' was reference to the Messiah, the prophesied Deliverer, who would come to deliver and rule over a restored Israel in the end times.

The prophet Nathan adds a further dimension to this as he comes to King David of Israel and, speaking of his son Solomon, he utters the most amazing prophesy about the future of David's throne:

"When your days are fulfilled and you rest with your fathers, I will set up your seed after you, who will come from your body, and I will establish his kingdom. He shall build a house for My name, and I will establish the throne of his kingdom forever... And your house and your kingdom shall be established forever before you. Your throne shall be established forever" (2 Samuel 7:12-13, 16).

Here we have an immutable promise of the everlasting continuance of the Royal House and throne of David. Henry Tudor in devising the motto of the Tudor Rose clearly affirmed that he considered himself to be of the line of those Davidic descendants seated on this prophesied throne of David that was to last forever. The divine promise is further confirmed in the book of Psalms and its absolute certainty is heavily emphasised once again:

"I have made a covenant with My chosen, I have sworn to My servant David. Your seed I will establish forever, and build up your throne to all generations" (Psalm 89:3-4).

Your seed, your throne and your kingdom will be established forever and to all generations! What could be clearer than that! This is what the Tudor family, being themselves of the line of David, had uppermost in mind when they devised the motto for the Tudor Rose. They considered the Tudor Rose to be *'that rose of virtue sent from on high'* as a sacred charge in that it represented the throne of David that *shall shine in sceptered state* (ruling over Israel) *eternally.'*

The Royal Thistle of Scotland

The 'Thistle' has for many centuries been associated with the Kings of Scotland. The emblem was first shown on silver coins dated 1474, during the reign of James III of Scotland. There are indications that it had been used as the personal badge of the Scottish sovereigns during previous reigns. Then in 1540, the Order of the Thistle was created, and ever since that time the 'thistle' has become uniquely associated with the Royal House of Stewart. As with most other royal emblems the authorities of heraldry are at a loss to explain the origin of the

Royal Thistle of Scotland (courtesy Wikimedia)

'thistle' as the pre-eminent heraldic device for Scotland. Once again it is only when we turn to the Bible that we discover the answer to the mystery. The Bible, Israel's history book records furious animosity between King Amaziah of Judah and King Joash of Israel, in which the King of Judah challenges the King of Israel to battle. King Joash responds by sending Amaziah, the King of Judah a sarcastic and most arrogant reply in which he refers to himself as a Cedar of Lebanon (the king of all trees), whilst at the same time referring to the King of Judah as a 'Thistle!' He goes on to say that a wild beast is going to trample the 'Thistle' (2 Chronicles 25:18; 2 Kings 14:9). Subsequently, in the inevitable battle that ensued, Amaziah, the King of Judah was taken captive and his armies suffered a terrible defeat at the hands of Israel. His enemy King Joash

broke down the walls of Jerusalem and took all the articles of silver and gold from the Temple and the King's treasuries in Jerusalem. Somehow, from that time forth the epithet given to the King of Judah has stuck for evermore and it has thus ended up in Scotland. The likelihood therefore is that the origin of the Royal Thistle of Scotland may well have been derived from the above incident. It seems that ever since that time the kings of Judah ended up with a new nickname and it appears they turned the 'thistle' epithet, which was meant as an insult, into a badge of pride. Might we thus in this emblem find an indication that the kings of Scotland are descended from that same illustrious Davidic line of the kings of Judah? There are quite a few people with some knowledge of the subject who would certainly say so. Currently, the Royal Scottish Thistle also features in the official Royal Arms of Great Britain.

The Arms of Westminster

Notice how the emblem of the breastplate of the High Priest is

Original Arms of Westminster

at the center of the Arms of Westminster. Thus the Coat of Arms of the Royal Borough of Westminster provides further incredible evidence of Britain's Israelite origins and identity. The emblem that more than any other identifies the London borough that has the Houses of Parliament at its center is a 'dead give-away' as to Great Britain's true origins.

Temple Mount Jerusalem and Westminster London

The Tribe of Levi was the priestly tribe of Israel. Their emblem was a representation of the Breastplate of the High Priest, who, like Aaron the brother of Moses, was the Head of the Tribe of Levi. Thus, the Breastplate containing Twelve Jewels representing the Twelve

Tribes of Israel, set in four rows of three jewels each, became the official tribal emblem of the Tribe of Levi.

This same emblem of the Tribe of Levi became the emblem of an enclave within Jerusalem in which the Temple of Solomon was situated. This great Temple and the area around it became, in effect a separate community. It became a city within a city. It was the headquarters of both the civil and religious governments of the nation, administered by the Tribe of Levi under the direction of the High Priest. The High Priest was not only the active religious head in absolute charge of the Levitical priesthood and the Temple worship, but he was also in charge of

High Priest wearing the
Breastplate
(courtesy Wikimedia)

the Civil Service of Israel, which was administered by the Tribe of Levi. King Solomon's massive Temple complex comprised no less than thirty-six acres, and in it were situated the offices and living quarters of the senior priests and civil servants. The Temple was the sacred place wherein on the High Holy Days of Israel *17 all services of national worship were held, and in which the coronation services of the Kings of the House of David took place. Again, let us note that the emblem of this separate area within Jerusalem was decorated with the symbol of the Breastplate of the High Priest. The garment upon which the Breastplate of the High Priest was fastened was called in Hebrew, *"choshen mishpat"*, which means the Breastplate of Judgement or Decision. It was in this central area of Jerusalem that all the religious, royal and civil authority of **the United Kingdom of Israel** was concentrated. This was the area where 'Judgement' and 'Decision' were the order of the day for the United Kingdom of Israel.

Replica of High Priest's Breastplate
(courtesy Dr. Avishai Teicher, Wikipedia)

Keeping this in mind, let us now turn our attention to Britain, the ancestral home of the Celtic and Anglo-Saxon family of peoples. There in London, just as in ancient Jerusalem, we see a distinct area or enclave, the Royal Borough of Westminster. Within this area we see a great and ancient Abbey, in which for a thousand years or more, England's – and later Britain's – national religious services have been held. Here, too, for the same period, the kings of Britain's ancient line have been crowned and anointed in a ceremony which is almost identical to that which was used in the Coronation of the kings of David's line in the Temple in ancient Israel. Furthermore, within this Royal Borough of Westminster, just a short distance from the Abbey, there are the Parliament buildings and the offices of the ministers of the Crown, from which the nation is governed. Within this same area we also find the Palace of the Royal House of Windsor. The arrangement and the location of the various offices of state are almost parallel to those of the Temple enclave in ancient Jerusalem. History confirms that during the successive reigns of King Saul, King David and King Solomon, **Israel was a "United Kingdom,"** comprised of thirteen tribes, each located in their own tribal territories. Today we see Great Britain described as **"The United Kingdom,"** composed of four kingdoms e.g. England, Scotland, Wales and Ulster, also known as Northern Ireland.

The Moses Room

In the Palace of Westminster, the seat of the British Parliament, we find in the House of Lords a most spectacular room called *"the Moses Room"*. On the facing wall of this chamber there is a huge oil painting picturing Moses coming down from Mount Sinai carrying two stone tablets with the Ten Commandments, (the Ten Words). As you enter the chamber the massive painting dominates the facing wall, as it covers nearly the entire surface. In the elaborately carved surface of its frame, a brass plate is affixed, imprinted with the following lines: *"Moses brings down the tablets of the Law to the Israelites".* There is no other parliament building in the world in which there is a Moses Room dedicated to the giant lawgiver of the Bible. You will not even find a Moses Room in the Knesset, the Israeli parliament building in Jerusalem! Yet, the House of Lords, which is the top legislative authority in the nation, does contain such a room. In this we have yet another pointer and this in Britain's very seat of government, to the special association that exists between Great Britain and ancient Israel.

The Jerusalem Chamber

Adjacent to Westminster Abbey is Lambeth Palace, which is the official London home of the Arch Bishop of Canterbury, who is the head of the Church of England, the official church of the United Kingdom of Great Britain. In some respects his office is comparable to that of the High Priest in ancient Israel. Just as the palace of the High Priest was in close proximity to the Temple in Jerusalem, the palace of the Arch Bishop too was virtually next door to the great

Abbey of Westminster in London. Inside Lambeth Palace there is a very special room that is called the *"Jerusalem Chamber"*, which serves a unique purpose. It has to do with the coronation of a new king or queen. Throughout the year the St Edward's Crown is kept secure in the Jewel House inside the formidable fortress of the Tower of London. On the eve prior to the coronation of each monarch, the St Edwards Crown is taken from there under armed guard to Lambeth Palace, where it is placed in the center of the great oak table in the *"Jerusalem Chamber"*. Whilst it is there, during the night, the Crown is carefully guarded by a special contingent of Yeomen of the Guards both inside and outside the Chamber. Thus, **the Crown that represents the Camp of Israel and the Kingdom of God** is kept in the 'Jerusalem Chamber' prior to the Coronation of the kings and queens of Britain's ancient line.

The Jericho Passage

Furthermore, on the morning of the Coronation of a king or queen, senior bishops and prelates take the St Edward's Crown in solemn procession from the Jerusalem Chamber to the Westminster Abbey itself. On the way to the Abbey the Crown that represents the Camp of Israel has to pass through a room called *the 'Jericho Parlour'*. This name has a very high resonance for anyone of Israelite descent, as at the end of their forty years in the wilderness, God commanded the children of Israel to be circumcised before they could go forward to conquer the Promised Land. All males of every age underwent the *'Brit Milah'*, the 'Covenant of Circumcision'. Subsequently, Jericho was the first city of the Canaanites, which the children of Israel destroyed in their campaign to take the Promised Land. Jericho effectively was the gateway to the Land of Promise, and the victory at Jericho was the token that the whole land was being given into their hands. This makes Jericho a name that is highly symbolic and pregnant with meaning. One, the Coronation Crown has been carried through the *'Jericho Parlour'*; the simplest way to enter Westminster Abbey is to directly go through the door at the end of the *"Canaan Passage"*. However, tradition prohibits the Crown that represents the Camp of Israel and the Kingdom of God, from going into the Abbey/Temple through some side entrance! This Crown, which symbolises the Messiah of Israel, the Prince of Peace, ruling over the whole world through the United Camp of Israel, may only enter through the *"Eastern Gate"*. This gate holds a special holiness for Jews, who believe that the "Shekinah or Divine Presence used to appear through the "Eastern Gate" of the Temple. The Prophet Ezekiel confirms this as follows: *"And the glory of the LORD came into the Temple by way of the gate which faces toward the east".* (Ezekiel 43: 4). The Prophet Zechariah elaborates further on this by prophesying the future arrival of the King Messiah of Israel:

"And in that day His feet will stand on the Mount of Olives, which faces Jerusalem on the east. And the Mount of Olives shall be split in two, from east to west, making a very large valley; Half of

the mountain shall move toward the north and half of it to the south." (Zechariah 14: 4).

This is the reason the Crown is taken in solemn procession, come rain or shine, through an outside courtyard leading to the **Great Eastern Entrance** door of Westminster Abbey. Upon entrance to the Abbey the Crown is taken up the long isle towards the high altar, where the new royal candidate awaits his or her investiture, whilst seated in the Coronation Chair. The Crown is placed upon the Altar and on its way the Great West Window has greeted it.

The Twelve Sons of Jacob Window

On entering the great Abbey one cannot but notice the large west window of stained glass, which totally dominates the central transept of the building. In this massive window every single one of Jacob's twelve sons is portrayed in the most glorious colors with their respective names placed underneath each figure. Apart from those twelve tribal Patriarchs of Israel, the window also features the illustrious Patriarchal Fathers of Israel, Abraham, Isaac and Jacob, as well as Great Spiritual Giants, Moses and Aaron. Thus here in this most ancient and glorious Abbey we see yet further startling references to Great Britain's Hebrew origins. How truly amazing all this is that every aspect of this royal enclave in London so perfectly reflects the original Temple complex in Jerusalem in the days of King Solomon. When foreign tourists come to London, their main fascination is with the magical mystery of Britain's Royal heritage. How much more amazed they would be if they understood her heritage goes all the way back some three thousand years to King David of Israel and even beyond to the Hebrew Patriarchs Abraham, Isaac and Jacob.

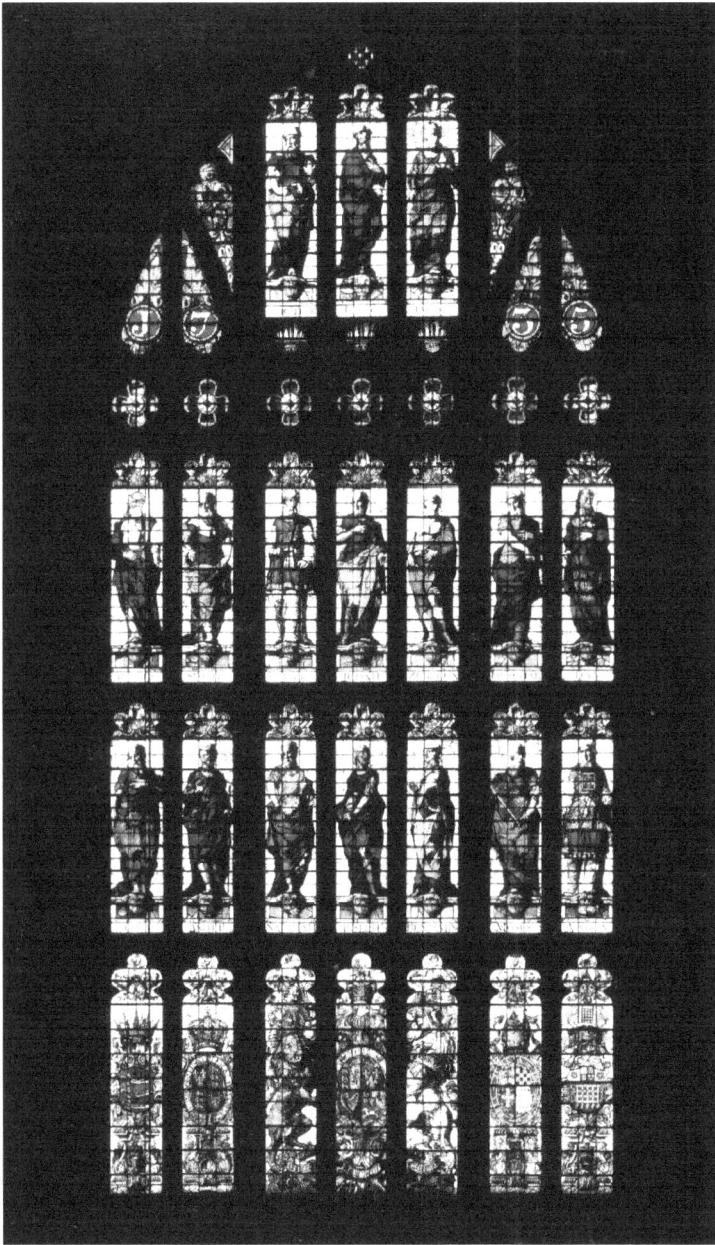

Westminster Abby Great West Window
(copyright Dean& Chapter of Westminster)

Amazing similarities

Thus, we have a capital city where, just as it was in ancient Jerusalem, there is a separate area in the center, from which the nation is governed, and in which there is an ancient Abbey in which the sovereigns are crowned and all the royal national religious services are held. This similarity with ancient Israel is truly amazing, but it becomes even more so when we see that the very emblem of the Royal Borough of Westminster, as well as the emblem that identifies both Houses of Parliament, is the same as that of the Temple area of Jerusalem. It is the emblem of the Tribe of Levi – the BREASTPLATE OF THE HIGH PRIEST OF ANCIENT ISRAEL. Remember how the garment backing onto the Breastplate of the High Priest was called the Breastplate of 'Judgement' or 'Decision'?

Just as the symbol of the Breastplate was placed upon all the major buildings in the central Temple area of Jerusalem, so we see a very similar symbol at Westminster in London. This same Breastplate of 'Judgement' and 'Decision' is placed upon the Houses of Parliament where 'Judgement' and 'Decision' are the order of the day for the United Kingdom of Great Britain. It is placed upon all the Borough of Westminster's public buildings—even upon the public lavatories within the borough. How can we possibly ignore evidence like this? Could this be just another coincidence? The answer surely must be a resounding NO, because just as with all the other signs of Britain's spectacular ancestry, there can really be only one explanation: Great Britain and her American and Commonwealth offspring truly are modern day Israel!

Current Arms of Westminster
(courtesy Wikimedia)

Houses of Parliament Emblem
(courtesy Charles, Barry, Wikimedia)

King and Priest United under One Crown

Incredible as it may sound, the prophet Jeremiah prophesied that there would be an everlasting connection between the continuous reign of the lineal descendants of King David over the House of Israel, and the Levitical priesthood. The prophet makes a direct link between the descendants of David and the Levites, as the two are mentioned in the same breath. Let us see exactly what Jeremiah has to say: *"For thus says the LORD: 'David shall never lack a man to sit on the throne of the house of Israel; nor shall the priests, the Levites, lack a man to offer burnt offerings before Me, to kindle grain offerings, and to sacrifice continually'"* (Jeremiah 33:17-18). Here we see clearly how the promise of continuous rule to David's descendants goes hand in hand with the promise of continuous administration of the priestly office by the descendants of Levi. Jeremiah then goes on to underline the absolute total permanence of God's covenant with the House of David, and as he does so he clearly brings the Levitical priesthood into it as well:

"Thus says the LORD: 'If you can break My covenant with the day and My covenant with the night, so that there will not be day and night in their season, then My covenant may also be broken with David My servant, so that he shall not have a son to reign on his throne, and with the Levites, the priests, My ministers'" (Jeremiah 33: 20-21).

The Covenant is clear; as long as there is a day and a night David will always have a son reigning over the house of Israel, and the Levites will continue to minister in their priestly office. The promise is absolute, as in the passage immediately following the above; the prophet brings in the sand and the sea and heaven and earth as timeless additional witnesses to God's Covenant with King David. In the whole passage, Jeremiah links the priestly Levites no less than four times with the royal descendants of David, and thus he completely includes them in this unbreakable and everlasting Covenant. Is this not the most astonishing revelation? It makes the extraordinary appearance of the emblem of the Breastplate of the High Priest on both Houses of Parliament, as well as in Westminster's Coat of Arms all the more intriguing. The question is: Where do we look for these Levites, whom God calls *"the priests, My ministers"*? The answer to this mystery is truly staggering.

History records that the Levitical priesthood that served in the Temple at Jerusalem came to an end in AD 70, when Titus destroyed and burned the Temple and expelled the Jews from the region of 'Palestine'. Again it is a fact of history that the Levitical priesthood has not practiced its sacrificial temple worship since that time. This almost mortal blow to Judaism caused a major rethink in Jewish circles at the time, but as history has shown time and again, you cannot kill man's religious beliefs. Thus despite this near lethal blow by the utterly pagan, ruthless and most unholy Roman Empire, Judaism has flourished with the advent of rabbinical Judaism, which is still the oldest monotheistic religion in the world. Where though, you may well ask, are these priestly Levites that Jeremiah spoke of? It truly is a mystery! Of course there are a number of Jews whose very names portray their descent from Levi. They will go under names such as Cohen, Levene, Lefevre, Levy or Levi. There are quite a few rabbis, who are aware of their descent from the tribe of Levi, and the dream of most Orthodox Jews is to see a new Temple built on the Temple Mount in Jerusalem. In fact the Temple Institute in Jerusalem is busily training Jews of Levitical descent, as priests in readiness and expectation of the new Temple that is to be built on the Temple Mount. Most of the golden artefacts of the Temple are already awaiting their future use, such as the golden Menorah, the Table of the Showbread, and the golden Altar of Incense, to mention but a few. *17 All of this is done in preparation for the 'Geulah', the Great Deliverance spoken of by the prophets, and is occasioned by the return of all the tribes, led by the Messiah of Israel, leading to the restoration of the Whole House of Israel.

Nevertheless, the prophet Jeremiah is referring to a priesthood that is somehow linked to the royal house of King David. What is the connection? Where should we look for the answer to this mystery?

The Priest-Kings

The answer is found in the history of the present day royal descendants of David. It was King Henry VIII, who united Church and State under his crown, and it is to him we must look for the answer. We all know the much-rehearsed account of secular history of how Henry became the Supreme Head of the Church of England, and therefore there is no need for us to go over this ground again. Nevertheless, what happened was extremely significant, as in uniting both the offices of the Church and the State under his Crown he was unwittingly fulfilling prophecy. He was fulfilling the prophecy of Jeremiah that David will always have a lineal descendant reigning over the house of Israel, and that the Levites will continue to minister in their priestly office. Jeremiah had connected the continuation of the royal descendants of David directly with the priestly Levites. The prophet had mentioned them in the same breath no less than four times and in effect he placed them together. This is what happened during the reign of Henry VIII, where the office of King and the office of High Priest were put together!

Celtic Christianity was *Torah*-observant

Even before Henry VIII united the offices of King and High Priest, the establishment of 'priest-kings' had been the tradition of the Scottish kings for many centuries. King Duncan I, who ruled from AD 1034 to 1040, was the son and heir of Crinan, Archpriest of the sacred Kindred of Saint Columba. Not only was Duncan King of Scots, but he also became the hereditary High Priest of the Celtic Church. Early Celtic Christianity was very close to the original *Torah*-observant teachings of Jesus. It had emerged within a few years of the crucifixion, as the foremost Church of the Christian world. These Celtic Christians adhered to the teachings of Jesus, as in following His example they observed the seventh day Sabbath, as well as the

Passover. Unlike their Christian successors they resisted the pagan ways of Rome, and were generally faithful to the Mosaic laws of the Old Testament. Great Britain became the center for this Celtic Christianity, and the influence of this religious movement spread far and wide. The Bible stood center stage, and both the Old Testament, as well as the New Testament received equal status within this Celtic church. The movement became so powerful that the Pope sent St Augustine to Britain in 597 to destroy the Celtic Church that was hindering the empirical designs of Rome. St Augustine, having been duly installed as the Archbishop of Canterbury, succeeded in suppressing and dismantling the Celtic Church in England. Nevertheless, Rome failed to subdue the faithful in Scotland, Ireland and Wales, where the people refused to let go of the Hebrew roots of their faith. Thus the Celtic Church in those lands prevailed for many more centuries to come.

Robert de Bruce—the Priest-King of Scotland

Robert de Bruce, the great patriot King of Scotland, like King Duncan I before him, was not only formally invested with the powers of kingship, but he was also ordained as the Chief Priest of the Columban Kindred, *e.g.* the Celtic Church. Sadly, the writers of secular history have largely ignored this highly significant fact. Robert II, the first king of the illustrious House of Stewart, succeeded him not only as king but also as hereditary priest of the royal line. The format of the royal investiture of the Scottish kings was highly unusual in that the king-designate had first of all to pass through a ritual of purification to become an ordained people's priest. After this he would appear at the Abbey of Scone (near Perth) dressed in white garments as a symbol of integrity. Once he had arrived there, a bishop followed by seven priests would conduct him to the *'Fealty Stone'*. This 'Fealty Stone' was none other than the *'Stone of Destiny'* upon which he was to swear his allegiance to God, as well as his Oath of Fealty as the people's champion. It was only after this that he would be anointed with oil and crowned as King of the Scots. *18

Anointed like Solomon

The British Coronation ceremony, according to heraldic authorities, is at least a thousand years old, yet the scholars admit that it is so old that it its origin has been lost in the past. The Coronation is conducted in front of the High Altar in Westminster Abbey, an Abbey that was mainly designed for the use of the Monks of Westminster, but its design was also specially applied to serve as a Coronation church. There is an almost mystical part to the ceremony. The British monarchs are consecrated almost like a bishop would be. The truth is that the Sovereigns of Great Britain are *'anointed with oil'*. This really is the most sacred part of the rite where Britain's kings and queens appear to be hallowed by this 'anointing'. It is almost as if the Sovereign is acquiring some priestly authority by this. It is the anointing that in one sense sets the Sovereign apart and in another sense makes the sovereign the consecrated head of the Commonwealth. Most relevant of all, it is only after the anointing that the Sovereign can receive the Crown. Notice, this practice of anointing the Sovereign at his or her coronation is unique to Great Britain, as the other royal families of Europe do not include it in their coronation services.

The Archbishop of Canterbury, assisted by the Dean of Westminster, anoints the Sovereign on the hands, the breast, and the crown of the head with the words:

"And as Solomon was anointed King by Zadok the priest and Nathan the prophet, so be you anointed, blessed and consecrated Queen over the Peoples, whom the Lord your God hath given you to rule and govern ... "

Why mention Solomon, Zadok the priest and Nathan the prophet? Why mention these biblical figures unless there is some pertinent reason for doing so? Judging by the words spoken by the officiating prelates, they might almost be in Solomon's Temple in Jerusalem, administering this anointing to one of the Kings of Israel.

The Tudor descendants of Aaron the High Priest

After the Anointing, the Sovereign moves to the Coronation Chair, containing Jacob's Pillar Stone, which faces the Altar. The choir at this point sings the anthem *'Zadok the Priest'* (now to the setting of Handel), yet it is an anthem that has been sung since the earliest known English Coronation service. The words of this hymn are yet another incredible telltale give-away to Britain's Israelite origins. The Sovereign is then invested with various garments, which most closely resemble ecclesiastical vestments! One of the last of these garments is called the *Armil*, which is much like a stole in appearance. It was King Henry VIII who first introduced this garment. This *'Armilla,'* as it was then called, in reality was a reference to the *'Breastplate of the High Priest'*. The **Armilla** with which the King was invested at his Coronation is essentially the Breastplate in another form. Its very name is derived from the Hebrew for the **'Urim'** or **'Lights of God.'**

It was the Tudors who first introduced this vestment. It was also the Tudors who introduced the 'Portcullis' as a badge, which at a glance is clearly identifiable as the Breastplate of the High Priest. An excellent example of this Tudor emblem of 'Levitical' origin can be seen in King Henry VII Chapel at Westminster Abbey. These Tudor monarchs were direct descendants not only of the royal line of David, but also of the priestly line of Aaron, who was the very first High Priest of Israel. The office of High Priest in Israel could only come to the direct descendants of Aaron, as it was a hereditary office. Thus here we have the fulfilment of the promise that continuous rule to David's descendants goes hand in hand with the promise of continuous administration of the priestly office by the descendants of Levi. The staggering fact is that Queen Elizabeth II is not only the 144th direct lineal descendant of King David, but she also is the 107th direct lineal descendant of the priestly line of Aaron. *19 This explains why the prophet Jeremiah mentioned the descendants of David and those of Levi in the same breath. This explains the close link Jeremiah said would exist between the two for all time; that is to say, for as long as there is a day and a night. Since Henry VIII came to the throne, the same person has held the two offices of King and Priest.

Our Queen today unites the Davidic function as Sovereign of Great Britain and Head of the Commonwealth, with the Aaronic priestly office of being the Supreme Head of the Church of England. What an extraordinary significance there is in the Royal House of Windsor! After all these reams and reams of evidence, how can anyone possibly doubt that the House of Windsor is in reality a continuation of the ancient and most illustrious House of David? Thus, just as was prophesied by Jeremiah, the House of David has, like the day and the night, continued to exist, its latest manifestation being the House of Windsor. What a gloriously meaningful and historic revelation this is!

Is it a breastplate or portcullis?

Heraldic authorities will refer to the Emblem of the Tribe of Levi depicting the Breastplate of the High Priest of Israel as a Portcullis. Not aware of its true origins and meaning, they have come to refer to it as a Portcullis because of its supposed resemblance to the iron gratings, which were once used to strengthen the gates of castles and walled cities. It is also claimed that this emblem was adopted by Westminster from the Arms of the Beaufort family. Both claims are open to serious doubt. If this emblem came from the Beaufort's, then the question is: Where did *they* get it from, and why would *their* emblem be chosen in preference to the emblems of other ancient and influential families? Further, why must it be assumed that, because the emblems are the same, Westminster adopted its emblem from the Beaufort family? The reverse is equally possible! The Beaufort family could have adopted the emblem of Westminster.

Actually this question is really not that relevant or important. The fact is that all the available evidence clearly indicates that both Westminster and the Beaufort family derived this emblem from a single and much older source – that is from Levi, the Priestly Tribe of Israel. We find this same, or at least a very similar, emblem in the Bayeux Tapestry, which was made between 1066 and 1072 to commemorate the Norman conquest of England after the Battle of Hastings. In this 900-year old tapestry we find depicted knights in full armour and on their chests an emblem very closely resembling the Westminster (Portcullis) emblem. They appear to be rectangular in shape, have a border, and within the border are displayed twelve objects, which could be representations of the twelve stones of the Breastplate of the High Priest of Israel. It may be that these are only part of the knights' armour but, if they are actual replicas of the 'Portcullis' emblem, it follows that this emblem was in use long before the time of the Beaufort family.

The reason for qualifying and explaining the background to the use of this emblem is that whenever one dares to go against the accepted wisdom of the authorities, there will always be a lot of flak. Some will deny that the Westminster 'Portcullis' emblem that is so prominently displayed in the Arms of Westminster, as well as on both Houses of Parliament, is in any way derived from the emblem of Israel's High Priest. To prove their case they have pointed to the spikes at the bottom of the emblem to indicate it is nothing more than a representation of a portcullis as used in castle gates. They say that when the portcullis was lowered these spikes would go into the ground making it more secure. The truth is that these spikes were not a part of Westminster's ancient emblem, as they were nothing more than a heraldic embellishment added in modern times! According to an official at the College of Heralds, the oldest known form of this emblem has **no** spikes. Further, a portcullis is made of iron and in true heraldry would be shown as such, whereas in the Grant of Arms to Westminster (which formally legalised the ancient usage of this emblem) it is definitely stated that the 'portcullis' and its two chains and rings are to be a representation of 'gold.' *20

Another most significant point is that whereas a real portcullis has many openings, the emblem of Westminster has only **twelve**, which is the exact number of openings in the Breastplate emblem of the Tribe of Levi. We can see therefore, that except its openings have no jewels, the emblem of Westminster is a near exact replica of the emblem of the tribe of Levi. Just like the emblem of Levi, it is a plate, it is made of gold, it has twelve openings, it has two golden rings fastened to it on each of its upper corners, and to each of these rings a golden chain is attached. Apart from the missing jewels there are no less than five similarities that confirm that the 'Portcullis' symbol on our Houses of Parliament and in the Arms of the Royal Borough of Westminster, is **identical** to the Breastplate of the High Priest of ancient Israel. Could this yet again be just coincidence? *21

The Union Jack

Our present Union Jack was created on January 1, 1801 in direct consequence of the Parliamentary Union between Great Britain and Ireland. Incredible as it may seem, even Great Britain's Union Jack is a symbol that goes right back to our ancestral father, Jacob of Israel. The pole is commonly referred to as the 'Jack', whereas the flag represents the 'Union'. 'Jack' is short for Jacob! In fact the very term 'Union Jack' in the Hebrew language is synonymous with the same words that mean *'Covenant of Jacob'*, and it also would be written in exactly the same way. Thus even the U.K.'s national flag points back to her origins in ancient Israel. Yes, even the flag is an emblem of Great Britain's Israelite ancestry!

(courtesy Jonund, Creative Commons usage)

Remember how Jacob blessed the two sons of Joseph, as recorded in Genesis 48. At the deathbed of his beloved father, Joseph had been most careful to place his younger son Ephraim with his right hand towards Jacob's left hand, and his older son Manasseh with his left hand toward Jacob's right hand. He knew that as Manasseh was his firstborn son, that accordingly he should receive the primary blessing of the firstborn. When you read the account you discover how Jacob, even though his eyes were dim with age, knowingly guided his hands the other way. He actually crossed his hands and put his right hand upon the head of Ephraim and his left hand upon the head of Manasseh. As Jacob started to bless the lads Joseph was displeased. He protested and intervened by taking hold of his fathers' right hand to remove it from Ephraim's head and put it on Manasseh's head. Jacob however insisted that the primary blessing of the birthright should go to Ephraim the younger son of Joseph. It was a prophetic act that in these 'latter days' has been manifested in Great Britain and in her Commonwealth.

Note that Jacob crossed his arms when he pronounced his blessing upon the lads, and he specifically did so in order to place the primary blessing upon Ephraim. Thus he blessed him under the sign of a cross! Even this act was prophetic! The fact that Jacob/Israel blessed Ephraim/England under the 'Sign of the Cross' is most significant because it is under the Sign of the Cross on the Union Jack that the British built their Empire. It was under the Sign of this same Cross that her Christian missionaries distributed hundreds of millions if not billions of Bibles and evangelised the four corners of the globe. What an awesome revelation this truly is.

It is the red cross of St George, the diagonal white cross of St Andrew, and the diagonal red cross of St Patrick that make up the Union Jack. The cross of St Andrew on its blue ground was the national flag of Scotland and was added at the beginning of the seventeenth century, when the crowns of England and Scotland were united. The cross of St Patrick on a white ground was added at the beginning of the nineteenth century, at the time of the union with Ireland.

Crosses of St. George, St. Andrew, and St. Patrick (left to right)

The colors of the Tabernacle were red, white, and blue

Yet another fascinating pointer to the Israelite origins of the Anglo-Saxon and Celtic peoples is that the national colors of the Kingdom of the Ten Tribes of Israel were red, white and blue, as well as purple! These colors were derived from the Tabernacle that stood at the center of the Camp of Israel in the wilderness. Even the veils in front of the Holy of Holies of the Tabernacle, as well as the garments of the High Priest, his Ephod, and the Breastplate of Judgement were all in this same color scheme. *22 The Tabernacle was constructed out of wood, precious metals, and various colored textiles. Apart from purple, the overwhelming colors of the Tabernacle to an external viewer would have been red, blue and white. Famous commentators such as Nachmanides, one of the greatest of the Jewish Sages, have noticed and commented upon this fact.

The national colors of the Kingdom of Israel were red, white, and blue

According to Rabbi Samson Raphael Hirsh, an eminent nineteenth century Sage and biblical commentator, the relevant colors of red, white and blue were the national colors of the Kingdom of Israel. Now notice a curious fact of history that even today most nations of Israelite descent employ these same colors in their national flags. It is no accident, therefore, that most of the nations that have Israel as their ancestor have at least two out of the three tri-colors of red, white and blue. Just look at the table below:

The national flags of Britain, USA, France, Netherlands, Luxembourg, Norway, Iceland, Australia and New Zealand are all red, white and blue. The flags of Denmark, Canada and Switzerland are red and white; whereas Israel's national colors are blue and white. The only exceptions to this rule are Sweden, Belgium and Ireland, who have only one of the Israelite colors in their respective flags, even though they too are decidedly nations of Israelite descent.

Having come this far on our journey of discovery, we have seen how every single symbol of British nationhood and identity points back to their roots in ancient Israel. The hidden ancestry of Great Britain and America are no longer hidden. Understanding their true origins should make a difference to all English-speaking people of British descent.

CHAPTER SEVEN

❧

11ᵗʰ Sign
A People Unaware of their True Origins

*"I said, I would scatter them into corners, I would make the
remembrance of them to cease from among men."*
(Deuteronomy 32:26 KJV)

The overwhelming majority of the Celtic and Anglo-Saxon
descendants of the ancient Israelites have forgotten their origins.
They do not know that in reality they are Israelites and tribal brothers
to the Jews, and hence they have lost so much of their precious
heritage. There is one scripture in the book of Isaiah that perfectly
describes the condition of these people:

*"The ox knows its owner and the donkey its master's crib; but
Israel does not know, my people do not consider."* (Isaiah 1:3)

The Ox was the tribal standard of the tribe of Ephraim, and it
was Ephraim who was the leader of the Northern Kingdom of Israel.
The prophet Isaiah is clearly referring here to the sad state of the 'Ox',
e.g. the Lost House of Israel, who does not know its owner and who
has forgotten where he came from. This is as true of Great Britain and
America today as it is of the Commonwealth nations of Canada,
Australia and New Zealand, as well as the Israelite nations of
northwestern Europe. Moses too prophesied that the children of
Israel would be scattered and that over time they would lose their
identity. This is how he phrased his warning:

"I said, I would scatter them into corners, I would make the remembrance of them to cease from among men." (Deuteronomy 32:26 KJV)

Moses gave this prophetic warning some three and a half thousand years ago, and yet it has been fulfilled in every detail. The Lost House of Israel has been scattered into the four corners of the earth, and any remembrance of her Israelite origins has completely ceased. They themselves do not know who they are and neither does the rest of the world. The modern day descendants of Joseph have been veiled in darkness, and this is why they are referred to as the 'Lost' House of Israel. Yet, even so, they are nations of people that have been carefully preserved. The world does not recognize their true heritage because of the superb disguise they wear.

Joseph's disguise

Remember the biblical account of the brothers of Joseph, how they had come to him to purchase food to alleviate the terrible famine in their land? Their father Jacob had sent them on this errand into Egypt. They never even thought about Joseph any more, as they had sold him into slavery some 21 years earlier. It had happened such a long time ago, that they assumed he was dead. In fact this is what they told their father Jacob, that a wild beast had devoured him. They never thought they would meet him again. Even so, as fate would have it, there they stood before their brother Joseph, in an official audience with the all-powerful Viceroy of Egypt, and they did not recognize him. They stood right in front of their brother and they simply did not recognize him because he was clothed in Egyptian garments. They also could not ever have imagined that their brother, whom they sold as a slave, could possibly be the effective ruler of Egypt. The whole thing was too ridiculous to imagine. This analogy can be applied to America, Great Britain, and her Commonwealth daughters as well, as they too have adorned themselves with foreign 'Egyptian' clothes, and consequently the whole world perceives them to be Gentiles. Even their Jewish brothers do not recognize them anymore! They themselves even think they are Gentile nations, as they have forgotten their Israelite ancestry. Joseph named his eldest son Manasseh. The meaning of Manasseh is most revealing, as the true meaning of the name is: "CAUSING TO FORGET"!

Joseph named his firstborn son Manasseh, because the birth of his son and his marriage to his Egyptian bride had 'caused him to forget' his pain at being rejected by his own brothers. Joseph, as the effective ruler over the world-dominating Egyptian Empire, had become so absorbed in the great affairs of state, that any thought of his own origins were buried deep in his past. Today, the modern day sons of Joseph have also forgotten their Israelite origins. They have forgotten their patriarchal fathers Abraham, Isaac and Jacob and their matriarchal mothers Sarah, Rebekah and Rachel. They are orphans cast out of their ancestral land just like Joseph. Just as Joseph made a great success of his life in exile in Egypt, so his modern day descendants have also made a great success of their lives in exile, as they have become Great Nations, who much like Joseph have become the rulers of the world.

It seems like a giant veil has been drawn over their collective memory, as they all have forgotten who they really are and from where they originate. They are suffering from a collective amnesia. It also seems that the truth of their incredible ancestry has been deliberately buried by the historians of the past. In fact it appears that they have almost, as if by magic, been literally edited out of the history books. It is as if a cloud of darkness has descended over them.

In the Bible, as well as in rabbinical tradition, the Lost Ten Tribes became associated with darkness, clouds and concealment in general. One of the places to which the Ten Tribes were exiled was Habor in Mesopotamia, which adjoined a river of the same name, (modern Khabor in Iraq). For the ancient Sumerians of Mesopotamia, the 'Hubur' (*ie.* Habor) had been a mythical river in the West over which the dead had to cross. Procopius, a Byzantine historian (in the 500s BC), reported that on the North Gaulish coast, fishermen were exempt from taxation since they had the task of rowing the souls of the dead across the Channel to Britain. In classical literature Britain was known as the "Isle of the Dead" and Saturn (Dis Pater, the god of the dead) was said to rule there. Remember, Joseph's brothers of old thought that their brother was dead. By abstract general reasoning can we not see that these notions fit Britain, as being the place of the Lost Ten Tribes? After all, had they not been taken away from their land to an inaccessible place, and were their whereabouts not shrouded in mystery?

The Celts too believed in two worlds: This world and the 'Otherworld'. A constant exchange of souls took place between the two worlds: Death in this world took a soul to the Otherworld; death in that world brought a soul to this world. These ideas make sense when you relate them to the experience of the Israelites, who had been uprooted from one sphere of existence and artificially transplanted into another stranger one.

The Hidden Secrets of the Book of Esther

Most of us will be familiar with the Purim story in which the evil Haman planned genocide against the Jewish citizens of the Persian Empire, which stretched across 127 Provinces from India to Ethiopia and from Turkey to Arabia. Haman planned an empire wide attack, which had it been successful, would have annihilated the Jewish race in one fell swoop and in one single day! His plan was:

"To destroy, to slay, and to cause to perish, all Jews young and old, little children and women, in one day, the thirteenth of Adar, and to plunder their possessions," (Esther 3:13 NKJV).

Of course we know that Haman's plans were thwarted – the terrible edict was rescinded. The Jews then turned the tables on their enemies, culminating in the hanging of Haman on his own gallows, as well as the subsequent hanging of his ten sons.

Recent history has shown the timeless relevance of the Purim story, as Haman was the ultimate role model, inspiration, and

forerunner of Adolph Hitler. The German Fuehrer was hell bent, much like Haman, on the eradication of the Jews from the face of the earth. Mordecai and Queen Esther were not around to save six million Jews from Hitler's extermination camps. Yet the God of Israel, did provide a rescue plan in the form of the British, Canadian, Australian, New Zealand and South African sons of Ephraim, who for a time stood alone in stubborn resistance against the fearsome Nazi regime. We know that later on they were joined by the Americans, (sons of Manasseh), and together the two sons of Joseph defeated the modern manifestation of Haman.

The rebellious queen

The book of Esther in the Bible contains an interesting analogy that relates to the story of Israel's enforced exile from the land, as well as to her eventual glorious return. The Jewish people celebrate the festival of *Purim* in February/March each year, and their joyful celebration revolves completely around the book of Esther. You only have to read the book of Esther, one of the shortest books in the Bible, and you will get a complete picture of what *Purim* is all about. *Purim* is sometimes criticised as a Jewish form of Halloween. This is because part of its tradition is that people, especially the children in Jewish families, dress up in costumes and wear masks. Nothing could be farther from the truth. Just as the Jewish Passover Festival celebrates the Exodus and the glorious deliverance of the children of Israel from their bondage in Egypt, so the festival of *Purim* is also about a miraculous deliverance from certain and inevitable genocide in the days of the Persian Empire.

Just as the Jewish State of Israel today yet again faces in Islam a ruthless enemy bent upon the total extermination of the Jewish people, she faced a similar foe in Haman, the then executive ruler of the Persian Empire. One of the most beautiful things about the Jewish people is that they never forget their history, and thus the defeat of the evil Haman is still celebrated in the joyous festival of *Purim*. To the Jews Haman was a type of Satan, who, had he been

201

successful in his plan to eradicate all the Jews from the face of the earth, would have prevented the ultimate coming of Messiah. The simple truth is: no Jews – no Messiah, as the promised Messiah is to come from the House of David. *1 Thus Satan, through Haman, would have thwarted the future salvation of the whole world. *Purim* as such is a festival of the greatest significance and relevance not only to the Jew, but also to the rest of mankind.

The heroine of the story is Esther, chosen by King Ahasuerus to replace his rebellious Queen Vashti. Historians have identified King Ahasuerus as Xerxes I, who reigned over the Persian Empire from 485 to 465 BC. The King ruled over 127 provinces, and symbolically he represents the God of Israel, as he was King over the world of his day. The royal capital of the King was Shushan, which is a symbolic type of Jerusalem, the future millennial capital of the Messianic world to come. The name Shushan itself speaks of lilies (a reference to Solomon), of roses (a reference to the rose of Sharon, a symbol of Israel), and it also speaks of the color white, which is a reference to righteousness and harmony.

In chapter one of the book of Esther the King prepares a seven day feast for all great and small in the court of the palace garden. In the meantime Queen Vashti is planning her own feast, rather than attending the feast of the King. On the seventh day of the King's feast the King summoned seven servants to bring his bride before him. He loved her above all women and he wanted to see her. He desired to show his bride and his Queen to all of his royal guests at the citadel of Shushan. Queen Vashti point blank refused to come to the party, leaving the King completely humiliated and highly embarrassed in front of all of his guests, many of whom were senior dignitaries and envoys from his world-wide empire. The King then sends for his bride the second time, and still Queen Vashti stubbornly refuses to come to him. To cut a long story short, the King, after consultation with his senior advisors, writes a decree and sends the rebellious Queen Vashti away. The search is now on for a new queen, as Queen Vashti's position is to be given to another.

If we stay with the same analogy, with King Ahasuerus symbolically representing the Great God of Israel, whom can Queen Vashti possibly represent? The answer to this question can be found in the book of Jeremiah:

"'Surely, as a wife treacherously departs from her husband, so have you dealt treacherously with Me, O House of Israel,' says the Lord." (Jeremiah 3:20)

Queen Vashti therefore symbolically represents the rebellious House of Israel, which split off from Judah, and which, much like Queen Vashti, started to keep her own feast days. Remember how King Jeroboam, the newly appointed king of the northern Kingdom of Israel, after the split was so concerned about his people continuing their worship at the festivals in Jerusalem, that he erected two golden calves and instructed his citizens to worship them? Queen Vashti was banished from the court of the King and she was sent away, in the same way that the rebellious Northern Kingdom of Israel was forcefully removed from their ancestral lands and sent away into exile. The analogy fits perfectly.

Esther—the beautiful orphan queen

The stage is now set for the entrance of Mordecai, a Jew who was the son of Jair. The name Jair is a significant pointer to the symbolic role of Mordecai, as the meaning of the name Jair is *'that which illuminates or brings light'*. Mordecai's role is symbolically that of the Messiah of Israel. He has adopted his uncle's beautiful daughter called Hadassah. This name too is most significant as the meaning of the name "Hadassah" is, *'that which was diffused, such as light or wind, and/or that which was hidden and kept in secret'*. Hadassah's name is subsequently changed to Esther. The name Esther refers to a section of land, or people, which is preserved and brings healing. Hadassah was given a Gentile name because she too is a symbolic type of the Lost House of Israel. The difference being that, whereas Queen Vashti symbolised the rebellious House of Israel, Queen Esther was a type of a repentant House of Israel that is set to return in the end time. Just as Hadassah was *'diffused, hidden and kept in secret'*, so has the Lost House of Israel's ancestry become diffused, hidden and kept in secret. Just as Hadassah had to acquire a Gentile name, so likewise has the Lost House of Israel acquired a Gentile identity to the point where they even think of themselves as Gentiles. Having lost the knowledge of their true origins, their ancestry became hidden. Incredibly, **the name Esther also means 'that which is hidden or veiled in darkness'.** Esther, just like the Lost House of Israel, had lost her parents. The word for parents in Hebrew is *'horah'*, and it comes from the same root-verb as *Torah*. Mordecai, then, is a type of Messiah – he saved the orphan Esther, took her in, educated and looked after her, and it was he who led her to the King.

The King preferred Esther above all the women in his kingdom, and he chose her as his new bride and Queen. It was while she was in this position that she was able to fulfil her God-given destiny – to save the House of Judah from certain extermination. *2

The Lost Tribes of Joseph – Ephraim and Manasseh – have, like Esther, been 'veiled in darkness' and are often referred to as 'lost'. Yet, they are a Commonwealth of Nations and a Great Nation that have been preserved to this day. The world cannot distinguish them from the Gentile nations because they are wearing a disguise. This is the real reason that the Jews, mostly without knowing the reasons why, dress in costumes for their *Purim* Festival. It is not to frighten away evil spirits, or any such pagan nonsense. It is simply to serve as a reminder that when the children of Israel take up the rituals of their Gentile fellow travellers in the world of their exile, they assimilate and become like those people and consequently they become unrecognizable to their brothers.

The present-day disguise of the Lost Ten Tribes of Israel can be seen even in the Jewish custom of wearing masks during the festival of *Purim*. This is the deep-rooted spiritual reason why 'masks' are worn during the feast of *Purim*. It has absolutely nothing to do with a so-called Jewish version of Halloween. Instead, the deeper meaning of *Purim* is about the veil, the disguise, and the mask, that God himself has drawn over the face of the wayward House of Israel.

The disguise of the Lost Ten Tribes of Israel is seen even within the name of Joseph's son Ephraim. The first three letters of **Ephraim, ALEPH, PEY, REYSH,** add up to the numerical value of **ninety-five,** which spells the word *'APHER,* which means *"MASK"* or *"DISGUISE."* This is the reason for the masks that are worn, or held up at the feast of Purim; **it has everything to do with the veil, the disguise, and the mask that God Himself has drawn over the face of the wayward Lost and *HIDDEN* House of Israel. The feast of Purim therefore fundamentally is about the deliverance and glorious return of the Lost House of Israel. The day will come when their mask is removed to reveal their true face before the whole world.**

The Feast of *Purim* is therefore not only about the miraculous deliverance of the House Judah, but it is also about the equally miraculous ultimate reappearance of the Lost House of Israel.

God's 'unfaithful wife'

Hosea was the final prophet to the rebellious and idolatrous Northern Kingdom of Israel just prior to her exile. His book contains the most remarkable theme, which gives the reader the most extraordinary insight into the very heart of God with regard to his 'chosen' people. Hosea was a prophet to Israel – he was not a prophet to Judah. His book contains no less than thirty-seven mentions of the name Ephraim, the younger son of Joseph, who was the leading tribe of Israel and the primary inheritor of the Birthright, together with his older brother Manasseh. Ephraim in the Bible can refer just to the descendants of the younger son of Joseph, or it can refer to the whole House of Israel consisting of the Ten Tribes of Israel. It never refers to Judah. Hosea was commissioned by God to warn Israel, not Judah, and therefore in most cases when he uses the term Ephraim he is addressing the whole of the Lost House of Israel.

In the book of Hosea, God through His prophet likens Israel (the Northern Kingdom) to an unfaithful wife. The book gives a rare and most unusual example of God communicating his love towards his wayward people. God called his prophet Hosea to be a *'living illustration'* of his relationship with Israel. Hosea is asked to marry a prostitute called 'Gomer' from the kingdom of Israel. Hosea loved her fully and has children by her, but she is continually unfaithful to him. Time and again he would go after her and bring her back when she strayed with other lovers. On one occasion Gomer willingly enters into slavery, only to be rescued by Hosea, when he buys her back. Hosea's eyes are thus opened to the heartbreak that God himself endures when his 'chosen' people forsake His ways. Even though they resist him stubbornly and are therefore unworthy subjects of his love, the Lord in his mercy continues to reach out to them and welcome them back.

A Divine divorce — Israel has to leave home

Hosea had three children by Gomer, and by the names of his children he prophesied that judgement would come upon the House of Israel. His first child is a son whom he names *Jezreel,* which can mean *'to scatter.'* With the birth of Jezreel, he pronounces that God will scatter Israel and bring an end to the kingdom. His second child is a daughter and he is instructed by God to call her Lo-Ruhamah, which means **'no mercy'**, *"for I will no longer have mercy on the house of Israel, but I will utterly take them away. Yet I will have mercy on the house of Judah"* (Hosea 1:6-7). Notice how the Scripture differentiates between the House of Israel and the House of Judah. The kingdom of Israel is going to be brought to an end, it is going to be scattered, and it will be utterly taken away. According to the prophetic verdict God will have no mercy on Israel, whereas he will have mercy on Judah. Finally, Hosea's unfaithful wife conceived for the third time and gave birth to a son, and *"God said: 'Call his name Lo-Ammi, for you are not My people, and I will not be your God'"* (Hosea 1:9). *Lo-Ammi* means 'not my people'! It is clear from the context that the names given to the children of the prophet reflected

God's attitude towards Israel at the time. God refers to Israel as a female! Israel is his unfaithful wife. In the names of the prophet's daughter, Lo-Ruhamah – that is 'not having obtained mercy' – and his son, Lo-Ammi – that is 'not my people' – God indicated that he was disclaiming her as a wife. Because of Israel's continued rebellion and unfaithfulness God is repudiating his former relationship with her. God wrote them a bill of divorce and put them away! From that time Israel (not Judah) was under the curse of the law. The prophet Jeremiah confirms that God divorced Israel:

"Then I saw that for all the causes for which backsliding Israel had committed adultery, I had put her away and given her a certificate of divorce; yet her treacherous sister Judah did not fear, but went and played the harlot also" (Jeremiah 3:8).

From this we can conclude that God 'divorced' the Northern Kingdom of Israel and He put her away, by allowing the Assyrian invaders to transport her into captivity from which to date, after some 2,700 years, she has not yet returned. Of course, Judah should have learned a lesson from Israel's example, but the truth is that she behaved even more abominably than her unfaithful sister. Judah was subsequently punished, as about 130 years later, she like her Israelite sister before her, went into captivity to Babylon from which she was allowed to return after only seventy years of exile. Because Israel had been given a bill of divorce, and Judah had not, Israel was unable to return to her ancestral lands in the land of Israel. According to the law (Deuteronomy 24:1-4), when God gave the House of Israel a certificate of divorce, He sent her away out of the 'Promised Land'. So long as that bill of divorce was in force, He could not take her back into his House, that is to say, into His land.

It is a legal separation — not a divorce

There are indications that this 'certificate of divorce' spoken of by the prophet Jeremiah might not have been exactly what we today have come to understand as a *'decree absolute'*, or the final decree in divorce proceedings, which leaves the parties free to remarry.

Instead it may only have been a **'decree *nisi'***, that is a provisional decree, which effectively means a legal separation. A 'decree *nisi'*, or a 'legal separation', still leaves the door slightly ajar for a possible future reconciliation. The reason for this interpretation is that in the very same chapter and almost in the same breath, the prophet Jeremiah, speaking of a yet future time, makes the most remarkable statement:

"Return, O backsliding children," says the LORD, "for I am married to you. I will take you, one from a city and two from a family, and I will bring you to Zion." (Jeremiah 3:14).

It appears from this that the marriage between God and Israel has not been finally annulled. There are numerous other Scriptures that indicate a future reconciliation between God and his Covenant people of the Lost House of Israel. Once your eyes have been opened to the reality that there is such a thing as a Lost House of Israel, the biblical evidence becomes overwhelming. The plain fact is that God never divorced or separated from Judah, and Judah was restored to the land covenanted to Abraham, Isaac and Jacob for an eternal and perpetual Covenant. Here we have a clear statement of fact: Israel is issued with a 'decree *nisi'* and a legal separation took place, but Judah was not divorced. What a revelation! God never divorced the Jewish nation. He is still in covenant relationship with them! So much for Christian replacement theology teaching, that the Christian Church has replaced Israel! The irony is that much of the Christian Church, especially the Reformed Protestant part of it, is situated in the very nations that comprise the modern descendants of Israel, and yet they are completely unaware of their identity. They are part of Israel and yet they do not know it. They have forgotten their original husband and they do not remember him anymore. Thus, in this context, the Christian Church is the divorcee, or at least she is the one who is legally separated from him, whereas the House of Judah is still married.

Once your eyes have been opened to it you will see that much of *Israel's History Book*, the Bible, especially in the books of the prophets, continually stresses the difference between the House of Israel and the House of Judah. Yet in spite of this strong evidence of the distinction between the two houses, the teaching of the majority of theologians declares Israel and Judah to be the same people. Even though in the book of Kings and the book of Chronicles, the separate history of the two kingdoms, as well as the separate lineage of the two royal houses is meticulously recorded, yet somehow these 'learned' scholars cannot see the distinction. Once you begin to analyse God's dealings with the House of Israel, you will begin to understand that they are altogether different from his dealings with the House of Judah.

Promise of a yet future reconciliation

Most encouragingly, numerous Scriptures prophesy a yet future reconciliation between God and his 'unfaithful wife'. Perhaps the most outstanding of these is by the prophet Jeremiah. This prophet has been given a rather negative name in the Christian West, as on occasions, when a person is being particularly miserable and negative in his opinions, he may well be told, *"Don't be such a Jeremiah!"* Yet one of the most positive prophetic statements in the whole Bible comes from his pen. He speaks of a glorious new covenant, which represents a new marriage relationship, as well as the long awaited reunion between the houses of Israel and Judah.

"Behold, the days are coming, says the LORD, when I will make a new covenant with the house of Israel and with the house of Judah – not according to the covenant that I made with their fathers in the day that I took them by the hand to lead them out of the land of Egypt, My covenant which they broke, though I was a husband to them, says the LORD.

"But this is the covenant that I will make with the house of Israel after those days, says the LORD: I will put My law in their minds, and write it on their hearts; and I will be their God, and they shall be My people" (Jeremiah 31:31–33).

Restoration of the 'united' Kingdom of Israel

Even the prophet Hosea refers to this fantastic time in the future when the marriage covenant relationship between the Lost House of Israel and her God is going to be restored. At the same time he speaks of the day when the breach between Israel and Judah is going to be healed.

*"'Yet the number of the children of Israel shall be as the sand of the sea, which cannot be measured or numbered. And it shall come to pass in the place where it was said to them, "You are not My people," there it shall be said to them, **"You are sons of the living God." Then the children of Judah and the children of Israel shall be gathered together, and appoint for themselves one head'** "* (Hosea 1:10–11, emphasis added).

Notice how Hosea begins his statement, as he refers to the covenant that God made with Abraham regarding his descendants becoming an innumerable multitude of people. As we have already covered earlier on, this can in no way be a reference to the tiny Jewish population in the world. It therefore can only be a reference to the modern day nations of the House of Israel, as well as the Jewish people and to the myriads of scattered Israelites in the four corners of the world. Hosea then gives the sure and certain prophecy that the House of Judah and the House of Israel are going to be united under a new head. This new head is none other than the promised Messiah, the Son of David, who is to rule over the REUNITED KINGDOM OF ISRAEL!

They shall beat their swords into ploughshares

This in essence is the Messianic vision of the prophets of Israel, as this promised yet future Son of David takes the reign over a Kingdom comprising the Twelve Tribes of Israel. It is through this United Kingdom of Israel that the whole world shall be blessed, and it is in the days of that Davidic King that the prophecy of Isaiah will be fulfilled. For Isaiah prophesied that:

"For out of Zion shall go forth the law, and the word of the LORD from Jerusalem. He shall judge between the nations, and rebuke many people; they shall beat their swords into ploughshares, and their spears into pruning hooks; nation shall not lift up sword against nation, neither shall they learn war anymore" (Isaiah 2:3b–4).

A wake-up call—"Go back to your roots!"

A truly fantastic future lies ahead for the Twelve Tribes of Israel – but first of all we need to rediscover our ancient roots. Again, through the words of Isaiah, God is urging us to look to our origins. God truly is speaking to our nations:

"Listen to Me, you who follow after righteousness, you who seek the LORD: Look to the rock from which you were hewn, and to the hole of the pit from which you were dug. Look to Abraham your father, and to Sarah who bore you; for I called him alone, and blessed him and increased him" (Isaiah 51:1–2).

Could anything be clearer than this? God is saying: "Look to your roots!" "Look to your origins!" "Don't you know that Abraham is your father and that Sarah is your mother?" He is obviously not speaking to the Jewish people of the House of Judah, simply because they have never lost the knowledge of who they are. The Jews of all people know exactly what their roots are. The Jewish people know full well that Abraham is their patriarchal father and that Sarah is their matriarchal mother. In the above scripture, God is saying that he called Abraham alone, and blessed him and increased him. This is a reference to the 'Birthright' blessing, which has come upon the descendants of Abraham because of Abraham's faithfulness. The exceptional blessings of America and Great Britain's temperate climate, their rich soil, their healthy populations, their freedom, their inventive people, as well as their extraordinary and exceptional prosperity, are all due to Abraham's faithfulness. As Israelite nations, the American, the British and associated English-speaking peoples, have inherited the Birthright blessings of Abraham, and the time has come for these nations to acknowledge this indisputable fact.

America and Great Britain, Canada, Australia, New Zealand, as well as the coastal nations of northwestern Europe, need to start looking to their patriarchal Hebrew ancestors by returning to the ancient paths. This book is a prophetic wake-up call for all of these nations!

CHAPTER EIGHT

⤞⤝

12th Sign
Received a Deferred Inheritance

"And after all this, if you do not obey Me, then I will punish you seven times more for your sins"
(Leviticus 26:18 – emphasis added)

The question is why did America come into being at the specific time she did? Was there any significance in the timing of the birth of this 'Great Nation' that was destined to play such a pivotal role in the world in the centuries to come? Why did Great Britain rise to her position as the unchallenged ruler of the world exactly at the time she did? Is there something significant about the timing of these two great nations coming to their respective positions of global supremacy?

Seeing off the French enemy and rival

The peace between Great Britain and France was short lived, as just ten years after the Treaty of Paris, France declared war on Britain once again in February 1793. The French Revolution was in full swing and France, having executed King Louis XVI, had become a republic. Republican France now was at war with almost all of Europe, and it became a colossal clash of empires that spread around the whole world to all the parts where French, Spanish, Dutch and British had left their colonial imprint. It was a conflict that was to last for a full twenty-two years until Napoleon's final defeat at the Battle of Waterloo in 1815. At that final battle Britain administered a 'knock out' blow to her greatest rival for the crown of world supremacy. Consequently, at the end of this war, Great Britain emerged as the only global superpower on the face of the earth. In the meantime America, *alias* Manasseh, was growing in confidence and wealth and was waiting in the wings ultimately to take over the 'Birthright baton' of global leadership from younger brother Ephraim.

Why did they have to wait for their inheritance?

Thus at the dawning of the nineteenth century the world witnesses the sudden sprouting forth of two of the mightiest world powers ever seen. The first was a Commonwealth of Nations forming the greatest empire in the history of the world, while the second was to become the wealthiest, most powerful nation on earth today. These two 'Birthright' peoples being of the same genetic stock then acquired with an unprecedented suddenness, more than two-thirds of the cultivated wealth and resources of the whole world. It truly was a sensational spurt from relative obscurity to a position of total global dominance, first by the British, and then by the Americans. The question is why did it happen at this particular juncture of time? Why did this unprecedented national wealth and power come to these two 'sons of Joseph' at this time *circa* 1800? Why did it not come at an earlier time or in an earlier age? These Israelite tribes had been wanderers ever since they were cast out of their ancestral land in ancient Israel. The ancient Assyrians had taken them into captivity over 2,500 years previously. Why did they not come into their prophesied 'Birthright' inheritance in the earlier centuries of their exile? Come AD 1800, their exile had already lasted an incredible length of time, and surely this very fact must beg the question: Why was their promised inheritance deferred for such a long time?

'Birthright' prophecies applied to 'the Last Days'

Remember, Jacob's deathbed prophecies spoken out over his sons were applicable to *'the latter days', or to 'the times of the end'* (Genesis 49:1). Consider also the reason why they were exiled in the first place. That reason was multiple decades of continuous rebellion against God's rule and his laws. Those very laws were purposely designed to bring the most abundant blessings upon the nation. The God of Israel had put in place a *'cause and effect'* system for his chosen people, whereby obedience to his laws would bring wonderful blessings, and disobedience would bring terrible curses. Call it a national *'carrot and stick'* principle. Moses first expounded these principles in the book of Deuteronomy in chapter 30, where he spoke of two distinct ways of life. His words can be summed up in verse 19, where it is written: *"I call heaven and earth as witnesses today against you, that I have set before you life and death, blessing and cursing; therefore choose life, that both you and your descendants may live."* However, human nature being what it is, the Israelites consistently chose to go their own way. Frank Sinatra's famous song *"I did it my way"* sums it all up perfectly, as by all account, it was their theme song too.

The deferred inheritance

After being warned scores of times by the prophets who were sent to warn them, the promised curses inexorably came into effect, leading to the ultimate captivity and exile of the entire nation. In their own book of the Law (*Torah*), God, through the hand of Moses, laid out the principle that the punishment or the curses that were to come upon them would be in direct proportion to the extent of their rebellion. This *'cause and effect'*, *'you reap what you sow'* principle is best explained in the book of Leviticus, chapter 26. During the reign of nineteen kings in seven different dynasties, God had pleaded with them through his prophets to mend their ways. Had they done so, the blessings would have overflowed, yet they consistently continued their lifestyle of rank idolatry, witchcraft and rebellion. Despite the fact that they had been punished repeatedly, as the prophesied curses kicked in, yet the nation under its mindlessly stubborn leadership refused time and again to learn the lesson. It was this consistent rebellion of the nation that served to defer the promised 'Birthright' inheritance. In the end it led not only to the expulsion of the entire nation from the land, but also to the 'Birthright' inheritance itself being postponed for a very long time.

The seven prophetic times

The key to understanding for how long this 'Birthright' inheritance would be postponed is to be found in just two words that are repeated four times in chapter 26 of the book of Leviticus. The first mention is in verse eighteen where, after listing a whole range of curses which their rebellion will bring, the LORD gives the following warning: ***"And after all this, if you do not obey Me, then I will punish you SEVEN TIMES more for your sins"*** (emphasis added). This clearly is a prophetic utterance. What can it possibly mean? Most scholars and students of prophecy are agreed that almost invariably prophecy has a dual meaning and application. So what of this *'seven times'* prophecy that is clearly related to punishment that is repeated again in verses 21, 24 and 28? The fact that the original Hebrew word translated into English as *'seven times'* does itself have a dual meaning and confirms that the term has a dual application. The original Hebrew word Moses wrote is *'shibah'* which can mean *'seven times'* as well as *'sevenfold'*. Logically seven times implies a certain duration or continuation of punishment, whereas *'sevenfold'* indicates a seven times greater intensity of punishment.

In Daniel chapter three, we have an example of sevenfold referring to the intensity of the punishment. In the account, King Nebuchadnezzar in a blind rage commanded that the furnace, into which Daniel's friends were to be thrown, should be made seven times hotter (Daniel 3:19). The ultimate punishment that could be visited upon the Israelites was expulsion and exile from their land, and captivity by their enemies. This for them would be the most intense punishment, and especially after their previous experience in Egypt, it would be tantamount to a 'sevenfold' punishment. Thus we are left with the other meaning of the Hebrew word *'shibah'*, translated into English as 'seven times,' as referring to a period of time that would last for a certain duration. The nation of ancient Israel is dealing here with a definitive prophecy of what will befall them if they do not mend their ways. The seven times more punishment for their sins in effect is a prophecy of their fate. It is speaking here of seven prophetic 'times'. In prophecy, as most scholars in this field will tell you, a *'time'* is a prophetic three-360 day year in the Hebrew Lunar calendar. Seven prophetic times thus represents seven years of 360 days.

However, this is still not the whole story, as other passages of the Bible make it clear that God operated in the administration of his punishment on the **'year for a day'** principle. This same principle of punishment was used upon a previous generation of Israelites. After Moses had led them out of Egypt to the very borders of the Promised Land he sent twelve men, one leader from each tribe, to spy out the land and report back to him. It took the spies forty days to complete their mission. On their return, the spies brought back a positive report about a land flowing with milk and honey, but only two of them, Joshua and Caleb, declared that Israel was well able to overcome their enemies and possess the land. The other ten spies were unanimous in giving an extremely discouraging and negative report about the strength of the enemy. The people chose to believe the bad news rather than the good news, and things got so completely out of hand that they even threatened to stone Joshua and Caleb to death. They even wanted to return to their place of slavery in Egypt, rather than go forward and take the land that had been promised to them by the God of Israel.

The 'day-for-a-year' principle

After all the astounding miracles they had witnessed in their Exodus from Egypt, the attitude of the people at the very least represented a phenomenal lack of faith. The land was theirs by a sacred and immutable covenant God had made with their ancestral father Abraham. The land had been promised to them, but they disbelieved God. Hence God pronounced his sentence that for each day the spies had spied out the land they would have to bear their guilt for a year. The consequence of this sentence was that the Israelites were condemned to wandering in the wilderness for forty years, a year for each day the spies had been in the land. The punishment the Israelites received for their rebellion at the borders of their Promised Land was that the promise was simply being deferred. It was never cancelled! The promise was simply being withheld from them for forty years. By way of confirmation, this 'day-for-a-year' principle is also mentioned elsewhere in the Bible. *1

When we couple the *'seven prophetic times'* pronouncement with the *'year-for-a-day'* principle, the 'seven times' becomes 7 x 360-day years – a total of 2,520 days. As each day represents a year of punishment, the penalty for the rebellion of the ancient house of Israel was to last 2,520 years. Furthermore, as the punishment consisted of a withholding of a promised blessing, the obvious conclusion is that the blessing of the 'Birthright' would be deferred for 2,520 years from the time of their captivity. Could this be true? It should be relatively easy to prove. The various dates of the Assyrian invasion of the territory of the Northern Kingdom of Israel are recorded in history. It is quite a simple sum to take those dates and add 2,520 years to them to see if anything of significance occurs at those times. This exercise should deliver concrete answers to the mystery of the sudden disappearance of the 'Northern Kingdom of Israel'.

- **721 BC: Assyrian Captivity – AD 1801: Union of Great Britain**

721 BC was the year of the third and final invasion of the Assyrian Army, when the Birthright tribe of Ephraim, as well as the rest of the tribes that comprised the Northern Kingdom of Israel were uprooted from their land and deported to the Caspian Sea and Black Sea area within the Assyrian Empire. Appreciating that we cannot count the actual year of their deportation, as we have to count 'from' that year, we find that exactly seven prophetic times later, i.e. 2,520 years later, we come to 1801 AD, a most significant date in British

history. Remember Jacob's deathbed promise was that Ephraim was to become a Company or Commonwealth of Nations. On January 1, 1801, the current Union Jack flag was established in recognition of the Parliamentary Union of Great Britain and Ireland. Britain by this time had already emerged from her relative European obscurity to become a flourishing empire, yet from 1800 onwards she was to become the greatest imperial power the world had ever seen. At this time she was engaged in a life and death struggle with Napoleonic France for world supremacy, and it was her great victory at Waterloo that led to her global dominance.

741 BC was the year when the half-tribe of Manasseh together with the Israelite tribes of Reuben and Gad were taken into captivity by the Assyrians in their first invasion of Israelite lands east of the river Jordan.

- **741 BC: Captivity of Manasseh – AD 1780: United States of America**

Again, with divine precision, exactly seven prophetic times later, i.e. 2,520 years later, we arrive at AD 1780. The American Declaration of Independence was formally adopted by the Continental Congress on the, by now, famous July 4, 1776. The declaration was made in the heat of battle whilst the American Patriot forces were engaged in a life and death struggle with the British colonial armies. Although the declaration was made on this historic July 4, independence was not actually granted until 1783. This makes 1780 the central date in the dramatic birth of America, as Manasseh takes his first steps onto the world stage in direct fulfilment of prophesy. On June 14, 1777, the Continental Congress passed a resolution in which the American flag was officially adopted. The flag displayed 13 white stars on a blue field, and 13 alternating white and red stripes. Thus, with these 'Stars and Stripes', Manasseh's Israelite red, white and blue identity is formally established.

Here we see absolute historic proof of God's faithfulness to Abraham. The unconditional Birthright promise, having been withheld for 2,520 years, was finally fulfilled. Having fast-forwarded 2,520 years from the time of ancient Israel's captivity, we witness these two 'Birthright' brothers suddenly bursting forth as the greatest powers the world has ever seen. Remember, God had promised this Birthright to the descendants of Abraham unconditionally, because of Abraham's faithfulness and obedience (Genesis 26:5). Clearly the 'Birthright' blessing that Great Britain and America inherited was not given to them on merit. Their meteoric rise to national wealth and power did not come to them because they somehow deserved to receive it. They did not somehow qualify for this extraordinary blessing. It was simply conferred upon them because of God's unconditional promise to their ancestral father Abraham. God was bound by His promise to confer this stupendous national blessing regardless of the righteousness or wickedness of the descendants.

Yet God had not broken his promise by withholding the birthright blessing for those 2,520 years, as in his promise to Abraham he had not committed himself to bestow it upon any particular generation. Thus, precisely at the time the seven times prophecy had been fulfilled, the British and American sons of Joseph came into possession of more than two-thirds of all the cultivated resources and wealth of the world. It truly is a totally unique record in all of world history! The wealth of the whole world had literally fallen into the laps of the latter day descendants of Ephraim and Manasseh, the two sons of Joseph. As history is our witness, all the other nations of the world shared between them less than a quarter of the wealth. And ever since then, from the moment this Birthright inheritance was realised, these two sons of Joseph have dominated the world scene. The unprecedented prosperity the world has come to appreciate is, not only owing to, but also dependent upon these two brother nations, the descendants of Joseph. In this respect they have fulfilled their role of bringing physical blessings to the nations of the earth. It was said of Joseph that he was *'a prosperous man'*, and surely his British, Canadian, Australian, New Zealand, and American descendants are walking in the footsteps of their patriarchal father Joseph. Yes, it can truly be said that Great Britain, including her Commonwealth offspring, and the United States of America, have left an indelible mark upon the world.

The Louisiana Purchase

The Louisiana Purchase took place in April 1803. It was an event of the greatest importance in the history of America, as it signified the largest single gain in territory for the United States. This great territorial leap forward for the nation was the miraculous outcome of what at first appeared a desperate disaster for the fledgling Republic. The crisis was precipitated by the decision of the Spanish government to transfer Louisiana back to France. The decision hit the new Republic like a bombshell. Barely forty years had passed since the French had ceded their vast American empire in 1763. The alarming question in everyone's mind was: *"Are the French coming back to re-establish their rule?"*

Up to that time Spain had controlled New Orleans at the mouth of the mighty Mississippi River. New Orleans was the most important port in the whole of the North American continent through which all the cotton exports passed from the giant cotton fields of the south. The transfer of ownership was seen as a disaster. Whereas Spain was weak, the French were a formidable military power, which under Napoleon seemed hell bent on military conquest. President Thomas Jefferson referred to the crisis as being *"the embryo of a tornado"*! Much like the British, he too saw France as their *'natural and habitual enemy'*. He wrote to this effect in April 1802, when he stated: *"There is on the globe one single spot, the possessor of which is our natural and habitual enemy. It is New Orleans, through which the produce of three eighths of our territory must pass to market"*. Jefferson then sent his envoys to Paris to negotiate with the French government some sort of a deal whereby access to New Orleans could be guaranteed. The President had very low expectations and he did not expect the negotiations to succeed.

Then, in April 1803, the miracle occurred, as Talleyrand, the French Foreign Minister, offered America the whole of Louisiana including New Orleans for $15 million cash. It was the most astounding bargain of all time, as here America was being offered 530 million acres of mostly prime agricultural land for the derisory price of a less than three cents an acre. In the deal America got 828,000 square miles, which not only doubled the size of her territory but also, at the same time made her as large as Europe itself. The purchase also opened up the way to the Pacific coast and enabled the westward expansion of the United States. President Jefferson was obliged to go to the banks to find the cash, and there was only one place in the world that could finance a purchase of this magnitude. It was highly ironic that Barings, the famous merchant bank in London, provided the loan to the American Republic – this despite the fact that Great Britain was at war with France, her *'natural and habitual'* enemy.

It surely was no coincidence that this stupendous acquisition of land, which at one stroke had doubled the territory of the United States, occurred in the year 1803. This biggest single gain in territory opened up the vast Mississippi basin and included some of the richest farmland in the whole world. It presents yet further evidence of the 'Birthright' blessing kicking in just at the right time after it had been withheld for so long. After just twenty years of full independence for the new nation, the world witnesses Manasseh, the older son of Joseph, coming into his 'Birthright' inheritance. It is a truly historic moment, as from here on we see the steady progression of America to her current status as the richest, greatest and most powerful single nation on the face of the earth. Thus, at the very moment that the seven prophetic times had been fulfilled, Manasseh began to build a great nation that would soon extend from *'sea to shining sea'*, whilst at the same time his younger brother Ephraim was busily building an Empire on which the sun never set.

The Judah connection

Yet another remarkable proof of the true origins of the British and American people is their historic involvement with the State of Israel. The fact is that these two sons of Joseph, as the leaders of the House of Israel, have helped to re-establish their older brother Judah back in the Land of Promise. After the Assyrians had invaded the Northern Kingdom of Israel and taken the entire population into slavery, the Kingdom of Judah came to suffer the same fate at the hands of the Babylonian Empire, just over a century later in 604 BC. Once again the whole population was deported in three successive waves to Babylon. Then after seventy years of captivity a small band of some 50,000 Jewish captives returned to Jerusalem, with the official sanction and blessing of King Cyrus of Persia, to rebuild the Temple of Solomon, which the Babylonians had so utterly destroyed. Even though they rebuilt the Temple and the walls of Jerusalem and brought prosperity to the whole region of Judea, they were never again, apart from brief interludes such as occurred after the Maccabean revolt, to enjoy their freedom as an independent nation, until the State of Israel was established in 1948. After the return of that remnant from Babylon they became a mere province of successive empires – first the Persian Empire, followed by the Greek and Roman Empires. Then in AD 70, after a major Jewish rebellion against Roman rule, the Romans destroyed the Second Temple and brutally suppressed the revolt with murderous ferocity. Subsequently, after a second Jewish revolt in AD 135, the entire Jewish population was expelled from their land and they became scattered throughout the world. The tragic fact of their history is that ever since the Babylonians took them into captivity in 604 BC, the Jewish people lost their national independence—that is to say until 1948.

This brings us back to the *'seven times'* principle. Remember, under this principle the blessing would be deferred or postponed for a period of 2,520 years. As we have already seen, it clearly applied to Judah's brother tribes of the Northern Kingdom of Israel. Could it possibly be that this same *'seven prophetic times'* principle also applied to the Kingdom of Judah? The Bible tells us that God is not a respecter of persons, thus what is good enough for the one ought also to be good enough for the other. Shall we see what happens if we carry out the same experiment we did with the House of Israel? We need to measure the *'seven prophetic times'* which, based upon the *'year-for-a-day'* principle comes to a total of 2,520 years. Our departure point is 604 BC, as this was the year the House of Judah was taken into captivity to Babylon. Shall we see what we come up with when we fast-forward 2,520 years from that date?

604 BC: Babylonian Captivity – AD 1917: The British liberate Jerusalem

Is this not amazing? What a wonderful confirmation of prophecy this is! Incredibly it was at the Jewish Feast of Hanukkah that the British, together with Australian and New Zealand Anzac forces led by General Edmund Allenby, liberated the city of Jerusalem on December 9, 1917. The Jewish residents of Jerusalem had a special reason to celebrate the festival of Hanukkah that year, as it is a feast that signifies deliverance. Furthermore, in the previous month Great Britain had published the, by now, famous Balfour Declaration in which the greatest empire in the world recognized the right of the Jews to have their own homeland in Palestine. The British military administration ended starvation with the aid of food supplies from Egypt, successfully fought typhus and cholera epidemics and significantly improved the water supply to Jerusalem. They reduced corruption by paying the Arab and Jewish judges higher salaries. New railway and telegraph lines improved communications. *2 A few years later in 1920, Max Nordau, the co-founder of the Zionist Movement, was quoted in the London Evening Standard as having said: *"We thought that the Messiah would be an individual, but I feel now as if it were a collective entity, and that its name might be the British Nation"*. Without fully comprehending what he was saying, Max Nordau in effect confirmed that it was Judah's brother Ephraim, the son of Joseph, who had been used by God to restore the Jewish nation. In the same year the League of Nations gave the mandate to rule Palestine to Great Britain. From that moment on the Jewish people were on a countdown to the establishment of their own State. It was a year of the greatest historical significance, as Ephraim assisted in the rebirth of an independent Judah.

The victorious General Allenby dismounted, enters Jerusalem on foot out of
respect for the Holy City, 11 December 1917
(courtesy Wikimedia)

Can a Nation be born in one day!

Few people realise the enormous part that Christian British Zionists played in bringing the vision of a Jewish homeland into reality. The Balfour Declaration was the ultimate culmination that had flowed from nearly a century of pro-active interaction between the Jewish community and British society. The British Movement for the Restoration of Israel is a totally unique event in all of the recorded history of the world. Never before had one nation shown such continuous interest in the destiny of another people. This interest was led by eminent British figures from Queen Victoria on down to

King Edward VII, Lloyd-Jones, Lord Palmerston, Lord Shaftesbury and Arthur Balfour, all of them enthusiastic proponents of Zionism. Michael Polowetzky, the author of *Jerusalem Recovered* asserted that the Balfour Declaration 'represented the culmination of half a century of active preoccupation with Jewish culture among British political and intellectual élites'. Just as Great Britain had been the 'mother' country that had brought about the births of America, Canada, Australia, New Zealand and South Africa, she now became the midwife assisting in the birth of the State of Israel.

On 30th September 1947, the British government decided to terminate her Mandate of Palestine. Subsequently on November 29, 1947, the United Nations General Assembly voted by 33-13 votes in favour of the 1947 U.N. Partition Plan. The prophet Isaiah prophesied the rebirth of the State of Israel some 2,700 years prior to the event, when he pronounced the following:

"Who has heard such a thing? Who has seen such a thing? Shall the earth be made to give birth in one day? Or shall a nation be born at once? For as soon as Zion was in labor, she gave birth to her children" (Isaiah 66:8).

This prophecy was fulfilled on May 14, 1948, when *'in one day'* the State of Israel was born.

Name of the 'Jewish' State was changed to Israel!

The common perception of all the parties involved in the process was that the name of the new nation was to be called the State of Judah. After all, this name perfectly confirmed its ancient history, as the Kingdom of Judah. It also overwhelmingly reflected the origins of its people from the tribe of Judah! Yet on that fateful day David Ben Gurion made the following formal declaration:

"WE DECLARE that, with effect from the moment of the termination of the Mandate being tonight, the eve of Sabbath, the 6th Iyar, 5708 (15th May 1948), until the establishment of the elected, regular authorities of the State in accordance with the Constitution which shall be adopted by the

Elected Constituent Assembly not later than 1ˢᵗ October 1948, the People's Council shall act as a Provisional Council of State, and its executive organ, the People's Administration, shall be the Provisional Government of the **JEWISH STATE, TO BE CALLED "ISRAEL."**

David Ben Gurion, the man destined to become the first Prime Minister of the new State of Israel, then goes on to make a statement of astounding prophetic significance. It seems most curious that even today almost no one has noticed the profound meaning of his words. The second part of his historic declaration is as follows:

*"**THE STATE OF ISRAEL** will be open for Jewish immigration and **FOR THE INGATHERING OF THE EXILES**; it will foster the development of the country for the benefit of all its inhabitants; it will be based on freedom, justice and peace as envisaged by the prophets of Israel; it will ensure complete equality of social and political rights to all its inhabitants irrespective of religion, race or sex; it will guarantee freedom of religion, conscience, language, education and culture; it will safeguard the Holy Places of all religions; and it will be faithful to the principles of the Charter of the United Nations."*

Did you get it? Not many people realise that the very foundational Declaration which brought the State of Israel into being calls not only for Jewish immigration e.g. the return of Judah, but that it also calls for THE INGATHERING OF THE EXILES e.g. the return of Joseph and his companions of Lost Ten Tribes of Israel. Is this not truly amazing! Those prophetic words spoken by Prime Minister David Ben Gurion were no accident, as the reunification of the two Houses of Israel is THE ultimate 'DIVINE' goal behind the reestablishment of the nation.

As we examine the final two paragraphs of the official 'Declaration of the Establishment of the State of Israel,' we discover further prophetic pointers to Israel's future.

"We appeal to the Jewish people throughout the Diaspora to rally round the Jews of Eretz-Israel in the tasks of immigration and upbuilding and to stand by them in the great struggle for the realization of the age-old dream – **THE REDEMPTION OF ISRAEL."**

"PLACING OUR TRUST IN THE **"ROCK OF ISRAEL,"** *WE AFFIX OUR SIGNATURES TO THIS PROCLAMATION AT THIS SESSION OF THE PROVISIONAL COUNCIL OF STATE, ON THE SOIL OF THE HOMELAND, IN THE CITY OF TEL AVIV, ON THIS SABBATH EVE, THE 5TH DAY OF IYAR, 5708 (14TH MAY 1948).*
DAVID BEN-GURION
Plus forty-one other signatories

Published in the Official Gazette, No. 1 of the 5th, Iyar, 5708
(14th May 1948).
Israel Ministry of Foreign Affairs

Did you notice those profound words about the REDEMPTION OF ISRAEL? This is so meaningful, as the 'Redemption of Israel' can only occur once the Two Houses of Israel have become united! It can only come about after the INGATHERING OF ALL THE EXILES.

How Great Britain gave Israel the Bomb!

According to an article in today's (March 10, 2006) The Guardian Newspaper, Great Britain secretly supplied the twenty tons of heavy water to Israel nearly half a century ago that enabled it to make nuclear weapons. According to the report the BBC Newsnight reporter Meirion Jones found a number of declassified files in an obscure Foreign Office counter-proliferation archive, which were lying unnoticed in the public records office. According to the files, officials in the MacMillan government deliberately concealed the transaction from the U.S. The full page Guardian article goes on to say that the deal was concealed from the U.S. which was hostile to proliferation, because the Eisenhower administration might have insisted on unacceptable conditions, and would have scuppered the sale. When Robert McNamara became U.S. Defense Secretary in 1961, he and President Kennedy strived to stop Israel from going on to build nuclear weapons. He told Newsnight that he had never known of Britain's behavior at the time. *"The fact Israel was trying to develop a nuclear bomb should not have come as a surprise to me,"* he said. *"It's very surprising to me that we weren't told because we shared information about the nuclear bomb very closely with the British."* Britain had got the heavy water from Norway for its own military purposes, but then chose a different technological route making the material surplus to requirement. Norway refused to cancel the heavy water contract, and it must have been tempting for those in charge of budgets to get their money back. The cover story was that the heavy water was "understood to be required by Israel for peaceful use in a reactor connected with desert irrigation". Accordingly, in June 1959, and again the following June, two lots of heavy water of ten tons each were, according to a note by Alan Brooke-Turner, then first secretary at the Foreign and Colonial Office in charge of disarmament, were "put on board Israeli ships at a U.K. port" and shipped out to Dimona.

According to a further authoritative article by Richard Norton Taylor of The Guardian Newspaper dated March 10, 2006, Britain also secretly supplied Israel with plutonium during the 1960s despite a warning from military intelligence that it could help the Israelis to develop a nuclear bomb. The deal made during Harold Wilson's Labor government, is revealed in classified documents released under the Freedom of Information Act and obtained by BBC 2's Newsnight Program.

The documents also show how Britain made hundreds of shipments to Israel of material, which could have helped in its nuclear weapons program, including compounds of uranium, lithium, beryllium and tritium, as well as heavy water.

Israel asked Britain in 1966 to supply 10mg of plutonium. Israel would have required almost 5kg of plutonium to build an atomic bomb, but British defense intelligence officials warned that 10mg had "significant military value" and could enable the Jewish state to carry out important experimental work to speed up its nuclear weapons program.

Documents show that the decision to sell plutonium to Israel in 1966 was blocked by officials in both the Ministry of Defense and the Foreign Office, who said: *"It is HMG's policy not to do anything which would assist Israel in the production of nuclear weapons."* But the deal was forced through by a Jewish civil servant, Michael Michaels, in Tony Benn's Ministry of Technology, which was responsible for trade in nuclear material, according to Newsnight.

Peter Kelly, who was a British defense intelligent expert on the Israeli nuclear weapons program, knew Mr. Michaels. He told Newsnight he believed Mr. Michaels knew that Israel was trying to build an atomic bomb, but that he had dual loyalties to Britain and Israel.

Mr. Tony Benn told the program that civil servants in his department kept the deals secret from him and his predecessor, Frank Cousins.

He had always suspected that civil servants were doing deals behind his back, but he never thought they would sell plutonium to Israel. He told Newsnight: *"I'm not only surprised, I'm shocked. It never occurred to me they would authorize something so totally against the policy of the government".*

"Michaels lied to me; I learned by bitter experience that the nuclear industry lied to me again and again." He thought that Prime Minister Harold Wilson might not have known that Britain was helping Israel to get the bomb.

Last year Newsnight showed that in the late 1950s Harold Macmillan's Conservative government provided Israel with twenty tons of heavy water to start up its Dimona reactor. Newsnight said it learned that Jack Straw, the Foreign Secretary, had admitted to the Liberal Democrat leader, Sir Menzies Campbell, that Britain knew the heavy water was destined for Israel, and that in 1961, Macmillan even made a failed attempt to get it back. *3

It certainly is a most remarkable revelation and without a doubt one of the best kept secrets of the twentieth century. Thus Great Britain, not only instigated the very conception and subsequent birth of the Jewish State, but also helped her subsequently to steal the most strategic military march on her enemies. Israel's nuclear weapons are to be seen as her *'Sampson option'* to be used only as weapons of last resort. The development of Iran's Nuclear Bomb program having reached an advanced stage has created great alarm throughout the West, as well as in Israel and the entire Middle East. Furthermore, the fact that she has perfected the missile technology to deliver those fearsome weapons of mass destruction indicate that the State of Israel may one day be forced to use her nuclear *'Sampson option'* in order to avoid total annihilation by her Islamic enemies.

Once again we witness exactly the same pattern we have seen before in the history of those two birthright sons of Joseph. Great Britain, *alias* Ephraim, arrives on the scene first, to assist in the birth of the new Jewish nation, whereas America, *alias* Manasseh, then takes over to protect and maintain her with his might. The plain facts of history are that without Great Britain's initial assistance the Jews would never have obtained their national independence. It is also a fact of life that without the consistent protection of the United States of America it is doubtful whether the Israeli State would still exist. It is wonderful to see the outworking of prophecy in history as these two 'Birthright' sons of Joseph are used to help their older brother Judah on his feet as an independent nation. In this we have yet another mighty proof of the true identity of the English-speaking peoples.

CHAPTER NINE

⤜⤏

12ᵗʰ Sign
What Now, America & Great Britain?

*"For there shall be a day when the watchmen will cry on Mount
Ephraim, "Arise, and let us go up to Zion, to the Lord our God."*
Jeremiah 31: 6

A Unanimous Verdict from Twelve Witnesses

In the previous chapters twelve major signs have given powerful
witness with each sign speaking with great authority. Thus these
twelve witnesses have given their testimony. They have produced a
unanimous verdict. There has not been a single disagreement among
them. To a man they have each in turn confirmed that America and
Great Britain and her Commonwealth offspring are definitely
descended from ancient Israel. Each witness has delivered his own
major sign or testimony. The twelve witness statements in turn have
contained not just one major piece of evidence, but in every one of
their respective statements they have produced scores of additional
proofs as well. Much of the evidence given can be categorised as hard
evidence. In addition a veritable mountain of corroborating, as well
as hundreds of pieces of circumstantial evidence has also been
examined. When we put it all together, we have in effect been
presented with close to a thousand pieces of evidence, each of them
pointing in exactly the same direction.

Galileo's approach vindicated once again

Having employed the same open-minded attitude Galileo displayed towards the accepted wisdom of the world, we too have discovered a whole new world. Galileo started with a premise, and so have we. He had the courage to go against the commonly held views of the opinion makers of his day. This is exactly the procedure we have followed in this book. Like him we have had the kind of enquiring mind that was prepared to start with a premise very few of our generation are prepared to consider. Having posed the question, we, like him, went out of our way to see if there was any evidence to support the idea about the possible Israelite origins of the English speaking peoples. Galileo by his approach discovered new things about our planet. We too have uncovered an unexpected mountain of irrefutable evidence. We have discovered something that almost certainly will have significant geopolitical implications and consequences. We have uncovered the long hidden ancestry of America and Great Britain!

This study into the ancient hidden ancestry of our nations has taken us into uncharted territory. Like Galileo before us, we have gone in the face of entrenched prejudice against the mainstream wisdom of the majority of our establishment. Galileo's world was not prepared to accept his conclusions in his day and they accused him of heresy. It is more than a possibility that our conclusions will meet with the same response. Like Galileo we will discover that majority opinion is frequently wrong. The nineteenth century Polish born philosopher Arthur Schopenhauer observed that, **"All truth passes through three stages:**

Firstly, it is ridiculed; Secondly, it is violently opposed; Thirdly, it is accepted as self-evident."

An ancient Secret now stands revealed

We have established that our Anglo-Saxon/Celtic civilization is over four thousand years old. It is a secret of our most ancient roots and independent nationhood. We have effectively proved that British, American and affiliated peoples are descended from a civilization every bit as ancient as the Egyptian, Persian and Babylonian civilizations of old. Why should this surprise us? The fact is that the British and the American people originate from a civilization that is much older than that of ancient Greece or Rome! This understanding is bound permanently to change our perspective of whom and what we are as a people. It will also change the perspectives of our friends and our enemies alike. Frankly, this long hidden secret changes almost everything generally believed about the ancestry of the English-speaking nations.

To the extent that people are willing take on board the revelation of the Israelite origins of America and Great Britain, it is bound to make a high impact in the geopolitical sense. Can you imagine the reaction to this news in the Islamic nations? This revelation truly is a Geopolitical Game Changer! One thing you may be sure of; it will not be welcomed by most of the world. Once this truth is out into the open, the nations of the world are certain to look upon these two sons of Joseph with different eyes. It is especially when you consider our nation's history over the past two centuries that the truth about our ancestry becomes so obvious. At the same time it is likely that it will become a cause for much debate and controversy.

The Veil over the Face of Israel is removed

The veil that has been placed over the face of the Lost House of Israel is being removed. As this veil vanishes the world will discover the true face of Israel. America and Great Britain form an intrinsic part of that face, and their Israelite heritage and identity in time will become recognized by the entire world. The reality of America and Great Britain's Israelite ancestry will become self-evident to the point where no one will question it any longer. The probability is that the people outside our border, yes, even our enemies, will get the picture before our own people will. These 'birthright' sons of Joseph today unfortunately have lost the vision that once drove them on to such unmatched achievement. This is especially true since the onset of the Obama era, where surrender and appeasement have become the policy of America. Joseph's historic mission to fight against tyranny and oppression to deliver whatever justice, freedom and prosperity they can deliver has become but a dim memory. Fresh in the minds of the ruling political class are the terrible disasters of the U.S. involvement first in Iraq and subsequently in Afghanistan, which have led to ignominious defeat in both wars. The outcome today is that America does not want to be the world's policeman any more, and Great Britain simply has not the means to do so even if she had the will. It needs to be understood that these two brother nations are after all only human and therefore any justice, freedom and prosperity they deliver will of necessity be of an imperfect kind. Nevertheless, it is a better kind of justice and freedom or prosperity than could ever be expected under the evil rule of either the likes of the Taliban, Saddam Hussein, the theocratic regime of Iran, the Muslim Brotherhood, or indeed of the EU, Russia or China for that matter.

The revelation of the Israelite origin and identity of America and Great Britain and her Commonwealth daughters, does present a challenging scenario. In the light of this new understanding about our nations' Israelite roots, it is surely fair to ask the question, "What now America, and what now Great Britain?" "What now, Canada?" "Where do we go from here, Australia & New Zealand?"

What do you think the consequences might be for this Anglo-Saxon family of nations, once the whole world finds out who you really are? Consider what your Jewish brothers have had to put up with these past two and a half thousand years! They have suffered three invasions and expulsion, followed by seventy years of captivity in Babylon, after having witnessed the burning of Jerusalem and the utter destruction of Solomon's glorious Temple. After the return of a remnant they then have to put up with occupation by the Greeks, who were hell-bent on destroying their ancient faith with the most godless and cruel decrees. Having invited the Romans to help them against the Hellenes of Greece, they then have to endure the harsh yoke of the Roman Empire. Having fallen from the frying pan into the fire they then lose their Second Temple in the flames at the hands of Titus, the Roman General, when they suffer their first genocide at the hands of Rome, with close to a million Jews crucified outside the walls of Jerusalem. Then just sixty-five years later in AD 135, after the second Jewish revolt, they suffer their second Roman genocide with most the survivors, mainly women and children being sold into slavery. After this they experience the persecutions of the Roman Catholic Church, culminating in the Crusades, expulsions from many countries, and the unspeakable cruelties of the Inquisition. Beyond this the Jews experience persecutions and pogroms almost wherever they go, ultimately leading to the ghastly-systemized industrial murder of six million Jews in the Nazi death camps. Even today, sixty-six years after the foundation of their own State in the Land of their Fathers, they are still hated and despised and spat upon by it seems most of mankind. Why, oh why is this so?

There can be only one reason! It is not really the Jews that the world has a problem with; their problem is with the God of the Jews!

It is the fact that, of all the twelve tribes of Israel, which have sprung from the loins of the twelve sons of Jacob, the Jews alone have remained faithful to the Covenant God made with Abraham, the Founding Father of the nation. Scripture has made it very clear that there is BUT ONE SIGN that identifies His people. We read this in the Book of Exodus:

"Speak also to the children of Israel, saying: 'Surely MY SABBATHS you shall keep, for it is a SIGN between Me and you throughout your generations, that you may know that I am the LORD who sanctifies you." (Exodus 31:13, emphasis added).

The Scripture then goes on to give us a second witness providing us an even clearer definition:

'It is A SIGN between Me and the children of Israel forever; for in six days the LORD made the heavens and the earth, and on THE SEVENTH DAY he rested and was refreshed'" (Exodus 31:17, emphasis added).

The Jews are the only people in the world, who have been faithful to this command. For some two thousand five hundred years, ever since their return to their Land of Promise after their captivity in Babylon, the Jewish people have been largely faithful to the Sinai Covenant. More than anything else it is their adherence to the seventh-day Sabbath of Rest that has *identified* them in the eyes of the world as the people of Israel. Thus the account of history has absolutely proved the above Scriptures to be true. The seventh-day Sabbath is indeed the **IDENTIFYING SIGN** between the Creator God of the Universe, and His 'chosen' people, the children of Israel. This is the 'sign' that makes the Jews stand out from the rest of mankind. The fact that most of the other tribes of Israel have not kept this 'SIGN' has caused them to lose their identity, and consequently the world does not perceive them as being of Israel descent! Furthermore, it has also caused them to forget their own Hebrew origins. The only way back to proper recognition of their true heritage for them therefore, is to turn around full circle and re-embrace the Covenant of Sinai. To heal the breach between the Two Houses of Israel, Ephraim needs to return to the Torah, which they and their ancestors have rejected ever since their separation from the House of David, some three thousand years ago.

The revelation that Israel has two identities and is comprised of the Jewish nation, as well as a whole host of other nations, truly is a major catalyst for change. Even though the Hebrew credentials of America, Great Britain and her Commonwealth offspring are not recognized in the world, WATCH OUT when that recognition dawns on the rest of mankind! This is the time when the veil, which YHVH, the God of Israel, has placed over the face of the House of Israel, will finally be removed. You may be sure that this revelation will not go down well in the Muslim street!

What is so desperately sad is to see the respective political masters of our nations turn against their beleaguered brother Judah in the Holy Land. Both the British Foreign Office and the U.S. State Department are known to be seasoned practitioners of 'Arabism.' Whereas the White House itself has become a leading organ of anti-Semitism, as it constantly sides with the genocidal Jew-haters of Hamas and the Muslim Brotherhood. All of this is done in an effort to appease the advance of the evil Islamic juggernaut that seeks to destroy our hard won freedoms. Whilst our plucky Jewish brothers are holding off this Islamic tidal wave of total evil, the leaders of our nations stand on the side lines criticizing the State of Israel for daring to fight back, and thus, oh my, oh my, causing casualties among her enemies that are attacking her. What spineless hypocrites they are! Not only this, but at the height of Israel's recent 50-day 2014 "Protective Edge" War with Hamas in Gaza, both the Prime Minister of Great Britain and the Secretary of State for the U.S. stated that they would cancel their contracts for essential military supplies to the State of Israel, whilst the Israeli bombardment of Gaza continued. The question surely is: With contract breaking friends like that, who needs enemies? Even though both announcements were made in the full glare of publicity, nobody in the west batted an eyelid at the news. Yet, none the less, it was an act of rank treachery and a disgusting betrayal of a friend in great need. All of this is done in the name of appeasing an enemy that cannot be appeased. The literal meaning of the word Islam is "submission," and the only way for any so-called Western infidel not to have his or her head cut off at the neck, is to submit to Islam and Sharia law. No doubt Hamas and Iran, the Muslim Brotherhood, Al Qaeda and Hezbollah, all of America's "new friends," were greatly blessed by the news. The great Winston Churchill once famously said: *"An appeaser is one who feeds the crocodile hoping it will eat him last!"*

It is just as well that the God of our Fathers, Abraham, Isaac and Jacob is in control of world events, and that He has everything in hand. He has His plan for the restoration of His Kingdom here upon this earth in the Land of Israel, which He has promised to the children of Israel by a perpetual and unbreakable covenant. Even though our nations are fighting Him in open rebellion against His plan and purpose, He will nevertheless prevail, as He will bring all of us to heel. Part of His method is to remove the veil, which He has placed over the face of His rebellious children of the House of Israel some two thousand plus years ago. It is through His agency that the world in time will come to marvel at the recognition that Judah (the Jews), have hundreds of millions of Hebrew relatives, who are their brothers, even though they are not Jews. This is the real Game Changer! This revelation will really set the cat among the pigeons. The cat can come in a number of disguises. At the moment it looks like it may come at us in the guise of Jihadist Islam and woe betide all of us. Maybe it appears in the form of the European Union, who, as it happens, is allied to Islam in the EURABIA Covenant. Maybe the cat that is out to catch us is a Russian or Chinese cat, or even a combination of several of these nasty critters. One thing is for sure, there is much trouble ahead for our nations. Maybe we need to receive some of the medicine our Jewish brothers have had to swallow these past two and a half thousand years. Maybe, just maybe, our wayward nations and our prodigal peoples deserve nothing less.

We have all heard the saying; *"No pain, no gain!"* Once our nations have tasted the bitter fruits of their disobedience to the Mosaic Covenant, and suffered the things which our enemies are permitted to do to us, the Prophets of Israel unanimously proclaim a great deliverance. Even though the whole world will unite and muster all its energies and powers to prevent God's purpose, as do our politicians today, they will fail utterly in their futile attempt. Our Creator God, the Holy One of Israel, will achieve His purpose for the restoration of the Whole House of Israel, as the United Kingdom of

Israel, in which all of our twelve tribes have once again been united. This is our glorious destiny! The Prophet Jeremiah describes this event most eloquently:

Thus says the Lord God: "Surely I will take the stick of Joseph, which is in the hand of Ephraim, and the tribes of Israel, his companions; and I will join them with it, with the stick of Judah, and make them one stick, and they will be one in my hand."

"And the sticks on which you write will be in your hand before their eyes.

"Then say to them, 'Thus says the LORD God: "Surely I will take the children of Israel from among the nations, wherever they have gone, and will gather them from every side and bring them into their own land; "and I will make them ONE NATION in the land, on the mountains of Israel; and ONE KING shall be king over them all; they shall no longer be TWO NATIONS; nor shall they ever be divided into TWO KINGDOMS AGAIN."' (Ezekiel 37:19 & 21-22, NKJV author's emphasis)

END NOTES

⊷∾⊶

CHAPTER ONE

*1) en.wikipedia.org/wiki/Five_Eyes

*2) en.wikipedia.org/wiki/Five_Eyes

*3) en.wikipedia.org/wiki/United_States_Navy_in_World War_II

*4) The National World War II Museum New Orleans

*5) Stockholm International Peace Research Institute, Yearbook 2014

*6) Cambridge Illustrated Atlas WARFARE IN THE MIDDLE AGES - 768-1487; Cambridge Illustrated Atlas – WARFARE – Renaissance to Revolution – 1492-1792; peninsulawar200.org/history.html; www.historyofwar.org/articles/wars_napoleonic.html

*7) William Pit – the Younger: A Biography, by William Hague, Harper Perennial, U.K. 2005

*8) Cambridge Illustrated History – The British Empire, Edited by P.J. Marshall, pp. 384-388, Cambridge University Press, Great Britain, 1996

CHAPTER TWO

*1) (Dupin, M: *Force Commerciale de la Grande Bretagne*).

*2) (*British Empire*, vol. 1, p. 274).

*3) (*Our Island Story, by H.E. Marshall,* pp.455/6).

*4) (*Pax Britannica* – The Climax of Empire, by James Morris, p. 46).

*5) Genesis 49: 3-4

*6) www.thetelegraph.co,uk/news/defence/10173740/Where-are-the-worlds-major-military-bases. Html

*7) Chalmers Johnson, author of The Sorrows of Empire

*8) Copyright, Nick Turse of TomDispatch.com

*9) Genesis 48:15-20

CHAPTER THREE

*1) E J Hobsbawn - *Industry and Empire*, p. 13

*2) (Statistics from *The Harmsworth Universal Atlas and Gazetteer*, 1909 edition.)

*3) (Statistics from *The Harmsworth Universal Atlas and Gazetteer*, 1909 edition.)

*4) Adam Smith, - An Inquiry Into the Nature and Causes of the Wealth of Nations, 1786

*5) www.bankofengland.co.uk/education/pages/inflation/calculation/flash/defaults.aspx

*6) *The Decline and Fall of the British Empire – 1781-1997*, by Brendon Piers, pp. 5, 7-8, 12-13

*7) Genesis 35:10-11 & Genesis 48:17-20

*8) Statistical conclusion compiled from: *The Harwin Chronology of Inventions Innovations Discoveries – from pre-history to the present day*, by Kevin Desmond; Book of Inventions & Discoveries, by Valerie-Anne Giscard d'Estaign, MacDonald, Queen Anne Press, 1990; Mark Tanner, Great British Inventions, published by Fourth Estate, 1997

*9) Statistical conclusions compiled from *The Harwin Chronology of Inventions Innovations Discoveries – from pre-history to the present day*, by Kevin Desmond; Book of Inventions & Discoveries, by Valerie-Anne Giscard d'Estaign, MacDonald, Queen Anne Press, 1990; Mark Tanner, Great British Inventions, published by Fourth Estate, 1997

*10) Lord Palmerston (Political Portraits), by M E Chamberlain

*11) Cambridge Illustrated History, *British Empire*, Ed. By P. J. Marshall, pp, 32-33

*12) The Essential Writings of Ralph Waldo Emerson, p 501, Modern Library Classics

*13) Excerpts from: The Space Race – From Sputnik to Shuttle: The Story of the Battle for the Heavens, Jon Trux, New English Library/Hodder & Stoughton, London, 1985

*14) Excerpts from: The Space Race – From Sputnik to Shuttle: The Story of the Battle for the Heavens, Jon Trux, New English Library/Hodder & Stoughton, London, 1985

*15) Source: Zenith International

*16) Source: CIA

*17) *Comets, Jews and Christians*, by John Hulley, Published by The Root & Branch Association, Ltd., Jerusalem, 2001

*18) Genesis 49: 1

CHAPTER FOUR

*1) Josephus Antiquities 11.5.133

*2) (from: *The 'Lost' Ten Tribes of Israel . . . . . Found!*, by Steven Collins).

*3) *Genetically Modified Prophecies – Whatever Happened to the Sand and the Stars God Promised to Abraham? by Victor Schlatter*

*4) www.jewishinternetlibrary.org/jsource/Judaism/expultion.html

*5) *Genetically Modified Prophecies – Whatever Happened to the Sand and the Stars God Promised to Abraham? p.78, by Victor Schlatter*

*6) A TEST OF TIME – *The Bible – From Myth to History, by David Rohl, Century Ltd., Random House, London, 1995*

CHAPTER FIVE

1) According to the Book of Mormon, one of his sons escaped to the Yemen and sailed from there to N. America

*2) *History of the Anglo-Saxons*, Vol. I., by Sharon Turner

*3) (*Prince Michael 2000*: pp. 12, 70, 198-199.)

*4a) Genesis 17:5; 25:23

*4b) Geneses 25:23

*5) 2 Chronicles 13:5

*6) *Our Ancient Throne, by W.H. Bennett, FRGS*

*7) *Israel's Lost Empires, by Steven Collins, p., 119*

*8) Ibid p. 120-121

*9) *the Annals of the Four Masters*

*10) The *Annals of the Four Masters*, the *Chronicles of Eri*, and the *Annals of Clonmacnoise*

*11) Ye Have Been Hid – *Finding the Lost Tribes of Israel*, by Leslie Pearson Rees, p. 150

*12) *OLLAMH FODHLA – Ireland's Famous Monarch and Lawmaker Upwards of Three Thousand Years Ago, by Eugene, Alfred Conwell, p.26, Dublin, 1873*

*13) *Daily Telegraph, July 25, 2014*

*14) 1Chronicles 3:16-17

CHAPTER SIX

*1) (Quoted from: *Symbols of our Celto-Saxon Heritage* by W.H. Bennett.)

*2) (Quoted from: *Symbols of our Celto-Saxon Heritage* by W.H. Bennett.)

*3) The Tribes, pp., 437-439, by Yair Davidiy

*4) (Quoted from: *Symbols of our Celto-Saxon Heritage* by W.H. Bennett.)

*5) (Quoted from: *Symbols of our Celto-Saxon Heritage by W.H. Bennett.)*

*6) *(Breshit Rabbah 39:11).*

*7) (Quoted from: *Symbols of our Celto-Saxon Heritage by W.H. Bennett.)*

*8) (Quoted from: *Symbols of our Celto-Saxon Heritage by W.H. Bennett.)*

*9) *(Genesis 41:42}*

*10) (Quoted from: *Symbols of our Celto-Saxon Heritage by W.H. Bennett.)*

*11) (Quoted from: *Symbols of our Celto-Saxon Heritage by W.H. Bennett.*)

*12) *(Who Are You America?- Time to Lift your Prophetic Veil, by Stephen Spykerman, Legends Library, New York, 2013}*

*13) (Quoted from: *Symbols of our Celto-Saxon Heritage by W.H. Bennett.*)

*14) *(Bronze Age Atlantis – The International Nautical Empire of the Sea Peoples, p. 45, by Walt Baucum, Brit Am, Jerusalem*

*15) (Quoted from: *Symbols of our Celto-Saxon Heritage by W.H. Bennett.*)

*16) (Quoted from: *Symbols of our Celto-Saxon Heritage* by W.H. Bennett.)

*17) Yair Davidiy; Rabbi Zvi Kalisher & Rabbi Israel Feld of Susia.

*18) *(Leviticus 23:4)*

*18) the templeinstitute.org

*19) *(From: The Forgotten Monarchy of Scotland by HRH Prince Michael of Albany.)*

*20) (Extract from: *The Royal House of Britain – an enduring dynasty,* by Revd W M H Milner, MA, FRGS.)

*21) (See *Boutell's Heraldry,* 1966 edition.)

*22) (Exodus 25: 1, 4 & 9; and Exodus 26:1, 31 & 36, and 28:5, 6 & 15.)

CHAPTER SEVEN

*1) (Isaiah 9:6-7.)

*2) Read the fascinating account in the book of Esther!

CHAPTER EIGHT

*1) (See Ezekiel 4:4-6, 9.)

*2) (Wikipedia).

*3) *Richard Norton-Taylor, Friday March 10, 2006, the Guardian Newspaper.*

CHAPTER NINE   Nil

Wikipedia Licenses and Fair Use Rationale

Certain reproductions of images used in this book were obtained from the English *Wikipedia* website (*Wikipedia, The Free Encyclopedia* at www.wikipedia.com) via the *Wikimedia Commons* (see http://commons.wikimedia.org/wiki/Main_Page). Credit for authors is given where authors are known. Some reproductions are licensed under the *GNU Free Documentation License* and/or the *Creative Commons Attribution-Share-Alike License*. Others are in the U.S. public domain, as noted under the image.

Any of the images licensed under the *GNU Free Documentation License* and/or the *Creative Commons Attribution-Share-Alike License* may be reproduced under the conditions of their respective licenses, which are documented in the web addresses given below—

- <http://en.wikipedia.org/wiki/Wikipedia:Text_of_the_GNU_Free_ Documentation_License>
- <http://creativecommons.org/licenses/by-sa/3.0/>

Fair use rationale for including these images is that their primary use is for informational and educational purposes; also that no free equivalents are available or could be created that would adequately give the same information. Reproduction of the images is not believed to limit the copyright owners' rights or profit in any way.

BIBLIOGRAPHY

᷒᷒

Adams, Andrew, - As Birds Flying – Isaiah 31:5 – Jerusalem 1917, Artisan Sales, U.S.A, 1993

Albany, HRH Prince Michael, - The Forgotten Monarchy of Scotland, - Vega, London, 2002

Allen, Rev. J.H., - Judah's Scepter and Joseph's Birthright, - 19th Edition, Destiny Publishers, Merrimac, MS, Original copyright: 1902

Anderson, - Royal Genealogies, - London, 1732

Andrews, Allen, - Kings and Queens of England & Scotland, - Marshall Cavendish Publications Ltd., Copyright & First printing 1976

Armstrong, Herbert, W., - The United States and Britain in Prophecy, - Publishers, Worldwide Church of God, Original copyright 1954

Aslet, Clive & Moore, Derry, - Inside the House of Lords, - HarperCollins *Publishers*, 1998

Bart, Herbert, Maxwell, MP., - Sixty Years A Queen, - Arranged & Printed by Eyre & Spottiswoode, Her Majesty's' Printers, London, 1897

Bennett, W.H., - Symbols of Our Celto-Saxon Heritage, - copyright 1976 W.H. Bennett, Herald Press, Windsor, Ontario

Bercovitch, Sacvan, - The Puritan Origins of the American Self, - U.S.A., 1975

Baucum, Walter, - Bronze Age Atlantis – *The International Nautical Empire of the Sea Peoples,* A Brit-Am Publication, Jerusalem, Israel

Black, Jeremy, - Cambridge Illustrated Atlas of Warfare – Renaissance to Revolution 1492-1792, Cambridge University Press, 1996

Boswell, James, - Samuel Johnson: March1776 – Dec. 13, 1784

Bourne, Russell, - Invention in America, - Fulcrum Publishing, Golden Colorado, 1996

Breeze, David & Munro, Graeme, - The Stone of Destiny – *Symbol of Nationhood,* - Publishers, Historic Scotland, Edinburgh, 1997

Brackman, Arnold C., - The Luck of Nineveh – the Dramatic Search for the Vanished Assyrian Empire, - Eyre Methuen Ltd, London, 1980

Brown, G.I., - The Guinness History of Inventions, - Guinness Publishing Ltd., 1996

Bruce, Alastair, - Keepers of the Kingdom, the Ancient Offices of Britain, - Published by Weidenfeld & Nicolson, 1999

Bryant, Arthur, - Protestant Island, - Published by Collins, 1967, London

Bryant, Arthur, - The Lion & The Unicorn, - Published by Collins, 1969, London

Bryant, Arthur, - Set In A Silver Sea - a History of Britain and the British People, - Volume One, Collins, London, 1984

Bryant, Arthur, - Freedom's Own Island - a History of Britain and the British People, - Volume Two, Collins, London, 1986

Burke, John, - An Illustrated History of England, - Published 1974 by Book Club Associates

Burl, Aubrey, - A guide to the Stone Circles of Britain, Ireland and Brittany, - Yale University Press, New Haven and London, 1995

Burl, Aubrey, - Prehistoric Henges, - Shire Publications, Great Britain, 1997

Burl, Aubrey, - Prehistoric Stone Circles, - Shire Publications, Great Britain, 2001

Burl, Aubrey, - Prehistoric Astronomy and Ritual, - Shire Publications, Great Britain, 1997

Capt, E. Raymond, - Jacob's Pillar – *A Biblical Historical Study*, - Published by Artisan Sales, Oklahoma, U.S.A., 1977

Capt, E. Raymond, - The Gem Stones of the Breastplate, - Published by Artisan Sales, Oklahoma, U.S.A., 1987

Capt, E. Raymond, - The Great Pyramid Decoded, - Published by Artisan Sales, Oklahoma, U.S.A., 1996

Capt, E. Raymond, - Stonehenge and Druidism, - Published by Artisan Sales, Oklahoma, U.S.A., 1983

Chadwick, Nora K., - The Druids, - University of Wales Press, 1966

Chamberlain, M. E., Lord Palmerton (Political Portraits), www.amazon.co.uk

Churchill, Winston, Sir – History of the English Speaking Peoples, - Volume 1, copyright BPC Publishing Ltd 1969, 1971, Published by Cassell, London

Colledge, Malcolm, - The Parthians, - Thames & Hudson, London, 1967

Collins, Steven, M., - The "Lost" Ten Tribes of Israel...Found!, - copyright Steven M Collins 1992, CPA Books, Oregon, U.S.A.

Collins, Steven, M., - Israel's Lost Empires, - Bible Blessings, Royal Oak, MI, USA, 2002, Copyright Steven M Collins

Collins, Steven, M., - The Origins and Empire of Ancient Israel, - Bible Blessings, Royal Oak, MI, USA, 2002, Copyright Steven M Collins

Collins, Steven, M., - Parthia – The Forgotten Ancient Superpower, Bible Blessings, Royal Oak, MI, USA, 2003, Copyright Steven M Collins

Collins, Steven, M., - Israel's Lost Tribes Today, Bible Blessings, Royal Oak, MI, USA, 2004, Copyright Steven M Collins

Cooke, Alistair, - Alistair Cooke's America, - Weidenfeld & Nicolson, London, 1973, 2002

Cooper, Bill, - After the Flood – *The early post-flood history of Europe traced back to Noah,* - New Wine Press, England, 1995

Crystal, David, - English as a Global Language, Cambridge University Press, 1997

Davies, Edward, - Celtic Researches – on the Origins, Traditions, and Languages of the Ancient British, - 1804

Davidiy, Yair, - Lost Israelite Identity – *The Hebraic Ancestry of the Celtic Races,* - A Brit – Am Publication, 1996, Russell-Davis Publishers, Jerusalem, Israel

Davidiy, Yair, - Ephraim – *The Gentile Children of Israel,* - Revised edition 2001, Russell-Davis Publishers, Jerusalem, Israel

Davidiy, Yair, - Joseph – *The Israelite Destiny of America,* - copyright Yair Davidiy, 2001, Russell-Davis Publishers, Jerusalem, Israel

Davidiy, Yair, - The Tribes – *The Israelite Origins of the Western Peoples,* - Russell-Davis Publishers, Jerusalem, Israel, 1993

Davidiy, Yair, - Biblical Truth – *The Lost Ten Tribes of Israel in the West according to the Book of Genesis,* - Russell-Davis Publishers, Jerusalem, Israel, 2002

Davidiy, Yair, - Origin – *You too are from Israel – You too are the People,* - Russell-Davis Publishers, Jerusalem, Israel, 2002

Davidiy, Yair, - The Khazars Tribe 13, Russell-Davis Publishers, Jerusalem, Israel 2004

Desmond, Kevin, - The Harwin Chronology of Inventions Innovations Discoveries – from pre-history to the present day, - Published by Constable & Company Ltd., London, 1986

Elder, Isabel, Hill Elder, Celt, Druid, and Culdee, The Covenant Publishing Co., Ltd., London, 1986

Encyclopaedia of Islam, www.brill.com/publications/onlineresources

Evans, Lorraine, - The Kingdom of the Ark, - Published by Simon & Schuster UK Ltd, London, 2000

Featherstone, Donald – Victorian Colonial Warfare – India, - first published in the U.K. 1992 by Blandford, a Cassell imprint

Featherstone, Donald – Victorian Colonial Warfare – Africa, - first published in the U.K. 1992 by Blandford, a Cassell imprint

Featherstone, Donald, - The Bowmen of England – Published by Pen & Sword Books Limited, Barnsley, Yorks, 2003

Fisher, David Hackett, - Albion's Seed – *Four British Folkways in America*, - Oxford University Press, 1989

Flick, Alexander, Clarence, The Rise of the Medieval Church and its influence on the Civilization of Western Europe from the First to the Thirteenth Century, Publisher, B Franklin, 1969

Foss, Michael, - Celtic Myths and Legends, - first published 1995 by Michael O'Mara Books Ltd, London

Fox-Davies, A.C., - A Complete Guide to Heraldry, - Revised by J.P. Brooke-Little, Copyright 1985, Thomas nelson & Sons Ltd, Published by Bloomsbury Books, London

Frederick von Schlegel, - Philosophy of History –

Garmonsway, G.N. (trans.), - The Anglo-Saxon Chronicle, - J.M. Dent, 1953

Gawler, Col. J.C., - Our Scythian Ancestors Identified with Israel, - MacLaren & MacNiven, Edinburgh, 1875

Gilbert, Adrian, - The Holy Kingdom, - Copyright – Adrian Gilbert, Alan Wilson & Baram Blackett, 1998, Corgi Books, London, 1999

Gilbert, Adrian, - The New Jerusalem, - Bantam Press, London, 2002

Giscard d'Estaign, Valerie-Anne, - Book of Inventions and Discoveries, - Mac Donald Queen Anne Press, 1990

Gow, Professor Andrew Colin, - "The Red Jews, Anti-Semitism in an Apocalyptic Age 1200-1600," published by Brill: New York, 1995

Grant, W.B., - We Have A Guardian, - Covenant Publishing Company, London

Green, John Richard, - A Short History *of the* English People, - Macmillan & Co, London, 1885

Grove, Eric, - Great Battles of the Royal Navy, as Commemorated in the Gunroom, - Britannia Royal Naval College, Dartmouth, Naval Institute Press, 1994

Hague, William, - William Pitt the Younger: A Biography, Harper Perennial, U.K., 2005

HaLevi, Rabbi Yehudah, - The Kuzari – In Defense of the Despised Faith, Feldheim Publishers, Jerusalem, Israel, 2009

Halter, Marek, - The Wind of the Khazars, Published by, Toby Press, London, 2006

Hannings, Bud, - A Portrait of the Stars and Stripes, - Seniram Publishing Inc., Glenside PA, U.S.

Harmsworth Universal Atlas and Gazetteer, 1909 edition, - The Amalgamated Press Limited, London

Hawkins, Gerald, S., - Beyond Stonehenge, - Published by Arrow Books Ltd, London, 1977

Henking, Frances, - The Tender Twig, - Published by, Covenant Publishing Co, Ltd., London, 1963

Hislop, Rev. Alexander, - The Two Babylons, - Published by, S.W. Partridge & Co, London

Hjelmslev, Dr. Louis, - Language: An Introduction, - Published by University of Wisconsin Press, 1970

Hodapp, Christopher, Freemasons for Dummies, Wiley Publishing, U.S.A. 2005

Hooper, Nicholas & Bennett, Matthew – Cambridge Illustrated Atlas of Warfare – The Middle Ages – 768-1487, - Cambridge University Press, 1996

Hulley, John, - Comets, Jews & Christians – Root & Branch Association, Ltd, Jerusalem, 1996

Hutton, Ronald, - The Pagan Religions of the Ancient British Isles, BCA, London – New York – Toronto, 1991

Hyde, Douglas, - A Literary History of Ireland, - London, (1899), 1967

Johnson, Paul, - A History of the American People, - Weidenfeld Nicholson, Great Britain, 1997

Jones, Gwyn, - A History of the Vikings, - Oxford University Press, Second Edition 1984

Josephus, Flavius, - Complete Works of Josephus, - Kregel Publications, Grand Rapids, U.S.A.

Jowett, George F. – The Drama of the Lost Disciples, - Covenant Publishing Co. Ltd., London, 1980

Keating, - History of Ireland, - Dublin, 1733

Kephart, Calvin, - Races of Mankind – *Their Origin and Migration*, - New York, 1960

King, John, - Kingdoms of the Celts – *A History and Guide*, - Published by Blandford Cassells & Co., Text copyright 1998, John King

King, Martin Luther, JR., - The Autobiography of Martin Luther King, - Edited by Clayborne Carson, Warner Books Inc., New York, 1998

Koestler, Arthur, - The Thirteenth Tribe – *The Khazar Empire and its Heritage*, New York, 1967

Knopf, Alfred, A. – Crucible of War, The Seven Years' War and the Fate of Empire in British North America, 1754 –1766, - Fred Anderson, Alfred A Knopf, 2000

Lapping, Brian, - End of an Empire, - Guild Publishing, London, 1985 edition

Lavoisne, - Genealogical and Historical Atlas, - London, 1814

Layard, Austin, Henry, - Nineveh and its Remains, - London, 1849

Mageoghagen, C., (Trans. By:) – Annals of Clonmacnois from the Creation to A.D. 1408, - Murphy University Press, Dublin, 1896

Margoliouth, Revd. Dr. Moses, - The History of the Jews in Great Britain, 3 vol. - 1851

Marshall, H. E. – Our Island Story, - Published by T.C. & E. C. Jack, Ltd, London

Marshall, P. J. – Cambridge Illustrated History of the British Empire, - Cambridge University Press, 1996

Massey, John, Dunham, - Tamar Tephi: or the Maid of Destiny – *The Great Romance of the Royal House of Britain,* - second and revised edition, - Covenant Publishing Co. Ltd, 1924

Massie, Robert, K., - Dreadnaught – Britain, Germany, and the Coming of the Great War, - Random House, 1991

Mee, Arthur, - Arthur Mee's Book of the Flag – Island and Empire, - Hodder and Stoughton Ltd, London, 1941

Milner, Rev. W.M.H., - The Royal House of Britain – An Enduring Dynasty, - Fifteenth Edition, Second Impression, The Covenant Publishing Co., Ltd

Monmouth, Geofrey of, - The History of the Kings of Britain, - trans. Lewis Thorpe, Penguin Books, 1979

Morris, James, - Heaven's Command – An Imperial Progress, - A Helen and Kurt Wolff Book, New York, copyright 1973 James Morris

Morris, James, - Pax Britannica – The Climax of an Empire, - published by Faber and Faber, London, copyright 1968 James Morris

Mozeson, Isaac, E., - THE WORD – The Dictionary that Reveals the Hebrew Source of English, Spi Books, New York, 1989

Macaulay, Thomas, Babington – The History of England, Vol. I – III, - published by J.M. Dent & Sons Ltd, London, 1906

McGovern, W., MacKenzie, Donald A. - Scottish Folk-Lore and Folk-Life – Studies in Race, Culture, and Tradition, U.K., 1935

Maclagan, Michael, - Lines of Succession – Heraldry of the Royal Families of Europe, - published by Little Brown & Co (UK) 1999

McKay, John P; Hill, Bennett D. & Buckler John, - A History of Western Society, - Third Edition, Houghton Mifflin Company, Boston, U.S.A., Copyright 1987 Houghton Mifflin Company

Mackenzie, Donald A, - Ancient Man in Britain, published by Senate, Random House UK Ltd, 1996

McNair, Raymond F., - America and Britain in Prophecy, – copyright 1996 Global Church of God

Noorbergen, R., - Secrets of the Lost Races, - 1978 New English Library, London

Olmstead, A.T., - History of Assyria, - London, 1923

O' Mara, Michael, - Tales of Old Ireland, - first published by Michael O'Mara Books Ltd in 1994

O'Rahilly, Thomas, - Early Irish History and Mythology, - Dublin, 1971

O'Cloirigh, H., (Recension by) Trans. By Macalister and MacNeil, Dublin, - Leabhar Cabkal, or the Book of the Conquests of Ireland

Parfitt, Tudor, - The Lost Tribes of Israel – *the History of a Myth,* - Weidenfeld & Nicholson, London, 2002

Patterson, Richard S & Richardson, Dougall, - The Eagle and the Shield: A History of the Great Seal of the United States, - 1976,

Published by the Office of the Historian, Bureau of Public Affairs, Department of State

Paxman, Jeremy, - The English – *A Portrait of a People*, - Penguin Books, Copyright Jeremy Paxman, 1998 & 1999

Phillips, Samuel, - Guide to the Crystal Palace and its Park and Gardens, - Crystal Palace Library, 1859

Pedersen, Holger, - The Discovery of Language: Linguistic Science in the Nineteenth Century: Methods and Results, translated by John Webster Spurgo, Cambridge, Massachusetts: Harvard University Press

Petrie, Sir Flinders, - Egypt and Israel

Pinches, Theophilus G., - The Old Testament in the Light of the Historical Records and Legends of Assyria and Babylonia, 3rd edition

Pritchard, James, Cowles, - Eastern Origin of the Celtic Nations, Houlston & Wright, London, 1857

Professor Gerald S Hawkins, Stonehenge Decoded, published by McGraw Hill, New York, 1965

Prucha, Francis, Paul, - The Sword of the Republic – *The United States Army on the Frontier* – 1783-1846, Macmillan, New York, 1969

Raphael, Ray, - The American Revolution: A People's History, -

Rawlinson, George, - Ancient History, - Barnes & Noble, New York, 1993 Edition

Rawlinson, George, - Parthia, - G.P. Putnam's & Sons, New York, 1893

Rawlinson, George, - The Origin of Nations, - London, 1877

Restall Orr, Emma, - Thorsons Principles of Druidry, - Thorsons an Imprint of Harper Collins Publishers, 1998

Rice, Tamara Talbot, - The Scythians, - Thames & Hudson, London, 1958

Richman, Chaim, - The Holy Temple of Jerusalem, - Published by the Temple Institute & Carta, Jerusalem, 1997

Rivoire, Mario, - The Life and Times of Washington, - The Hamlyn Publishing Group Ltd, England, 1967

Rolleston, T.W., - Myths and Legends of the Celtic Race, - London, 1911

Ruggles, Clive, - Astronomy in Prehistoric Britain and Ireland, Yale University Press, New Haven and London, 1999

Savage, Anne (trans.), - The Anglo-Saxon Chronicle, - MacMillan, 1982

Seitz, Raymond, - Over Here, - Weidenfeld & Nicholson, London, Copyright Raymond G H Seitz, 1998

Shakespeare, William, - The Complete Works of William Shakespeare, - Crown Publishers, Inc., New York

Shore, T.W., - Origins of the Anglo-Saxon Race, - London, 1906

Shoumatoff, Alex, - The Mountain of Names – A History of the Human Family, - New York, 1990

Skelly, David, James, - The Assyrian Empire, - Sidney, Australia 1996

Skene, William. Forbes - Celtic Scotland, A History of Ancient Alban - David Douglas, Edinburgh, 1886

Smith, Adam, An Inquiry Into the Nature and Causes of the Wealth of Nations, original publication 1786, 4th Edition, Corins Classic Inc.

Stanley, Rev., Arthur, Penrhyn, - Sinai and Palestine in Connection with Their History,

Stephens, - The Literature of the Khumry – The Language and Literature of Wales, - Longmans, Green & Co., 1876

Strong, James, - The Exhaustive Concordance of the Bible, - Mac Donald Publishing Company

Squire, Charles, - The Mythology of Ancient Britain and Ireland, - London, 1909

Tanner, Lawrence E., - The History of the Coronation, - published by Pitkin Pictorials Ltd in December 1952

Tanner, Mark, - Great British Inventions, - published by Fourth Estate, 1997

The Illustrated Bible Dictionary, - Vol. 1-3, Inter-Varsity Press, Tyndale House Publishers, 1980

Thorpe, Benjamin, F.S.A., - Lappenberg's History of England under the Anglo-Saxon Kings, - Vol. I & II; published by John Murray, London, 1875

Turner, Sharon, - History of the Anglo-Saxons, Vol. I, 6th Ed., - Longman's, London, 1836

Trux, Jon, - The Space Race – From Sputnik to Shuttle: The Story of the Battle for the Heavens, - New English Library/Hodder & Stoughton, London, 1985

Tysylio, - The Chronicles of the Kings of Britain, - trans. Kenneth Wellesley, Guild publishing, 1989

Waddell, L. A. – The Phoenician Origin of Britons Scots & Anglo-Saxons, - The Christian Book Club of America, Hawthorne, California, U.S.A. 1973

Wagner, Heinrich, - Studies in the Origins of the Celts and of Early Celtic Civilization, - Belfast, U.K., 1971

Wardle, W.L. - The History and Religion of Israel – The Clarendon Bible, Old Testament, Vol. I. - Clarendon Press, Oxford, 1936

Weber, Eugen, - Modern History of Europe: Men, Cultures, and Societies from the Renaissance to the Present (1971), p. 130.

Wegener, Alfred, Lothar, - The Origin of Continents and Oceans (4th Edition), published by: (Dover Earth Science), U.K. 2003

Wexler, Alan, - Atlas of Westward Expansion, - Facts On File Inc., New York, 1995

William of Malmesbury, - Chronicle of the Kings of England, - Bohn, 1847

William of Malmesbury, - History of the Kings of England, - trans. P.H. Norman

Williams, Jane, - A History of Wales, - Longmans, Green & Co., 1869

Wilson, Robert, - Life and Times of Queen Victoria 1837 – 1897, - Cassell and Co. Ltd

White, Craig, Martin, - The Modern Descendants of Dodanim and Tarshish, - Sidney, Australia, 1990

White, Craig, Martin, - The Nations of Central Asia and the Middle East, - Sidney, Australia, 1994

White, Craig, Martin, - *In Search of…* The Origin of Nations, - Copyright 2003 History Research Projects, Sidney, Australia

Woodman, Richard, - The History of the Ship, - published by Conway Maritime Press, 1997

Worrel, W.H., - A Study of Races in the Ancient Near East, - Cambridge, 1927

Wylie, J.A., - History of the Scottish Nation, - London: Hamilton, Adams & Co., 1886

Zuckerman, Arthur J, - A Jewish Princedom in Feudal France, - New York, 1972

All scriptural references are from the New King James Version, Copyright 1982, Thomas Nelson Inc., unless stated otherwise. Emphases are the author's.

Recommended Further Reading

Bennett, W.H., - Symbols of Our Celto-Saxon Heritage, copyright 1976 W. H. Bennett, Herald Press, Windsor, Ontario

Capt, E. Raymond, - Jacob's Pillar – A Biblical Historical Study, Published by Artisan Sales – 1977

Capt, E. Raymond, - Stonehenge and Druidism, - Published by Artisan Sales, Oklahoma, U.S.A., 1983

Collins, Steven, M., - The "Lost" Ten Tribes of Israel...Found!, Copyright Steven M Collins 1992, CPA Books, Oregon, U.S.A.

Collins, Steven, M., - Israel's Lost Empires, - Bible Blessings, Royal Oak, MI, USA, 2002, Copyright Steven M Collins

Collins, Steven, M., - The Origins and Empire of Ancient Israel, - Bible Blessings, Royal Oak, MI, USA, 2002, Copyright Steven M Collins

Collins, Steven, M., - Parthia – The Forgotten Ancient Superpower, Bible Blessings, Royal Oak, MI, USA, 2003, Copyright Steven M Collins

Collins, Steven, M., - Israel's Lost Tribes Today, Bible Blessings, Royal Oak, MI, USA, 2004, Copyright Steven M Collins

Davidiy, Yair, - Lost Israelite Identity – *The Hebrew Ancestry of Celtic Races*, Russell-Davis Publishers, Jerusalem, Israel, 1996

Davidiy, Yair, - Ephraim – *The Gentile Children of Israel*, Revised edition 2001, a Brit – Am Publication, Russell-Davis Publishers, Jerusalem, Israel

Davidiy, Yair, - Joseph – *The Israelite Destiny of America*, copyright Yair Davidiy, 2001, A Brit – Am Publication, Russell-Davis Publishers, Jerusalem, Israel

Davidiy, Yair, - Biblical Truth – *The Lost Ten Tribes of Israel in the West according to the Book of Genesis,* - Russell-Davis Publishers, Jerusalem, Israel, 2002

Davidiy, Yair, - Origin – *You too are from Israel – You too are the People,* - Russell-Davis Publishers, Jerusalem, Israel, 2002

Davidiy, Yair, - The Tribes – *The Israelite origins of Western peoples*, Third Edition, - Russell-Davis Publishers, Jerusalem, Israel 2004

Davidiy, Yair, - The Khazars Tribe 13, Russell-Davis Publishers, Jerusalem, Israel 2004

Grant, W.B., - We Have A Guardian, Covenant Publishing Company, London

Gilbert, Adrian, - The New Jerusalem, Bantam Press, London, 2002

White, Craig, Martin, - *In Search of...* The Origin of Nations, - Copyright 2003 History Research Projects, Sidney, Australia

ABOUT THE AUTHOR

STEPHEN J SPYKERMAN was born in September 1940 during the Nazi occupation of Holland. His parents were Catholics of Jewish origin and he was the fourth son of seven children with a Dutch father and an English mother. The family escaped the Holocaust due to his parent's Catholic religion plus the fact that his mother was English, and thus she was seen as the English rather than the Jewish woman. Stephen's early years were full of excitement and danger, as their house for some time became the emergency headquarters for the Dutch resistance in his region. His father was arrested by the Nazi authorities and held for a period of time in a special prison for people who were considered influential in their local communities. His parents also sheltered Henny Cohen, a Jewish woman, who was hiding whilst on the run from the Nazis. At the same time their formidable children's nanny worked as

courier for the Dutch resistance. At age seventeen Stephen had a major encounter with God, which resulted in his leaving the Roman Catholic Church for good.

Having received a solid general education, he spurned the higher education his parents had hoped for and entered the world of retail fashion at age nineteen. After working in his hometown for a few years he left to try his luck in London, where he trained as a tailor in various high-class fashion houses. Whilst he was aware that his maternal grandfather had been a renowned tailor in London, he did not realise at the time that he was following a family tradition going back for at least five generations. Then in 1965 he married Virginia Edwards, and after the second of his four children was born, he left the fashion industry to take up a more lucrative career in financial services. During a successful career he pioneered a number of new schemes and concepts in charitable giving and seminar selling, and became an international speaker in his field. His interest in public speaking led him to direct his own public speaking club. In the years prior to his retirement in 1997, he became involved in a Speakers Bureau, after which he and a colleague set up their own International Speakers Bureau in London.

Once retired from day to day business he started writing books and founded Mount Ephraim Publishing as a vehicle for his work. As an Elder and representative of the Mayim Chayim Messianic Community in England he visited Israel in 1998 and, whilst there he re-discovered his interest in the truth about the Two Houses of Israel. In his subsequent visit the following year many doors were opened for him into an Orthodox community, who much to his surprise embraced the same truth. On one memorable occasion he was given the rare privilege to teach some senior rabbis some of the aspects he had learned about the future restoration of the whole House of Israel. He first met his good friend Rabbi Avraham Feld at a conference at the Hilton Hotel in Jerusalem, where Stephen had been invited to speak in the year 2000, and they have been firm friends ever since. Stephen and Avraham, who is one of the Founder

Directors of the Maccabee Institute in Jerusalem, share the same vision for the restoration of the two divided houses of Israel and the establishment of the United Kingdom of Israel.

In the year of that same conference Stephen received the calling to become "A Watchman on Mount Ephraim! – as per Jeremiah 31:6. Then in 2010, Stephen, his wife Virginia and his daughter Melissa moved to Ariel, which is in the so-called "occupied territories" to study Hebrew at Ariel University, where the family remained for two years. Whilst in Israel, Stephen and his wife organized an eight-day Sukkot Festival in the Old City Quarters of Jerusalem, as a haven for Messianic believers, Hebrew Roots people and Ephraimites from all over the world. The family had hoped to remain in Israel for good and over the years they had made many dear friends. However, God ruled otherwise and it was a terrible wrench for the whole family to have to leave. The pill was softened somewhat, as within just one year, three of his books were published in the United States, and doors were opening in all directions for the work of Mount Ephraim. To this day he continues to give lectures, radio and T.V. interviews. Stephen Spykerman is a consummate communicator and has addressed audiences and conferences in Great Britain, Canada, the United States, Ireland, France, Belgium, the Netherlands, Israel, Malta and Cyprus.

www.ingramcontent.com/pod-product-compliance
Lightning Source LLC
Chambersburg PA
CBHW062203270326
41930CB00009B/1635